The Growth of Italian Cooperatives

The Italian Cooperative Sector is amongst the largest in the world, comprising over 60,000 cooperatives from all sectors of the economy and directly employing 1.3 million people. Cooperatives created close to 30 percent of new jobs in Italy between 2001 and 2011, demonstrating that democratic cooperative enterprises can successfully operate in a market economy combining economic success and social responsibility. These offer a viable alternative to profit-maximizing enterprises and an opportunity to create a more pluralist and democratic market economy.

The *Growth of Italian Cooperatives: Innovation, Resilience and Social Responsibility* comprehensively explains how the Italian cooperative sector has managed to compete successfully in the global economy and to grow during the global financial crisis. This book will comprehensively explain how the Italian cooperative movement has managed to grow into a large, successful network of cooperatives. It will examine the legislative framework and the unique business model that allows it to compete in the market as part of a network that includes central cooperative associations, financial and economic consortia and financial companies. It will explore cooperative entrepreneurship through a discussion of the formation of cooperative groups, start-ups, worker-buyouts and the promotion of entirely new sectors such as the social services sector. Finally, *The Growth of Italian Cooperatives* examines how cooperatives have managed the GFC and how their behavior differs from private enterprises. It will also analyze the extent to which cooperatives compete while still upholding the key cooperative principles and fulfilling their social responsibility.

This book is an interdisciplinary study of cooperative development and is designed to inform members of the academic community, government, public policy makers and cooperative managers that are primarily interested in economic democracy, economics of the cooperative enterprise, cooperative networks and economic development, cooperative legislation, democratic governance, job creation programs, politics of inclusion and how wealth can be more equitably distributed.

Piero Ammirato is Honorary Fellow, School of Humanities and Social Sciences, Faculty of Arts and Education, at Deakin University, Melbourne, Australia.

Routledge Studies in Social Enterprise and Social Innovation
Series Editors: Rocio Nogales, Lars Hulgård and
Jacques Defourny

A social enterprise seeks to achieve social, cultural, community economic or environmental outcomes whilst remaining a revenue-generating business. A social innovation is said to be a new idea or initiative for a social problem that is more effective, efficient, sustainable or just than the current process and which sees the society it is operating in receive the primary value created rather than a private organization or firm.

Routledge Studies in Social Enterprise & Social Innovation looks to examine these increasingly important academic research themes as a central concept for social theories and policies. It seeks to examine and explore the activities of social participation among civil society organizations, SMEs, governments and research institutions and publishes breakthrough books on the new frontiers of the field as well as state of the nation defining books that help advance the field.

The Growth of Italian Cooperatives

Innovation, Resilience and Social Responsibility

Piero Ammirato

Routledge
Taylor & Francis Group

NEW YORK AND LONDON

First published 2018
by Routledge
605 Third Avenue, New York, NY 10017

and by Routledge
2 Park Square, Milton Park, Abingdon, Oxon, OX14 4RN

First issued in paperback 2020

Routledge is an imprint of the Taylor & Francis Group, an informa business

Library of Congress Cataloging-in-Publication Data
A catalog record for this book has been requested

ISBN 13: 978-0-367-73490-9 (pbk)
ISBN 13: 978-1-138-06721-9 (hbk)

Typeset in Sabon
by Apex CoVantage, LLC

Contents

Tables and Figure

Tables

Figure

Acknowledgments

I would like to sincerely thank Mario Viviani for the many discussions we had in Bologna, for his constant encouragement, for sharing his knowledge on the Italian cooperative sector which he knows so well and for reviewing the manuscript. My warm thanks to Professor Vera Zamagni for reviewing the manuscript and the many insightful comments, which I have truly valued and appreciated; and to Professor Carlo Borzaga and Gianluca Laurini for their prompt and insightful comments in response to my many queries.

I would like to extend my gratitude to: Professor Borzaga and the European Research Institute on Cooperative and Social Enterprises team in Trento for making available their valuable research and analysis on the Italian cooperative sector and the Alleanza delle Cooperative Italiane for making available their data on the Italian cooperative sector. In particular, I would like to thank Francesco Linguiti (Legacoop Centro Studi) for kindly providing updated data on the cooperative sector and the Centro di Documentazione sulla Cooperazione e L'Economia Sociale in Bologna for publishing books on cooperatives' business history and biographies of key leaders of the cooperative movement, which have also been valuable.

A very sincere appreciation to: Alfredo Morabito and Barbara Moreschi (Coopfond) for sharing their knowledge of Coopfond and the innovative Coopstartup program, and for their encouragement; Igor Skuk and Alberto Alberani (Legacoop Emilia-Romagna) for sharing their experience and knowledge and for their constant support; Serena Bitossi and Fiorenzo Badalamenti (Legacoop Toscana) and Professor Luca Bagnoli (University of Florence) for the wonderful discussion we had in Florence on the cooperative movement and cooperative groups; and sincere appreciation to Tito Menzani and Antonio Zanotti for sharing their insights into cooperative history and cooperative governance during our discussions in Bologna.

During my visits to Emilia-Romagna, Trento, Florence and Rome, I held discussions with the following people, who shared their knowledge and insights into the cooperative sector: Marco Bulgarelli (Cooperare Spa); Roberto Genco (Coopfond), Pier Luigi Brunori (Legacoop Rome); Andrea Benini (Legacoop Ferrara); Daniela Cervi (Legacoop Reggio-Emilia); Piero Ingrosso and Luca Grosso (Legacoop Bologna); Guido Caselli (Unioncamere

Emilia-Romagna); Alessandro Viola and Iolanda Esposito (Cooperazione Finanza Impresa); Egidio Formilan (Federazione Trentina); Sara Depedri (Euricse); Luigi Angeloro and Giovanni Ottimo (Cooperfidi Italia); Walter Dondi (Unipol); Lara Furieri (Cadiai); Carlo Occhiali (Raviplast); Antonio Caselli (Greslab); Carlo Zibordi (Italstick); Alessandro Tortelli (Piazza Grande); Alessandro Gentilini (Banca Popolare Etica); and Filippo Bernardini (Emil Banca).

I would like to thank Giovanni D'Adda, coordinator of the Master of Economic Cooperative Studies, University of Bologna, for arranging for me to attend seminars led by Professors Stefano Zamagni, Antonio Matacena and Everardo Minardi. Thank you also to Professors Mario Ricciardi (University of Bologna) and Lucio Poma (University of Ferrara) for sharing their knowledge on industrial relations and cooperative groups respectively.

I am most grateful to Professor Brenda Cherednichenko and Professor Andrew Scott for welcoming me to the Faculty of Arts and Education at Deakin University and for providing a welcoming, professional and supportive academic environment.

Finally, I would like to thank my wife, Li-Jun Yao, for her continuous support, insightful comments and formatting the monograph. My wife and I are very grateful to Dino and Marina Terrusi for their wonderful friendship and the hospitality they gave us during our four-month stay in Bologna in 2016.

Abbreviations

AGA	Annual General Assembly. Also refers to the various general assemblies held before the AGA
Alleanza	Alleanza delle Cooperative Italiane. It represents the three major Central Cooperative Associations
BCC	Banche di Credito Cooperativo or Cooperative Banks
CCC	Consortium of Construction Cooperatives
CCFS	Consorzio Cooperativo Finanziario per lo Sviluppo, a financial consortium that finances small to medium sized cooperatives
Central Associations	Refers to the three major cooperative associations—Legacoop, Confcooperative and the Associazione, and the smaller Trentino Federation
CFI	Cooperazione Finanza Impresa, a national financial consortium that finances WBOs and other cooperatives
CNS	National Services Consortium
Confcooperative	The Catholic-inspired Confederation of Italian Cooperatives
Cooperare	A financial company that invests in large cooperatives, majority owned by cooperatives
Cooperative Group	A cooperative that owns a number of subsidiaries either directly or via a controlled holding company
Cooperfidi Italia	The national financial consortium that provides credit guarantees to cooperative members

Coopfond	Legacoop's cooperative development fund
Euricse	European Research Institute for Cooperatives and Social Enterprises
Federazione Trentina	The central federation for the cooperatives of the province of Trento
Federcasse	The national association of cooperative banks
Fincooper	Legacoop's financial consortium from 1969 until 1999, when it merged with CCFS
Fondosviluppo	The cooperative development fund managed by Confcooperative
ICA	International Cooperative Alliance
Invitalia	The public agency for economic development and investment attraction. It reports to the Ministry of the Economic Development
Legacoop	The Socialist/Communist-inspired Central Association (ex Lega Nazionale delle Cooperative e Mutue)
Marcora Law	Refers to the legislation named after Minister Giovanni Marcora that promotes worker buyouts
MFM	Manutencoop Facility Management, the holding company majority owned by the property maintenance cooperative Manutencoop
NPMC	Non-prevalent mutual cooperative
PMC	Prevalent mutual cooperative
Promocoop	The cooperative development fund of the Trentino Cooperative Federation
Public Companies	Joint stock companies
Unipol	Insurance group majority owned by Legacoop Cooperatives
WBOs	Worker-buyouts of private enterprises in crisis

1 Introduction

There has been a renewed interest in cooperatives and their potential in recent years as a result of both the limitations of the State and of the capitalist-led market economy. These limitations have manifested in the State's difficulty in providing social services and in managing the economy; the inability to prevent the Global Financial Crisis (GFC); persistently high unemployment and underemployment; higher levels of inequalities; and less cohesive societies. This book will explain how the Italian cooperative sector successfully competes in a global market economy and how it has managed to grow—demonstrating resilience, innovation and entrepreneurship—to meet community needs and expectations. It will also demonstrate that the Italian cooperative sector has operated in a socially responsible manner, created employment during the GFC, reduced inequalities and promoted social inclusion. The Italian cooperative model offers hope to everyone who wishes to promote economic democracy and a more just and equal society.

The Italian cooperative sector is large and operates in every part of the economy. In 2011 it comprised 79,949 registered cooperatives,[1] directly employing 1.3 million people and equaling 7.2 percent of the total Italian workforce and 8.5 percent of the Gross Domestic Product (GDP). The highly regarded Trento-based European Research Institute on Cooperatives and Social Enterprises (Euricse) estimates that if one considers the number of self-employed people that rely on cooperatives for their livelihoods (for example, farmers) and the indirect employment they create, the figures rise to 11 percent of the workforce and 10 percent of the GDP. The sector's significance is further highlighted by the fact that it created close to 29.6 percent of all new jobs created in Italy from 2001 to 2011. The same study estimated a total turnover of 130 billion euros (Borzaga 2015).[2]

The national presence, size, inter-sectoral dimension and diversity of the Italian cooperative sector demonstrates that democratically managed, socially responsible cooperatives can be considered a viable alternative to capitalist enterprises,[3] and that an alternative economic system is both possible and achievable. This is demonstrated by the following data:

- Cooperatives are present throughout Italy, including in the North-East, providing 30.7 percent of the total cooperative workforce; the

North-West, 27.9 percent; the Center, 19.4 percent; and the South, 22 percent (Fondazione Censis 2012).

- Cooperatives operate in all sectors of the economy, including banking and insurance, agriculture, retail, manufacturing and construction, maintenance, cleaning, catering, social services, medical services, tourism, culture and entertainment.
- They hold a substantial market share in some sectors: more than 50 percent in social services; 33 percent in the retail sector; 33 percent in insurance; 25 percent in agri-business (V. Zamagni 2017); 10.7 percent in construction and housing; 9.5 percent in the service industry (Borzaga 2015); and representing 9 percent of the total business loans and 8.5 percent of the total family loans (Federcasse 2016).
- The percentage of employment share is high in the following sectors: social services cooperatives employ 44.5 percent of total private sector employment; transport employs 20 percent; agri-business employs 13.2 percent; general services industry employs 11.6 percent; the construction business employs 6.1 percent; and the retail sector employs 4.3 percent (Borzaga 2015).
- Cooperatives are, on the whole, larger than the average Italian enterprise. While cooperatives make up only 1.5 percent of the total firms operating in Italy, they represent 17.3 percent of all medium-sized enterprises with a workforce between 50 and 250 employees and 14.8 percent of all large enterprises with a workforce of more than 250 employees (Alleanza delle Cooperative Italiane 2017). In addition, there are 250 cooperatives and consortia across Italy with turnovers of more than 50 million euros. They are market leaders in retail, insurance, agriculture, construction, manufacturing, general maintenance and social services (Alleanza delle Cooperative Italiane 2016).

This book will comprehensively explain how the Italian cooperative movement has managed to grow into a large, successful network of cooperatives. It will examine the unique cooperative business model that allows it to compete in the market as part of a network that includes central cooperative associations ('Central Associations' hereafter), financial and economic consortia, financial companies and friendly institutions. This book will explore cooperative entrepreneurship through a discussion of the formation of cooperative groups, start-ups, worker-buyouts and the promotion of entirely new sectors such as the social services sector. It will analyze how cooperatives have managed the GFC and how their behavior differs from private enterprises. Finally, it will examine the extent to which cooperatives compete while still upholding the key cooperative principles and fulfilling their social responsibility.

In so doing, the book will provide answers to the following key questions:

- Are cooperatives able to achieve economic performance in compliance with the law and in alignment with international cooperative principles?

- How has the cooperative business network model managed to overcome key obstacles to cooperative development such as access to finance, management expertise and democratic governance?
- Can cooperatives grow into large market players and form cooperative groups of companies without degenerating or demutualizing?
- Are cooperatives and their networks better suited than capitalist enterprises to managing an economic crisis, and what do the different approaches tell us about cooperative behavior as compared to that of a capitalist enterprise?
- To what extent has cooperative identity evolved, and what are the challenges associated with these changes?
- Does the current size, inter-sectoral diversity, multiple enterprise model and the network capability of the cooperative sector place it in a position to further expand economic democracy in a pluralist market economy?

1.1 Why Is This Study Important?

This book is an interdisciplinary study of cooperative development, supported by longitudinal case studies, and is designed to inform governments who wish to promote alternative democratic enterprises to guide economic development, leaders and managers of cooperative sectors, public policy professional and academics and theorists of economic democracy. This study is important for five major reasons. First, this book explains how the Italian cooperative sector evolved and succeeded and is offered as a model to consider when promoting cooperative sectors around the world. The book will explain its relationship with the political system, the importance of the cooperative legislative framework and the function and operations of the inter-sectoral cooperative networks. It will describe how new cooperatives are created and grow while describing the key events that highlight how limits were identified and overcome. The book will share with the reader the ways in which the various players operated in a concerted way to navigate the GFC as well as various enterprise and sectoral crises. The book, in parts, is explicitly detailed—for example, when explaining cooperative law or the workings of cooperative funds or the worker-buyout program. This will allow the reader to better familiarize themselves with the policies and processes that govern cooperatives and to better understand and consider their practicality.

Second, this book will demonstrate that the cooperative business model practiced in Italy provides an ideal model for the equitable redistribution of wealth between capital, labor and the community. Cooperatives can overcome the persistence of inequalities between people and communities. The capitalist-led market economy has demonstrated a great capacity to generate wealth, increase productivity, develop innovations and bring an abundance of goods and services to market. However, it also generated unemployment and a high level of inequalities. The unequal level of asset ownership and high salary differentials have all contributed to major inequalities (Krugman

2014; Atkinson 2015). Indeed, it is estimated that "1 percent of the people in the world own more wealth than the rest of the planet" (Oxfam 2017). Governments have used progressive taxation systems, social welfare payments and other means of transferring wealth such as social housing. While these are admirable, humane measures, they have failed to reduce inequalities (Picketty 2014; Atkinson 2015). This book will demonstrate that cooperative's unique way of distributing value-added, lower salary differentials and the fact that cooperative assets cannot be distributed to existing members but are instead passed on to future generations can reduce inequalities.

Third, cooperatives are the ideal economic enterprise to make communities and local economies more resilient to economic crises and capital movements. The current phase of globalization allows capital, jobs and people to move at great speeds wherever there are new opportunities to make more money or to find a job. Profit-maximizing firms transfer jobs and capital to any location in the world that offers the opportunity to make more money or to pay fewer taxes (or both) than their existing location (Oxfam 2016). This creates unemployment, alienation and disruption among individuals, families and communities. The research presented in this book and the case studies offered will present an alternative. It will show that cooperatives are democratically owned local companies that do not relocate to maximize returns on investment as this is not their goal. In a cooperative, capital is a means of achieving mutual goals, including job creation and maintenance. This book will also demonstrate that cooperatives invest in their local communities and promote both inter-firm collaboration and trade with local firms within a region. The cooperative development fund creates new firms and helps existing ones deal with difficult situations, further creating local resilience. This cooperative business culture creates trust between the cooperative and their communities and promotes social capital and many positive political, social and economic externalities (Putnam 1992).

Fourth, cooperatives promote economic democracy and can become the pillar of a more pluralist economic system within which democratically owned and managed cooperatives control a greater share of the economy. As Robert Dahl argues, market-capitalism also limits the further development of political democracy: "unequal ownership and control of major economic enterprises in turn contributes massively to inequality in political resources … and thus an extensive violation of political equality" (Dahl 1998). Tom Malleson defines economic democracy as a critique of the current society and a corresponding vision of an alternative that includes forms of direct ownership, ways to direct investments, power-sharing arrangements and holding accountable those who make investment decisions and hold economic power. The economic players that can promote and contribute to economic democracy are many, including national governments, local government, superannuation funds and local community banks; large socially responsible enterprises that operate with power-sharing arrangements; sovereign wealth funds; and citizenship having a direct influence over public spending (Malleson 2014). Cooperatives are democratically owned enterprises that encourage participation and shared ownership. They are governed by the principle that one-person-equals-one-vote. They re-invest most of the profits back into the enterprises and, most importantly, the assets are passed on to the next generation. Cooperatives promote economic democracy in perpetuity at the enterprise level and throughout society since cooperatives are present in every sector of the economy, including banking and insurance. Cooperatives can democratize the market because they can influence the flow of investments, work conditions, the food we buy, the houses we live in, the health services we need and the places in which we holiday.

Fifth, cooperatives are the ideal enterprise that can enter into public-cooperative partnerships to overcome some of the most difficult issues faced by our societies today. In Western democracies, States are having financial difficulties meeting the needs of citizens and society. They have resorted to privatization, public-private partnerships, outsourcing and the user-pays system to provide welfare services. Cooperatives are the ideal partner for governments to meet the needs of people, knowing that cooperative enterprises put people and communities first, just as an ethically minded State should. Cooperatives operate as quasi-public enterprises whose ultimate goal is to meet the needs of members and their communities. They ultimately operate for the common good. In line with the discussion on economic democracy, forms of public-cooperative partnerships could lead to cooperatives providing public services or job creation schemes without the profit motive that drives public-private partnerships or the outsourcing of government services. The book demonstrates that cooperatives already provide social services for the aged, the young and disabled on behalf of the State. The State is an investor in job creation schemes, cooperatives and a cooperative development fund. Joint ventures have been created for the provision of school meals and child care centers. This opens the opportunity for the State to become a partner, enabler or investor in the cooperative sector aimed at the provision of services and in solving important community issues such as food prices, housing affordability and unemployment, especially for the young and long-term unemployed. If expanded, such partnerships could become a key feature of economic democracy.

1.2 The International Cooperative Alliance: Principles, Cooperative Typology and Size

1.2.1 Cooperative Principles

The International Cooperative Alliance (ICA), established in 1895, represents all types of cooperatives. The ICA liaises with international bodies and governments, promotes cooperatives around the world and conducts research. The most important contribution of the ICA, however, is having established a definition of a cooperative along with a set of values and guiding principles for cooperative members. More specifically:

- A cooperative is defined as an autonomous association of persons united voluntarily to meet their common economic, social, and cultural needs and aspirations through a jointly-owned and democratically controlled enterprise.
- Cooperatives are based on the values of self-help, self-responsibility, democracy, equality, equity, and solidarity. In the tradition of their founders, cooperative members believe in the ethical values of honesty, openness, social responsibility and caring for others.
- Cooperatives operate by seven cooperative principles: open membership, democratic member control, member economic participation; autonomy and independence; education for members; cooperation among cooperatives and concern for their community.

(International Cooperative Alliance 1995)

1.2.2 Cooperative Typology

Cooperatives were developed to meet the needs of people and local communities. As the capitalist economy developed, inequalities, unemployment, low wages and a weak position in the market compared to their employers and competitors led workers and producers to form cooperatives. Over time many types of cooperatives developed:

- Consumers established consumer cooperatives so that they could have access to food and other items at reasonable prices.
- Workers or employees established worker cooperatives in the construction, manufacturing and, more recently, in the service industry especially cleaning, service and maintenance to ensure steady jobs, good pay and conditions and more control over their work.
- Agricultural producers (farmers) formed cooperatives so that they could achieve economies of scale and better compete against large capitalist firms. Cooperatives enabled collective and low-cost purchasing of inputs to share machinery and to market their primary and manufactured produce. Cooperatives provided a stable outlet for their produce.
- Artisans and farmers established popular and rural banks to access credit at reasonable rates as they could not access credit from larger banks and usurers charged very high interest rates.
- Welfare or social services cooperative or health cooperatives have emerged over the past 30 years in response to an aging population and the growing financial difficulties faced by governments to meet citizen's health and social needs. These provide aged care services, child care centers, jobs for the long-term unemployed and care for the mentally ill.

- Community cooperatives are multi-function cooperatives recently established to cater for the multiple needs of communities, usually in remote villages. Members of these cooperatives are multitasked and can deliver mail, work in a dairy cooperative and provide taxi, catering and accommodation services. In this way, cooperatives are reviving communities that faced extinction.

1.2.3 Size and Diversity

A study conducted by the International Organisation of Industrial and Service Cooperatives (CICOPA) considered the number of worker-members and employees working for the cooperative sector as well as employees working for producers who relied on a cooperative for most or all of their livelihood. The study estimates that cooperatives provide work for 250 million people on a full- and part-time capacity. The majority of people employed are producers (223.6 million), while 15.6 million are employees and 10.8 million are worker-members. CICOPA estimates that the share of the cooperative sector in a country's economy is as high as 10.9 percent in Italy, 8.6 percent in Japan, 6.4 percent in Germany, 3.9 percent in Canada, 1.36 percent in the United Kingdom, 1.32 percent in the United States and less than 1 percent in Australia (Roelands et al. 2014).

Some cooperatives are quite large. The annual World Cooperative Monitor Database revealed in 2016 that there are 1,420 cooperatives with a turnover of above 100 million USD. Of these, 96 percent belonged to three sectors: agriculture (32 percent); insurance and banking (45 percent); and wholesale and retail (19 percent) (Euricse 2016). A key factor is the low number of worker-cooperatives from the industrial sector.

Cooperatives also hold prominent positions in key sectors of a country's economy. Cooperative banks hold 40 percent of the market in France and Holland. Mutual insurance companies hold 25 percent of the world market. Agricultural cooperatives hold more than 70 percent of the market in Japan (Zamagni 2012). Consumer cooperatives hold more than 35 percent of the domestic market in Denmark (International Cooperative Alliance 2016). Energy cooperatives in the United States provide electricity service to 42 million people (America's Electric Cooperatives 2017).[4]

The Italian cooperative sector distinguishes itself from other countries by having three major politically aligned Central Associations that associate cooperatives from all sectors of the economy.[5] It also provides financial and business support via a network of consortia and financial companies and promotes inter-sectoral trade and cooperation. It further distinguishes itself by having the highest number of worker cooperatives. This is confirmed by the CICOPA study cited above, which notes that Italian cooperatives employ 57 percent of all worker-members employed in European cooperatives (Roelands et al. 2014).[6]

1.3 Chapter Outline and Content

The book will cover all key aspects that will enable the reader to appreciate, understand and value the Italian cooperative movement. To provide the reader with a deeper understanding of the cooperative sector and its history, institutions and programs, the book will use Legacoop's experience and institutions as case studies to complement the broader discussion. This is because Legacoop has been more open to public scrutiny, makes more information publicly available and has been more willing to engage with researchers and scholars. It has also been the Central Association at the forefront of promoting legislation, the indivisibility of reserves, the cooperative development funds, the large cooperative enterprises, national multi-sector consortia and social or sustainability reporting. It produces the highest turnover of any association[7] and almost 48 percent of the cooperative sector's total turnover.[8] One scholar referred to Legacoop as being so well organized that it became, ever since the post-war reconstruction, "the mind, heart and also the manpower of the entire national cooperative movement" (Williams 2015).

1.3.1 Chapter Outline

The book comprises 11 chapters, including the introduction. The following chapter, Chapter 2, examines how the cooperative legislative framework enables cooperative development and promotes cooperative principles. It discusses the concept of mutuality and how it discourages demutualization, enables cooperative economic development in a global market and promotes democratic governance practices, and how external oversight ensures cooperatives are genuine and operate in compliance with the law.

Chapter 3 will discuss the leadership qualities and the role of Central Associations. This chapter will demonstrate that Central Associations perform a more complex role than traditional employer associations that goes beyond the provision of political representation and business services. It will describe how Central Associations are governed, the services provided to members, political representation and the role of the State. It will then discuss Legacoop's system of authority and the role it performed in promoting cooperatives, cooperative development and managing crisis. A discussion on cooperative unification, which commenced in 2011, will complete the chapter.

Chapters 4 and 5 explain how the financial and economic networks have helped the cooperative sector grow, innovate and manage change in a global economy. Chapter 4 will explore the diverse and strategic use of finance, the inter-sectoral dimension of financial consortia and the lifecycle approach to funding, which enables cooperatives to access finance at every stage of their lifecycle. It examines the role performed by the various financial structures in helping cooperatives access loans, equity capital and long-term patient capital needed to enter and compete in global markets. Particular attention will be given to the role performed by cooperative development funds and the national financial consortia.

Chapter 5 will examine the role performed by the consortia in helping cooperatives improve their ability to compete. The key question here is to understand the extent to which the consortia model can meet the needs of the small, medium-sized and large cooperatives that are competing in world markets. It examines how consortia help cooperatives achieve economies of scale, access know-how, introduce quality management and access new markets. It provides an overview of consortia networks, the regulatory environment, the typology of cooperatives, their functions, how they have evolved and the impact they have on the cooperative sector.

Chapter 6 will assess the formation and governance arrangements of a cooperative group and their unique role within the cooperative sector. This chapter considers whether the formation of cooperative groups is a new type of cooperative model suitable for enterprises of large, complex dimensions, and the extent to which they uphold cooperative principles. This chapter introduces the concept of business groups and then examines the importance of cooperative groups, why they have formed and their key economic benefits. Five case studies will reveal the various strategies and pathways that led to the development of cooperative groups. The benefits and risks associated with their formation conclude this chapter.

Chapter 7 will focus on entrepreneurship. The formation of new cooperatives is important because it allows cooperatives to enter new markets, revitalize the cooperative movement and promote generational change. This chapter will explore how new cooperatives are promoted, explain how the Marcora program promotes worker-buyouts of private enterprises in financial difficulties and discuss the cooperative sector's ability to promote cooperatives in new economic sectors such as welfare services and community services.

Chapter 8 will assess how the cooperative sector has performed during the GFC. The chapter will demonstrate the anti-cyclic nature of cooperative enterprises and how their behavior differs from capitalist enterprises. It provides background information on the impact of the GFC on Italy and, specifically, on the cooperative sector, including details of how the cooperative sector performed following the GFC. This is followed by a comparison of the economic performance and behaviors of cooperatives and capitalist enterprises and the identification of key economic behaviors of the cooperative firm. Key factors that have enabled cooperatives to perform well during the GFC, the anti-cyclic role performed by the cooperative banks and the negative impact that the crisis had on some cooperative sectors will be discussed.

Chapter 9 will assess the extent to which the activities of cooperatives are aligned with the cooperative principles. The key question of this chapter is whether cooperatives have managed to compete in the market in alignment with the ICA principles. The chapter is divided into the four themes of mutuality, democracy, cooperation and community. Under each theme, the alignment of cooperative legislation, the policies and guidelines of Central Associations and the practices of cooperative enterprises in line with the ICA principles will be examined.

Chapter 10 will discuss cooperative identity by examining key features that have defined the Italian cooperative movement. These include broad-based, inter-classist, inter-sectoral movement; the relationship between politics and cooperative legitimacy; democratic management; equality; good citizenship; and jobs for all. The final part of this chapter explores how a united cooperative movement is dealing with today's key identity question: namely the development of a new vision for society and the cooperative movement's role within it.

The concluding chapter will bring together the evidence presented in the book, assessing the extent to which the cooperative sector can continue to compete in a global market while maintaining its unique set of cooperative principles and values. It will highlight the opportunities and challenges facing the cooperative movement and summarize a set of proposals relating to the cooperative governance, external oversight and long-term cooperative vision. Finally, the role that the cooperative sector could perform in promoting economic democracy in a pluralist market economy will be discussed, and public policy implications will be highlighted.

Notes

1. The Italian cooperative sector has developed a comprehensive data base. It includes information on registered cooperatives, active cooperatives, employment and regional data. More specifically:

   - Registered cooperatives are cooperatives registered with the Ministry of Economic Development. They need to be registered in order to access fiscal benefits (Bonfante 2011). The book uses registered cooperatives' data, which is collected via the Census of Industry and Services every ten years. This facilitates ten-year comparisons. The number of registered cooperatives, however, is higher than the number of active cooperatives. This is because some cooperatives do not get started, or soon fail, or merge, or are under administration, which whilst not trading (even for more than one year) are still registered until all creditors are paid and left-over assets transferred to the cooperative funds. For these reasons the number of registered cooperatives in 2011 was 79,949, but the number of active cooperatives was 61,398.
   - Active cooperatives are captured in the Statistical Register of Active Enterprises (ASIA), which is a unit of the Italian National Institute of Statistics (ISTAT). It is updated annually and merges data from the Italian Revenue Agency, business registers from the Chambers of Commerce and the National Institute of Social Welfare (INPS). The turnover of the cooperative sector will be based on this data, which is based on cooperative's financial statements.
   - Employment data is captured from INPS, which records all social security payments made to staff employed by cooperatives.
   - Regional data is provided by the regional chambers of commerce based on their regional business registers, which include cooperatives.

   (Borzaga 2015; Carini 2015)

The book uses data published by Euricse; Fondazione Censis; the Italian Cooperative Alliance's own study group and Unioncamere (the Italian Chamber of Commerce). All their data is based on the above sources.

2. The 130 billion euro turnover does not include turnover from banking and insurance activities.
3. The terms capitalist and private enterprise are used interchangeably and refer to enterprises whose assets or the means of production are owned by individuals or investors.
4. For further information on the world cooperative movement please refer to the following sources: Michie, Blasi and Borzaga (2017); Battilani and Schroeder (2012); Zamagni and Zamagni (2010); Borzaga and Defourny (2004); Nyssens (2006).
5. Chapter 3 discusses the role and functions of the Central Associations.
6. The study notes that in Europe there are 1,231,102 worker-members employed in cooperatives. Of these, 703,879 are employed by Italian worker cooperatives. These are manufacturing, construction, social and service sector cooperatives.
7. Legacoop members' total turnover, including finance and insurance, amounted to 82.9 billion euros in 2014 (Centro Studi 2015). Confcooperative's total turnover, including the finance, insurance, and banking sector, amounted to 64.2 billion euros in 2016 (Confcooperative 2017).
8. This figure was arrived at by dividing Legacoop's total turnover of 56.731 billion euros produced in 2014 (Centro Studi 2015), which does not include insurance and banking activities, with the total turnover of the cooperative sector of 116.343 billion euros, which also does not include banking and insurance activities (Ufficio Studi ACI 2015). This equals 48.8 percent of the total turnover.

References

Alleanza delle Cooperative Italiane. 2016. "Le Grandi Imprese Cooperative." *Osservatorio Grandi Imprese*, 2.
———. 2017. *Imprese Cooperative in Italia: Incidenza sul Totale delle Imprese per Classi di Addetti 1971–2011*. Cooperative Census. Rome: Alleanza delle Cooperative Italiane.
America's Electric Cooperatives. 2017. *Powering America*. Accessed December 22, 2016 and June 14, 2017. www.electric.coop/our-mission/powering-america/
Atkinson, Anthony B. 2015. *Inequality: What Can Be Done?* London: Harvard University Press.
Battilani, Patrizia, and Harm Schroeder. 2012. *The Cooperative Business Movement, 1950 to the Present (Comparative Perspectives in Business History)*. Cambridge: Cambridge University Press.
Bonfante, Guido. 2011. *Manuale di Diritto Cooperativo*. Bologna: Zanichelli.
Borzaga, Carlo. 2015. "Introduzione e Sintesi." In *Economia Cooperativa: Terzo Rapporto Euricse*, edited by Carlo Borzaga, 5–31. Trento: Euricse.
Borzaga, Carlo, and Jacques Defourny. 2004. *The Emergence of Social Enterprise*. London: Routledge.
Carini, Chiara. 2015. "Data Collection on Cooperatives: The Italian Case." In *Cooperatives for Sustainable Communities*, edited by Leslie Brown, Chiara Carini, Jessica Gordon Newbhard, Lou Hammond Ketilson, Elizabeth Hicks, John Mcnamara, Sonja Novkovic, Daphne Rixon and Richard Simmons, 48–59. Saskatoon: Centre for the Study of Cooperatives.
Centro Studi. 2015. *Legacoop in Cifre*. Annual Data, Rome: Legacoop.
Confcooperative. 2017. *Statuto della Confederazione Cooperative Italiane*. Rome, 18 February.

Dahl, Robert. 1998. *On Democracy*. New Haven: Yale University Press.

Euricse. 2016. *Exploring the Co-operative Economy: Report*. Trento: Euricse.

Federcasse. 2016. *Bilancio di Coerenza delle BCC*. Annual Report, Rome: Federcasse.

Fondazione Censis. 2012. *Primo Rapporto sulla Cooperazione Italiana*. Census Report, Rome: Alleanza delle Cooperative Italiane.

International Cooperative Alliance. 1995. "Cooperative Identity, Values and Principle." *International Cooperative Alliance Website*. Accessed December 13, 2015. http://ica.coop/en/whats-co-op/co-operative-identity-values-principles.

———. 2016. *Facts and Figures*. 22 December. Accessed December 22, 2016. http://ica.coop/en/facts-and-figures.

Krugman, Paul. 2014. "Why We Are in a Gilded Age." *New York Review of Books*, 8 May.

Malleson, Tom. 2014. *Economic Democracy for the 21st Century*. Oxford: Oxford University Press.

Michie, Jonathon, Joseph Blasi, and Carlo Borzaga. 2017. *The Oxford Handbook of Mutual, Cooperative, and Co-Owned Business*. Oxford: Oxford University Press.

Nyssens, Marthe. 2006. *Social Enterprise*. London: Routledge.

Oxfam. 2016. *Tax Battles*. Oxfam Policy Paper, Oxford: Oxfam.

———. 2017. *An Economy for the 99%*. Oxfam Briefing Paper, Oxford: Oxfam.

Picketty, Thomas. 2014. *Capital in the Twenty-first Century*. Cambridge: Harvard University Press.

Putnam, Robert. 1992. *Making Democracy Work*. Princeton: Princeton University Press.

Roelants, Bruno, Eum Hyungsik, and Elisa Terrasi. 2014. *Cooperatives and Employment a Global Report*. Brussels: Cicopa.

Ufficio Studi ACI. 2015. *Il Movimento Cooperativo Italiano 2008–2014*. Note e Commenti, Rome: Alleanza delle Cooperative Italiane.

Williams, Walter. 2015. "Per un Progetto Riformatore all'Insigna della Cooperazione." In *Giovanni Bersani: Una Vita per gli Altri*, edited by Fondazione Giovanni Bersani, 85–120. Bologna: Bonomia University Press.

Zamagni, Stefano, and Vera Zamagni. 2010. *Cooperative Enterprise: Facing the Challenge of Globalisation*. Cheltenham: Edwin Elgar Publishing Limited.

Zamagni, Vera. 2012. "A World of Variations: Sectors and Forms." In *The Comparative Business Movement, 1950 to the Present*, edited by Patizia Battilani and Harm Schroeder, Chapter 2. Cambridge: Cambridge University Press.

———. 2017. "A Worldwide Historical Perspective on Co-Operatives and Their Evolution." In *The Oxford Handbook of Mutual, Co-operatives and Co-owned Business*, edited by Jonathon Michie, Joseph Blasi and Carlo Borzaga, 97–114. Oxford: Oxford University Press.

2 The Legislative Framework
Enabling Growth and Promoting Cooperative Principles

The study of cooperative law is fundamental to understanding the history, principles, values and economic development of the cooperative sector. Cooperative law defines cooperatives and specifies what they can and cannot do. These laws provide for a variety of organizational and legal structures that are suitable for all types of economic activities, taking into account size and complexity. They regulate the relationship between members and non-members, between cooperatives operating within a consortium, between cooperatives and the Central Associations, between existing and future co-operators and between the cooperatives, their Central Associations and the State. Cooperative law does this by attributing powers, rights, duties, responsibilities and obligations to all stakeholders.

Laws passed by parliaments in liberal democratic states embody values and standards that reflect society's views as mediated through political compromises (Chisolm and Nettheim 1997). Cooperative laws are also an expression of society's views expressed through political parties and representative bodies operating within civil society. As a result, cooperative laws are constantly changing in their attempts to balance upholding original cooperative values and principles with meeting the needs and expectations of their members and communities. These needs and expectations are usually met by finding a way to compete in the global markets and maintaining or redefining cooperative principles and values.

The first Italian law to cover cooperatives was the Commercial Code of 1882. While it provided for a limited number of shares per member, equal voting rights and non-transferability of shares, it was silent on the distribution of profits.[1] Since then, cooperative law has been updated regularly to reflect the political climate and the needs of cooperatives. The most significant Italian cooperative laws include the following:

- The Law of 1909 allowed cooperative consortia to bid for public contracts.
- The Basevi Law of 1947 was a comprehensive law dealing with democratic management, profit distribution, indivisible reserves, shares remuneration, and supervision.

- The Law of 1971 allowed members to provide loans to cooperatives in addition to shares.
- The Law of 1977 declared that profits deposited in indivisible reserves were not taxable.
- The Law of 1983 allowed cooperatives to invest in private companies.
- The 1991 Law defined social cooperatives.
- The 1992 Law allowed external shareholders to invest in cooperatives and for cooperatives to deposit 3 percent of their profits into a cooperative development fund.
- The Law of 2001 clarified the dual rights of workers as cooperative members and as workers.
- The Law of 2002 enhanced the way Central Associations conducted reviews of their members.
- The Civil Code of 2003 (Civil Code hereafter) provided a more precise definition of a cooperative as well as allowing cooperatives to demutualize.

(Bonfante 2011; Fici, Italy 2013)[2]

It is important to note that the law has always reflected the democratic nature and the economic and financial needs of cooperatives. In reviewing the law in more detail, we would expect that an effective cooperative law would simultaneously promote cooperative principles and cooperative economic development by facilitating their formation, consolidation and growth. More specifically, this chapter examines the extent that the cooperative legislation:

- Defines a cooperative enterprise that promotes principle of mutuality and protects cooperatives from demutualization.
- Promotes democratic management based on the principle of one-person-one-vote and appropriate democratic practices.
- Facilitates cooperative economic development so that cooperative enterprises can compete in global markets.
- Provides adequate oversight of all cooperatives to assure the public that cooperative enterprises are authentic and operate in compliance with the cooperative law.

This chapter is divided into four sections, each assessing and analyzing a key cooperative theme. Section one examines the definition of cooperatives and the issue of demutualization. Section two focuses on democratic governance, including the open door principle, together with voting and governance arrangements. Section three discusses economic development, including access to capital, networks and flexible management arrangements. Section four discusses supervisory and oversight functions. The final section draws some conclusions as to the effectiveness of the law in promoting cooperative growth, innovation and resilience.

2.1 Definition of Cooperatives

Italian law did not initially provide a concise definition of cooperatives; rather, it provided a series of regulations defining the character of cooperatives. These defined how cooperatives dealt with their members, distributed profits, remunerated shares, cooperative registration and government oversight. The Italian Constitution provided for a broad definition of cooperation that was later qualified by the Basevi Law of 1947, the law on social cooperatives of 1991 and the Civil Code.

The Italian Constitution of 1947, Article 45, raised the profile of cooperatives and provided its first legal definition: "the Republic recognizes the social function of cooperation with its mutual character and without any private speculative objectives. The law promotes and facilitates its growth with the most suitable means and ensures its character and objectives through appropriate controls" (Ajani 2011). This broad definition of cooperation highlighted the principle of mutuality and non-speculative objectives. It also placed responsibility on the State to promote cooperatives. The Basevi Law of 1947, provided content to these two principles. It required cooperatives to:

- Operate under the principle of one-person-one-vote;
- Deposit at least 20 percent of profits into the indivisible reserve;
- Limit remuneration on members' shares
- Limit members' rebates to 20 percent of total salaries;
- Prohibit the distribution of assets to members in case of winding-up (also known as 'asset lock').[3]

It was the Civil Code of 1942, updated in 2003, which provided a more precise definition of a cooperative enterprise according to Italian law. The Civil Code defines cooperatives as societies with variable capital (new members are free to join) and with a mutual purpose (cooperatives needed to demonstrate their engagement with their members). Most importantly, for the first time, the law makes a distinction between prevalent mutual cooperatives (PMCs) and non-prevalent mutual cooperatives (Non-PMCs). To demonstrate their PMC status, cooperatives need to:

- Demonstrate that they mostly engage with their members. To this end, consumer cooperatives need to demonstrate that sales to members exceed 50 percent of total sales. Additionally, worker-cooperatives need to demonstrate that the labor cost of members exceeds 50 percent of total labor costs. Meanwhile, producer cooperatives (including agriculture, dairy and fishing sectors) need to demonstrate that the production costs for goods and services provided by members exceed 50 percent of total production costs.
- Comply with the following requirements: dividends paid on members' shares do not exceed the postal bond rate by more than 2.5 percent;

dividends paid to investor members do not exceed members' dividends rate by more than 2 percent; and cooperative reserves cannot be distributed to members. In case of dissolution, all cooperative assets, minus debts, are to be deposited in a cooperative development fund.[4]

In return for complying with the above principles of mutuality and capital restrictions, PMCs receive tax concessions. The Non-PMCs do not have to comply with any of the above requirements and do not receive tax concessions. They are, however, still regarded as cooperatives and have to comply with all the remaining cooperative legal requirements.

The Law of 1991 on social cooperatives further expanded the concept of mutuality. It defined the purpose of social cooperatives as "the pursuit of the general interests of the community in the promotion of humankind and the social integration of citizens"[5] through the promotion of two types of cooperatives. Type A Cooperatives provide social, health and educational services. Type B Cooperatives can operate in any sector of the economy with the aim of integrating disadvantaged persons into the labor market.[6] This law has expanded the concept of mutuality: from the principle of mutual help between cooperative members to one that includes the interests of the whole community. The latter is seen as a much broader concept (Borzaga and Tortia 2009; Tavaglini 2009).

2.1.1 Demutualization

Demutualization reduces the number of cooperatives and hurts the reputation of the cooperative sector. It is a brake on further cooperative development. The Italian Constitution, and later the Basevi Law of 1947, promoted a cooperative sector that was based on the principles of mutuality with a clear social function. To this end, the Basevi Law introduced the concept of indivisible reserves, which meant reserves could not be distributed to members and that a cooperative's assets (minus members' shares) were to be deposited to a mutual fund supporting mutuality should the cooperative cease to operate. In support of this legal requirement, in 1959, the Italian High Court ruled that cooperatives could not be transformed into capitalist enterprises. Therefore, demutualization was not permitted (Menzani 2015).

The Civil Code, while making it difficult to do so, has re-introduced the possibility for members to demutualize their cooperative. To demutualize, a cooperative needs to be a Non-PMC. The existing Non-PMCs can demutualize if at least 50 percent of their members support demutualization. Cooperatives with fewer than 50 members require two-thirds of the votes to demutualize. Should cooperatives demutualize, their indivisible reserves need to be deposited into a cooperative mutual fund.[7]

The PMC can demutualize via a two-step process. Firstly, they have to become a Non-PMC. This step can happen when a PMC either does not comply with the PMC requirements for two consecutive years or if the majority of its members vote in favor of becoming a Non-PMC. Secondly, the majority of members must vote in favor of demutualization. This process is discouraged because the law requires accumulated assets to be transferred to the indivisible reserve fund before becoming a Non-PMC. Further, in cases where a prevalent cooperative becomes a Non-PMC, it is a requirement that any gap in the indivisible reserve at the time of the change to a Non-PMC be made up before any profits are distributed to members. The funds accumulated in the indivisible reserve fund need to be transferred into a cooperative development fund once demutualization occurs (Fornasier 2010).

2.2 Democratic Governance

Democratic governance based on open membership and the principle of one-person-one-vote is a key principle of the cooperative movement (International Cooperative Alliance 1995). The principle of one person being entitled to only one vote was enshrined in the 1882 Commercial Code.[8] The principles concerning democratic governance, however, have been refined over the years. Of particular note is the Law of 2001, which specifically defines the rights of worker members to participate in the formation of the leadership and management group and the decision-making process relating to strategic and operational decisions.[9] Key areas that define democratic governance include open membership, voting rights, voting procedures and governance models.

2.2.1 Open Membership

Open membership is a key principle of cooperation. The ICA principle states that "cooperatives are voluntary organizations, open to all persons able to use their services and willing to accept the responsibilities of membership, without gender, social, racial, political or religious discrimination" (International Cooperative Alliance 1995). Thus, anyone can join a cooperative provided they use its services and accept the responsibility that comes with membership. More specifically, a member is required to invest in the cooperative (members' shares) and be willing to engage in the democratic processes. Therefore, membership is not automatically granted but is offered to employees who are willing to invest and actively participate in the life of the cooperative.

The Civil Code is aligned with the open door principle. It states that any person can become a member provided they use the cooperative services and support its principles of mutuality. The Civil Code requires members to actively contribute, invest and participate in the management of the cooperative (Genco 2005). This law prohibits anyone who exercises an activity in competition with a cooperative to become a member (for example, a shopkeeper could not become a member of a consumer cooperative). To facilitate open membership, the law requires the Board to decide within 60 days whether a membership application is accepted. The annual report must note all decisions made and, in cases where an application is not accepted, the applicant can ask the general assembly to review the decision. It is important to note that the Central Associations, when conducting their annual review of cooperatives, review the procedures used to assess membership applications and can intervene if applicants are being discriminated against or refused membership without due cause.[10]

The Civil Code has also introduced a new category of members aimed at encouraging open membership. These are 'probationary members' who, after five years, will automatically become members if they have performed adequately and have paid-up the minimum share requirement. Probationary members cannot exceed one-third of total members.[11]

The social cooperatives Law of 1991 and the Law of 1992 introduced two other type of members. The social cooperative law promotes a stakeholder governance model, and as such it allows voluntary personnel to be admitted as members provided they do not exceed 50 percent of the total cooperative membership (Borzaga and Loss 2006). The 1992 Law allows external investors (individuals or institutional investors) to become cooperative members with voting rights and the right to elect candidates to the Board.

2.2.2 Voting Rights

Voting rights are based on the principle of one-member-one-vote, with some variations depending on the member status:

- Each member is entitled to one vote regardless of the number of shares held.
- Individual investor members each have one vote.
- Institutional investors[12] can hold a maximum of five votes.
- At all times, however, members always hold at least two-thirds of the total votes cast at the annual general assembly, with investor members holding the remaining one-third.[13]

In the case of a cooperative consortium whose members include other cooperatives, voting is based on a weighted system which allocates more votes to those cooperatives that have a greater level of engagement with the consortium. This allows the large cooperatives, who have more members, to hold up to 10 percent of the total votes cast at the annual general assembly (Genco 2005).

2.2.3 Voting Procedures

The voting procedures encourage member participation in elections. The law requires large cooperatives that operate in some provinces or that manage different activities to hold separate general assemblies. These assemblies may debate issues or elect a representative to participate at the annual general assembly. Voting can also be arranged via email, post or other telecommunication devices. Members may nominate another member as a proxy, but no one member can hold more than ten proxy votes.[14]

Elections are held every three years. Board members can be elected for three consecutive terms, after which they can once again stand for elections. The Civil Code initially held that members could not stand for election after three terms, but this clause was removed in 2004 because it was deemed difficult for smaller cooperatives to replace board members. This is a topical issue, with Legacoop promoting limited terms to encourage generational change (Legacoop 2008).

2.2.4 Governance Models: Tripartite, Monistic and Dualistic

Cooperatives can choose between three governance models through which members can exercise their democratic rights and govern their cooperative. These include the tripartite, the monistic and the dualistic models. The differences between these three models relate to the distribution of powers between the members (via their powers exercised at the annual general assembly), the board of directors and the oversight board (a body with broader functions than an audit committee).

The first model—the tripartite model—consists of the general assembly (*assemblea generale*), the board of directors (*consiglio di amministrazione*) and the oversight committee (*consiglio di sorveglianza*). Their roles and responsibilities are distributed as follows:

- The Annual General Assembly (AGA) is a powerful body. It elects the board of directors and the oversight committee and holds them to account; approves the annual budget; approves policies and procedures regarding mutuality objectives, including the annual dividend and members rebates. It can review all decisions made on membership applications.
- The Board of Directors, of whom at least 50 percent must be members, are responsible for managing the cooperative and implementing the strategy approved by the AGA. It appoints the senior management team, some of whom may have been elected to the board at the AGA. It reports to the AGA on economic performance, compliance with the law and the cooperative statute. The Board also reports to the AGA on how they promoted and complied with the principles of mutuality and membership applications.
- The Oversight Committee is a stand-alone committee elected by and reporting to the AGA. It comprises professionals of whom one is a registered accountant. Its role is to supervise the operations of the Board by reviewing the quality of management practices and ensuring that

decisions are aligned with the principles of mutuality. It must appoint the external auditor, review member complaints against management and report to the AGA on performance, compliance and application of mutuality principles.

(Legacoop 2010; Bonfante 2011)

The key unique features of the tripartite model rest in the power of the AGA to elect the other two bodies. The AGA is the body where members express their will. It elects the Board and the Oversight Committee and has exclusive powers over mutuality matters such as membership, dividend payments and rebates. Its authority is further enhanced by having the power to approve the annual budget where discussions on cooperative strategy, dividends and rebates are discussed (Genco 2005). The other key feature is that both the Board and the Oversight Committee need to report on how they promoted mutuality and what criteria they used to make decisions. This model also allows independent members to be elected to the Board, but they need to be nominated and elected by the AGA.[15]

The second model is the monistic model. The monistic model operates similarly to the tripartite model, with the only difference being that the Oversight Committee is a sub-committee of the Board and it is the Board that appoints the external auditors. Other than this, the AGA retains the same powers, but it is argued that much power is concentrated in one body, whereas in the tripartite model the Oversight Committee is a separate body. In practice, this model is rarely used.

The third model is the dualistic model. It has clearer separation of powers between the AGA and the Board and between the Board and senior management. The AGA, however, has less authority under this model. Key features of this model are:

- The AGA elects the Board of Directors and decides on matters relating to dividends and member rebates.
- The Board of Directors is responsible for approving the strategy and appointing senior management. It appoints the external auditors and approves the financial statements. It reports to the AGA on economic performance, compliance and on the criteria used to further mutual goals and membership. The Board also appoints the Oversight Committee.
- The Oversight Committee is a sub-committee of the Board. It performs the same functions as those performed in the tripartite model. The only difference is that it has the authority to approve the budget.

(Bonfante 2011)

This model has the merit of making the lines of accountability between the Board (representing members and ownership) and management (who cannot be elected to the Board) quite clear. This makes it easier for the Board to hold management to account. Critics have noted that this model dilutes the power of the AGA as it no longer elects management and the oversight committee. AGA's powers are further diluted because it does not approve the budget and does not deal with general membership issues as before (Fici 2010). Indeed, Roberto Genco argues that not having members approve the budget removes them from decisions on key aspects of cooperative principles such as the open door policy, alignment with mutual goals, and preservation of the prevalent mutual nature of the cooperative (Genco 2005).

2.3 Economic Development

2.3.1 Access to Capital

Access to capital is indispensable for any business organization. The amount of capital needed by a business will vary depending on the size, markets presided over and whether the business is capital or labor intensive. Cooperatives are of different sizes, operate in different sectors of the economy and have different capital requirements. Italian cooperative law has facilitated access to capital by facilitating investment from members, retained earnings and external investors, which is supported by appropriate regulations and tax policies.

Investment from members includes member shares and member loans. Members are required to purchase shares as a condition for membership. The maximum amount they can invest is 100,000 euros, and dividends paid cannot exceed the postal bond rate by 2.5 percent. Member loans were first allowed in 1973. Members can invest 36,000 euros for all cooperatives except those operating in the manufacturing, agri-business and housing sectors, whose members can invest up to 66,000 euros (Bonfante 2011).

Retained earnings consist of profits after tax that are re-invested in the cooperative. Profit distribution is highly regulated and includes a set amount to be destined for the indivisible reserve. Profit distribution is divided as follows:

- 30 percent of profits must be allocated to the cooperative indivisible reserves.
- 3 percent must be deposited into a cooperative development fund.
- The remaining profits can be used for paying a dividend on members' shares within the legal limits[16] or paying members a rebate for their services. There is no limit on how much can be paid in rebates, other than for workers in a workers cooperative where the rebate cannot exceed 30 percent of their salary (Fici 2013).
- Remaining profits not distributed as dividends or rebates can be placed in the reserve fund and cannot be distributed to members during the life of the cooperative and even in case of closure.[17]

The tax laws have facilitated internal capital raising. The Basevi Law of 1947 provided tax concessions on cooperative profits ranging from

25 percent for consumer cooperatives to 100 percent for agricultural cooperatives (Balboni 1991). In 1977, all profits deposited into the indivisible reserve fund were 100 percent tax exempt. Since 2004, however, at least 40 percent of cooperative profits are taxed, other than agricultural cooperatives (20 percent of profits are taxed) and consumer cooperatives (65 percent of profits were taxed) (Fici 2013).[18] Social cooperatives are exempt from paying taxes and pay value-added tax of 5 percent instead of 26 percent (Legacoop 2010).

The law has encouraged internal capital raising through compulsory allocation, indivisible reserves, asset lock, limiting dividends payments on member shares and tax concessions. This approach, in addition to the cooperative business model's inherent propensity to re-invest their profits, has led cooperatives to re-invest over 88 percent of their profits (Petrucci 2009).

Since 1992, cooperatives have also been allowed to attract investments from external investors—individuals or legal entities—including cooperative development funds.[19] The law does not place any limit on the amount that external investors can invest. Capital return, however, is set at 2 percent above members' dividends return.

2.3.2 Cooperative Networking

The cooperative law allows cooperatives to use a variety of legal entities to promote their development and new cooperatives. These entities include consortia and holding companies. They also provide the opportunity to invest and own private enterprises, joint groups of companies, worker buyouts, social cooperatives and small cooperatives (formed by three instead of nine members).

The consortia have been the first business model that cooperatives have used to integrate their activities. This economic entity allows cooperatives to achieve economies of scale and improve their market competitiveness. The first law passed to promote consortia goes back to 1909. This law permitted cooperatives to form consortia to bid for public contracts. The Basevi Law of 1947 allowed the formation of consortia for promoting a common activity. This was usually to facilitate access to raw materials and machinery, manufacturing and marketing cooperative products, and for bidding for public works. A consortium can be formed by at least three cooperatives, with a minimum capital requirement of 500 euro, and is subject to the same regulations, tax laws and oversight requirements as individual cooperatives (Bitossi and Simion 2008).[20]

The Visentini Law of 1983, for the first time, allowed cooperatives and consortia to form groups of companies in which cooperatives own (or partly own) private companies either directly or via a holding company. Cooperative groups of companies are now well established, and they are required to produce consolidated annual reports. This organizational model allows large cooperatives to grow through acquisition or partnership or by attracting capital from private enterprises in a controlled company or a holding company. The law, however, is silent on how the principles of mutuality apply to holding companies and their subsidiaries (Bonfante 2011; Zamagni and Felice 2006).[21]

The Civil Code provides for cooperatives to form a cooperative-led 'joint group of companies,' which can include privately owned companies. The unique features of the joint group are that, via contractual arrangements, one or more cooperative members are given the authority to lead and coordinate the group's activity. The joint group acts as a holding company without having any formal controlling interest in its members. The contract is required to state the powers of the lead cooperative(s), its mutual aims and the duration of the agreement. It needs to be registered and reviewed annually. Any member can leave the joint group at any time without incurring punitive sanctions. This new entity seems to give cooperatives an opportunity to be part of a cooperative-led group of companies while maintaining their autonomy (Genco 2008).

A unique feature of the Italian cooperative legislation is the establishment of cooperative development funds. The Law of 1992 required all cooperatives to deposit 3 percent of profits into a cooperative development fund. These funds are managed by an approved Central Association or the government. Currently, there are four approved funds[22] managed by the three major Central Associations and by the Trentino Cooperative Federation.[23] The law allows funds to be used for: establishing new cooperatives; promoting existing cooperatives; investing in consortia; investing in cooperative-owned companies; and funding educational activities. Considering that cooperatives can now attract external capital, this instrument can perform an important role for cooperative development (Bulgarelli 2006).

2.3.3 Entrepreneurship

The law has also encouraged the formation of new types of cooperatives. These include:

- Worker Buyouts (WBOs). These are cooperatives formed from private enterprises in crisis. The Marcora Law of 1985, updated in 2001, provides for a mechanism by which employees can take over private enterprises in crisis. In brief, the State allows employees to use their redundancy payments to buy the whole or part of the company. The cooperative sector via the financial consortium Compagnia Finanza Impresa, the cooperative development funds and other financial structures provide financial and non-financial support (Cooperazione Finanza Impresa 2016).
- Social cooperatives. They have been operating in Italy since the 1970s but were formally recognized in 1991.[24] The Law of 1991 provided a formal definition and a governance structure to social cooperatives. Two types of social cooperatives were identified. Type A provide for

the provision of social, health or educational services. Type B undertake activities in other sectors such as agricultural, manufacturing or commercial for the purpose of integrating vulnerable or disadvantaged persons into the workforce. They both have a stakeholder governance model where employees, voluntary personnel and institutions can be board members (Legacoop 2010). Social cooperatives have been the fastest growing cooperative sector since 1991.[25]

• Small cooperatives. The Civil Code allows the formation of cooperatives, as limited companies, with three members instead of the normal nine members. This can facilitate the formation of new cooperatives as it is easier to form a cooperative with three persons.[26]

2.3.4 Flexible Workplace Arrangements in Times of Crisis

The Law 2001, n.142, contains a unique set of regulations that facilitates flexible workplace arrangements in times of crisis. It formalizes a process that allows a cooperative to declare that it is experiencing a crisis. This, in turn, allows a cooperative to activate solidarity contracts with its workforce, enabling it to place employees (members and non-members) on the temporary unemployment list or to reduce working hours or their pay for a limited period. Solidarity contracts can be activated subject to the cooperative having a restructuring plan in place and agreeing not to distribute profits to members or investors for the duration of the crisis.[27]

2.4 Cooperative Sector Oversight and Supervision

The Italian State and approved Central Associations have formally supervised the operations of cooperatives since 1947. The Italian Constitution, Article 45, placed responsibility on the State to assure itself and the public that cooperatives operate according to their mutual aims and in compliance with cooperative law. The demonstration that cooperatives comply with mutual aims and the law has always been a pre-requisite to access tax concessions. This requirement has also been a way to discourage spurious cooperatives from being formed that damage the reputation of the cooperative sector.

The law requires the larger cooperatives to be reviewed annually and the smaller ones reviewed every two years.[28] Those Central Associations with more than 2,000 cooperative members have the authority to review their members,[29] while the cooperative branch of the Ministry of Economic Development reviews the remaining cooperatives. The Ministry has responsibility for how all cooperatives reviews are conducted. The reviews consist of:

• Making recommendations to improve internal democracy and to promote the effective participation of members in the enterprise. In doing so the reviewer ascertains whether AGAs and elections were held, budgets were approved, key decisions on mutuality and executive salaries were made, reports on mutuality were tabled and so on.

- Ensuring that cooperatives complied with the principles of mutuality via reviewing financial statements, board minutes and other documentation. This would include noting whether transactions with members or labor costs exceed 50 percent of total transactions or labor costs. It would also include ensuring that the payment of dividends and member loans are made within the legal limits, that worker-cooperative members' rebates do not exceed salaries by 30 percent, that 3 percent of profits are paid into cooperative development funds and at least 30 percent of profits deposited into the indivisible reserve fund.[30]
- Ascertaining whether cooperatives, in compliance with the Law of 2001, apply to worker-members the same conditions as they apply to non-member employees as per agreed national industry collective agreements.

(Bonfante 2011; Legacoop 2016)

The law also requires the Central Associations to take action should they find acts of non-compliance. It can take a variety of action depending on the finding. It can ask the cooperative to attend to items of non-compliance within 90 days. It can persuade the cooperative to voluntarily cease activity if found that it will not be able to become profitable (this option precedes the declaration of bankruptcy). It can recommend to the Department for Economic Development that administrators should be called in to administer the cooperative assets should it find the cooperative to be insolvent. It can also recommend to the Department for Economic Development to de-register the cooperative should it find that the cooperative is not pursuing mutual aims, is not able to achieve their stated mutual aims or have not deposited an annual report or conducted any activity for two consecutive years (Bonfante 2011).

The Ministry of Economic Development can initiate its reviews by randomly choosing cooperatives, or it can conduct an in-depth review after considering findings from other reviews.[31] Cooperative members can request that the tribunal conduct an independent review should they suspect irregularities in the way their cooperative is managed.[32]

2.5 An Innovative Legislative Framework That Promotes Growth and Resilience

The law provides a definition of cooperatives (prevalent and non-prevalent) that is based on the level of transactions they have with their members, limited return on capital and inability to distribute reserves to members. This definition is backed by some laws that support the cooperative principles of open membership, democratic management and inter-cooperative support via the formation of consortia and cooperative development funds. The law has made possible demutualization since 2003, but it has made it difficult to implement it by preventing the transfer of assets to the demutualized business. The Central Associations' oversight functions also ensure that their cooperative members comply with the cooperative law and associated principles.

The legislative framework has also been demonstrated to be innovative, to facilitate cooperative growth and to strengthen cooperative resilience. A key innovation is a provision that allows cooperatives to attract external capital with limited voting rights. This has allowed cooperatives to attract capital from more sources. The law on social cooperatives has introduced a stakeholder governance model allowing volunteers and other categories of members the right to vote and to be elected to the board. The three governance structures provide cooperatives with a choice and the opportunity to further divide the role of the board (direction and control) with that of management (implementation of the strategy and operational responsibility). Finally, the promotion of cooperative development funds promotes external mutuality between cooperatives and the cooperative sector and local communities.

Cooperative law has enabled cooperative growth through various provisions that have facilitated cooperative access to capital, the formation of consortia and the ownership of holding companies. It has facilitated access to capital via internal means through being able to attract member shares, member loans and equity capital from external shareholders. Internal capital accumulation was also encouraged by the taxation law which exempted from the corporate income tax all profits allocated to the indivisible reserves from 1977 to 2003. The law enables cooperatives to own private enterprises directly as subsidiaries or via a holding company, which allows cooperatives to attract private partners and institutional and retail shareholders through the co-owning of subsidiaries or via listing companies on the stock market. The law allows the formation of consortia and a 'joint group of companies' that help cooperatives compete in the market via achieving economies of scale. It has promoted new types of cooperatives such as WBOs and social cooperatives.

Resilience is defined as the ability to recover from setbacks, adapt well to change and keep going in the face of adversity (Ovens 2015). The legal framework promotes resilience through various provisions. Large cooperatives that own holding companies have a better chance of dealing with adversity and can manage change better than smaller companies. The Law of 2002 allows cooperatives to formally promote flexible workplace arrangements in times of crisis, enabling them to manage difficult situations via activating solidarity contracts. The Law of 1992, which simultaneously allowed cooperatives to access external capital and to establish the cooperative development funds, helps cooperatives become more resilient. This is because the funds can provide equity capital—as well as loans—in times of crisis in order to implement a restructuring plan designed to help the cooperative overcome the crisis and become profitable again.

Italian cooperative law has met the needs of cooperatives in a changing market. It has attempted to find a balance between the needs of the market and principles of cooperation, member control and effective governance, the need to make a profit and limit returns on capital, the needs of members and those of investors and the needs of current and future generations. It provides the basis to build sound, democratic and socially responsible cooperative enterprises. The law, however, also provides the possibility for cooperatives to demutualize and to own private enterprises directly or via holding companies. In the latter case, the law does not place any obligations on cooperatives to demonstrate how they comply with the principles of mutuality when managing private enterprises. This book will expand further on these questions in later chapters and consider whether a new cooperative identity is emerging.

Notes

1. Refer to Commercial Code 1882, Chapter IX, Section VII, Articles 220–227.
2. All the Italian cooperative-related laws can be found at: www.cooperazione.net/pagina.asp?pid=77&uid=11.
3. Please refer to Article 26 of the Basevi Law of 14 December 1947, Number 1577: Provvedimenti per la Cooperazione.
4. These regulations are found in the Civil Code (1942) which was amended by the Legislative Decree of 17 January of 2003: Titolo VI. Delle Societa' Cooperative e delle Mutue Assicuratrici.
5. Refer to Law of 8 November 1991, 381: Disciplina delle Cooperative Sociali, Article 1.
6. The Law of 8 November 1991, Article 4, defines disadvantaged persons as those in need of psychiatric treatment, alcoholics, drug addicts and minors with family difficulties and ex-prisoners.
7. Refer to Civil Code 2003, Articles 2545–10 and 2545–11.
8. See Commercial Code 1882, Part Nine, Section Seven, Article: b 225.
9. See Law 2001, 142, Article 2.
10. Refer to Law 2002, Number 220, Articles 4 and 5.
11. See the Civil Code 2003, Articles: 2527, 2528 and 2545.
12. Institutional investors are cooperative development funds, financial consortia and cooperative-owned financial companies.
13. See the Law 31.1.1992, Number 59, Article 4.
14. See the Civil Code 2003, Articles: 2538, 2539, 2540, and 2541. Those cooperatives that employ more than 3,000 staff and operate in many provinces and those that employ five hundred staff and manage a number of activities are required to hold separate assemblies.
15. See Civil Code 2003, Articles: 2542, 2543. 2544.
16. See Civil Code 2003, Articles: 2545.
17. In case of closure, after debtors are paid, the amount of money left in indivisible reserve fund is deposited in the cooperative development funds.
18. When they were first introduced in 1973, interest on member loans was taxed at half the rate of bank deposits (12.5 percent instead of 25 percent). Today they are taxed at the same rate of 26 percent (Unicoop 2016).
19. See Law 1992/59, Articles 5 and 11; Civil Code article 2526.

20. Chapter 5 will discuss the role of consortia in depth.
21. Chapter 6 will discuss the role of groups of enterprises in depth.
22. Refer to Law 1992/59, Articles 11 and 12.
23. Chapter 4 provides further information on cooperative development funds.
24. There is also another category of social businesses called social enterprises. These are privately owned firms that operate for a social purpose. As per Law 2006/155, they must generate at least 70 percent of income from business activities and cannot distribute profits (European Commission 2014).
25. Chapter 7 will discuss social cooperatives and WBOs.
26. Refer to Civil Code 2003, Article 2522.
27. Please refer to Law 2001, n. 142. 2001.
28. The larger cooperatives are those cooperatives that have a turnover of 21 million euros, own a controlling interest in a public company or have indivisible reserves or member loans that have a value above 2 million euros (Bonfante 2011).
29. The Federazione Trentina conducts reviews with its own staff. Legacoop outsources this function. Confcooperative uses a network of reviewers throughout Italy.
30. Refer to Law 1947, 1577: Articles 3 and 4; and the Civil Code 2003, Article: 2513 and 2514.
31. Refer to Law 1992, 220: Articles 5–10; Civil Code 2003: Articles 2545, paragraphs 14, 16, 17, 18.
32. Five percent of members in a cooperative with 3,000 members or 10 percent of members for all other cooperatives can request the Tribunal to conduct a review. Refer to Civil Code: Article 2545, paragraph 15.

References

Ajani, Gianmaria. 2011. *La Nascita della Republica e la sua Costituzione*. Turin: UTET.

Balboni, Michele. 1991. "L'impresa Cooperativa: Aspetti Legislativi e Fiscali." In *Il Movimento, Il Sistema, La rete: Un Decennio di Cambiamenti nelle Imprese Cooperative*, edited by Carella Francesco, 56–58. Bologna: Editrice Emilia Romagna.

Bitossi, Serena, and Marco Simion. 2008. "Gli Strumenti Della Crescita per le Cooperative dal Consorzio al Gruppo: La Realta' Cooperativa Toscana." In *I Gruppi Cooperativi: Strategie, Risultati, Criticita' delle Cooperative Holding*, edited by Bitossi Serena, 153–198. Bologna: Il Mulino.

Bonfante, Guido. 2011. *Manuale di Diritto Cooperativo*. Bologna: Zanichelli.

Borzaga, Carlo, and Monica Loss. 2006. "Multiple Goals and Multi-Stakeholder Management in Italian Social Enterprises." In *Social Enterprise*, edited by Marthe Nyssens, 72–84. Abingdon: Routledge.

———, and Ermanno Tortia. 2009. "Cooperativa (Impresa)." In *Dizionario di Economia Civile*, edited by Luigino Bruni and Stefano Zamagni, 240–246. Rome: Citta' Nuova Editrice.

Bulgarelli, Marco. 2006. "Coopfond e la Nuova Promozione Cooperativa." In *La Promozione Cooperativa: Coopfond tra Mercato e Solidarieta'*, edited by Marco Bulgarelli and Mario Viviani, 39–80. Bologna: Il Mulino.

Chisolm, Richard, and Garth Nettheim. 1997. *Understanding Law*. Sydney: Butterworths.

Cooperazione Finanza Impresa. 2016. "CFI, Foglio Informativo." *Cooperazione Finanza Impresa*. September. Accessed January 6, 2017. www.cfi.it/public/wp-content/uploads/2016/09/CFI-foglio-informativo.pdf.

European Commission. 2014. *Country Report Italy*. A Map of Social Enterprises and their Eco-Systems in Europe, Brussels: European Commission.

Fici, Antonio. 2010. *Italian Cooperative Law Reform and Co-operative Principles*. Euricse Working Papers, 1–27.

———. 2013. "Italy." In *International Handbook of Cooperative Law*, edited by Dante Cracogna, Antonio Fici and Hagen Henry, 479–502. Heidelberg: Springer.

Fornasier, Edi. 2010. "Differenza fra Cooperative a Mutualita' Prevalent e non Prevalente." In *Manuale per Nuove Cooperative*, edited by Legacoop, 73–81. Bologna: Legacoop.

Genco, Roberto. 2005. "Il Governo dell'Impresa Cooperativa." *La Nuova Disciplina delle Societa' Cooperative*. Firenze: Fondazione Cesifin Alberto Predieri. 1–18.

———. 2008. "Mutualita' di Gruppo e Corporate Governance di Gruppo." In *I Gruppi Cooperativi: Strategie, Risultati, Criticita' delle Cooperative Holding*, edited by Serena Bitossi, 99–134. Bologna: Il Mulino.

International Cooperative Alliance. 1995. "Co-operative Identity, Values and Principles." *International Cooperative Alliance*. Accessed December 13, 2015. https://ica.coop/en/whats-co-op/co-operative-identity-values-principles.

Legacoop. 2008. *Linee Guida per la Governance delle Cooperative Aderenti a Legacoop*. National Governance Guidelines, Rome: Legacoop.

———. 2010. *Manuale per le Nuove Cooperative*. Bologna: Legacoop.

———. 2016. *Vigilanza sugli Enti Cooperativi ai Sensi del Decreto Legge 2 Agosto 2002 N.220: Verbale di Revisione*. Rome: Legacoop.

Menzani, Tito. 2015. *Cooperative: Persone oltre che imprese*. Soveria Mannelli: Rubbettino Editore.

Ovens, Andrea. 2015. "What Resilience Means and Why It Matters." *Harvard Business Review Digital Articles*, January 5: 1–4.

Petrucci, Paola. 2009. *La Distribuzione degli Avanzi di Gestione e la Pratica del Ristorno nelle Imprese Cooperative*. Rome: Centro Studi Legacoop.

Tavaglini, Claudio. 2009. "Cooperativa Sociale." In *Dizionario di Economia Civile*, edited by Luigino Bruni and Stefano Zamagni, 247–250. Rome: Citta' Nuova Editrice.

Unicoop, Firenze. 2016. *Prestito Sociale*. January 4. Accessed January 4, 2016. www.e-coop.it/web/unicoop-firenze/il-prestito-sociale.

Zamagni, Vera, and Emanuele Felice. 2006. *Oltre il Secolo: Le Trasformazioni de Sistema Cooperativo Legacoop alla Fine del Secondo Millennio*. Bologna: Il Mulino.

3 Central Associations
Leadership and Economic Development

Business associations are an important part of the political and economic landscape. Business associations and trade guilds, in one form or another, have existed since the Middle Ages, but it was not until 1870 that the first trade associations were formed. Employers' associations followed some 30 years later. Trade associations represent their members' interests in the political arena but also provide services such as legal, marketing, fiscal advice and research. Employers' associations represent their members in industrial relations and focus on influencing public policy and social issues. At times, one national body can perform both functions (Lanzalaco 2007).

In Italy, there are three major national Central Associations and one from the autonomous province of Trento. The three largest Central Associations are: Legacoop (Communist/Socialist), formed in 1886; Confcooperative, the Confederation of Italian Cooperatives (Catholic), formed in 1919; and the General Association of Italian Cooperatives (Republican/Social Democratic), formed in 1952. These Central Associations claim to represent 39,000 registered cooperatives[1] that in turn produce 90 percent of the total cooperative sector turnover and 88 percent of total employment, and have 12 million members.

The previous chapter noted that Central Associations are responsible for conducting reviews of cooperatives to ensure they comply with the cooperative law and to manage the cooperative development funds. This chapter explores how Central Associations are governed, how they influence public policy and how they promote economic development.

This chapter will describe how all Central Associations have contributed to cooperative growth. However, to provide a more in-depth explanation of the association and its cooperative members, it focuses more on Legacoop.[2] This chapter comprises six sections. The first section explains how the Central Associations are governed. The second describes the various services provided to members, and the third examines political representation and the role of the state. An analysis of Legacoop's system of authority is described in section four, while the fifth section explains how it promotes new cooperatives, cooperative development and its approach to crisis management.

Finally, the sixth section considers the reasons that led the three major Central Associations to commence a journey toward unification.

3.1 Governance Arrangements

Legacoop is comprised of one national body, 20 territorial structures and ten industry sector associations.[3] There are also four provincial bodies, all of which are located in Emilia Romagna. Legacoop's key body is called the Congress. The Congress is the principal representative body and is made up of delegates chosen by the regional bodies, consortia and cooperative-owned companies of national significance. Cooperative representatives must fill at least 50 percent of the national board positions. The Congress meets every four years, and its key roles include the election of the national board, the oversight committee, and the audit committee. The Congress approves any strategic directions and changes to the statute and the values charter. The oversight committee ensures that the board complies with the statute and the values charter, and it deals with conflicts between members and the board. The audit committee reviews its financial statements (Legacoop 2014).

The Board elects the CEO (called 'President') and the executive committee. The Board effectively leads the Central Association's activity and implements its strategic directions. It approves the annual program, the budget, establishes member fees and approves policies and procedures (other than those relating to the oversight committee). It approves the establishment of sectoral associations, establishes the equal opportunity commission and reviews the industrial relations agreements entered into by the sectoral associations. The CEO's role is to appoint an executive team, coordinate the activity of the national, territorial and sectoral associations, provide regular progress reports and engage with the government (Legacoop 2014).

Legacoop does not engage in any direct economic activity. This is left to cooperatives and consortia, with the Central Association having a comprehensive mandate and scope. It has the responsibility of promoting cooperative values; economic development; democratic management; and inter-cooperative relations. It is also responsible for leading public policy debates on issues such as well-functioning markets, social cohesion, equal opportunity, the integration of new migrants, working rights and protecting the environment (Legacoop 2014).

The regional bodies have a similar structure and are elected by cooperatives headquartered in each region. Their role is to represent cooperatives vis-à-vis the regional and local government and in industrial relations matters. The regional bodies promote new cooperatives and inter-sectoral cooperation and ensure their activities are aligned with the national strategy. The regional bodies also promote cooperative research, management training and social responsibility. They also coordinate the reviews of cooperatives on behalf of the national Association (Legacoop Toscana 2013).

The ten sectoral associations represent cooperative members from the following sectors: consumer, retail, production and labor (construction and manufacturing), agriculture, services, welfare, culture, media, housing and tourism. Their role is to engage with ministers and government departments (in consultation with the CEO and executive team). They engage with trade unions and negotiate national collective industrial agreements. A key role is promoting networking, alliances and cooperative consolidation and expansion in areas of low cooperative economic density (Legacoop 2014).

Legacoop's governance rules emphasize the autonomy of the association from political or other influences. To this end, it prohibits anyone from holding a position within Legacoop structures if they simultaneously hold executive positions in political parties; executive positions in local, regional or national governments; or the position of mayor of a city with a population of more than 15,000. Also, a member of any other employer association cannot be an office holder (Legacoop 2012). This is something that has been strongly emphasized since the 1990s.[4]

3.2 Provision of Services

All Central Associations have always provided a variety of services to their members. These services meet the needs of cooperatives throughout their lifecycle: from the moment a cooperative is established until they reach maturity. Services are provided at their service centers or offices or through other cooperative-owned or jointly owned companies. Non-cooperative companies are also used if required.

The first type of advice is provided to new cooperatives. It includes information about what a cooperative is, how they work, the type of cooperative statute to use and how to develop a business plan. Once cooperatives are formed and join the association, they are then either linked up with other cooperatives or can join a consortium.

The second type of services are legal, industrial relation and accounting services. Legal services include dealing with contractual arrangements or compliance with legislation and legal compliance regarding administrative, environmental and contract law. The industrial relations unit provides advice on collective agreements and pay and conditions. Accounting services include tax advice, payroll support and assistance with the preparation of financial statements. These would mostly suit small to medium-sized enterprises, as the large enterprises typically have their own divisions that provide these services.

The third type of services provided by the Central Associations is consultancy and training. These include consultancy services aimed at making cooperatives more competitive or developing export strategies or restructuring, including mergers and acquisition. Specialist companies helping cooperatives enter and manage international trade have been established. Companies owned by each of the Central Associations provide professional training, while Fon.Coop, jointly owned by the three Central Associations and the trade union movement, provides continuous training, including focusing on reskilling, especially for those at risk of market exclusion.

Financial support is another service provided via a number of national consortia servicing the whole cooperative sector. Cooperfidi Italia helps cooperatives access loans via acting as a guarantor with third parties. Cooperazione Finanza Impresa supports the formation of cooperatives from enterprises in crisis and the consolidation and growth of existing cooperatives. All Central Associations manage their own cooperative development funds. More specifically, Legacoop has established:

- Consorzio Cooperativo Finanziario per lo Sviluppo, a national consortium that provides loans and makes strategic investments on behalf of the cooperative sector.
- Cooperfactor, a company that provides factoring services to cooperatives dealing with the public sector.
- Cooperare Spa, which invests in large cooperatives.

Legacoop, Confcooperative and the Trentino Federation have their own insurance companies. Confcooperative and the Trentino Federation can count on cooperative banks. The Trentino Federation has its own finance company in Fincoop Spa.[5]

3.3 Political Representation: Influencing the State

One of the unique features of cooperatives is that they are very versatile and can meet the needs of various social classes. As a result, people and parties of all political persuasions have supported the cooperative sector. In Italy, Liberals, Republicans, Socialists, Communists and Catholics have all supported cooperatives. They have supported them because they could meet the needs of their constituents, be it urban middle classes (via the formation of consumer cooperatives and mutuals), farmers (via agricultural cooperatives and rural banks) or workers (via consumer, worker cooperatives and housing). These groups have also supported cooperatives because they were part of their political projects. The Liberal and Conservatives wanted cooperatives to support the Liberal State. Giuseppe Mazzini, a key figure in Italian unification, wanted them to support universal suffrage and a new democratic state. The Socialists wanted cooperatives to join the trade union and the party to create a socialist society. The Catholics did not have their party until 1919 but followed the *Rerum Novarum* (Rights and Duties of Capital and Labor) teachings, which led to their support of farmers in the countryside and artisans in the cities. It is not surprising, therefore, that Central Associations have had close relations with political parties and have been able to influence the State (Zangheri, Galasso and Castronovo 1987).

The cooperative sector has always exerted political influence. In 1905 it had already created a 'friends of cooperation' group that numbered 60 members of parliament (Galasso 1986). This approach was interrupted by fascism, but when democracy resumed following the defeat of fascism, in 1946, the three major Central Associations could count on 108 deputies as friends of cooperatives (Earle 1986). It became a common practice for ex-cooperative CEOs or executives to be elected to Parliament (Zamagni and Felice 2006; Cafaro 2008). In 2014, Legacoop's President, Giuliano Poletti, became Minister for Labor and Social Policies in the Renzi Government (February 2014 to December 2016). This was the first time that a President of a Central Association was appointed as a minister.

The cooperative sector's influence extended to all spheres of public policy. The first success was gaining access to public works in 1899. After 1945, it successfully influenced cooperative legislation (including the Constitution) so that it reflected the economic and social needs of cooperatives. It successfully lobbied for the establishment of Cooperbanca, the cooperative branch of the Banca Nazionale del Lavoro, to access unused land to form agricultural cooperatives and to bid for public works in infrastructure, schools and housing to meet baby-boom demands. It influenced planning laws to facilitate the expansion of cooperative supermarkets in the 1970s (Ammirato 1996). In the 1990s, the cooperative sector lobbied to have social cooperatives formally recognized and became a major player in the provision of welfare services (Marzocchi 2012).

Influencing the State has not been an easy task, nor has the State always been responsive to cooperative needs. A closer look reveals that cooperatives have been most influential when three interrelated factors converged: first, the state is either facing serious challenges or managing an economic crisis; second, Left-wing parties who supported the cooperative sector have gained a greater level of political influence; and, third, the cooperative sector positioned itself for growth and demonstrated a capacity to create employment and to promote public policies to deal with a crisis.

The State supported cooperatives in three key periods. The first period took place during the Giolitti Governments of 1901–14. It provided cooperatives access to public works at a time when the state was facing an economic crisis and the Socialist Party was in ascendancy. The second period was the post-war reconstruction period of 1945–47. The Committee of National Liberation promoted cooperatives because they supported democratic ideals, could contribute to lowering food prices and could create local employment in a time of crisis. The third period commenced from 1971 until 1992. During this time, the State experienced fiscal problems, unemployment and social unrest at a time when the Communist Party's popularity was rising and national solidarity governments were formed. At the same time, the cooperative sector was growing and promoted itself as the third sector of the economy alongside the private and state sectors. The state passed favorable legislation enabling cooperatives to access capital, facilitate WBOs and form holding companies. Even during this favorable phase, however, the State's support did not extend to granting Legacoop any banking or insurance licenses.

The State was hostile to cooperatives during three key periods, which distinguished themselves for their hostility towards Left political parties. The first period took place during Fascist rule between 1922 and 1943. A dictatorship was established, and cooperatives were either destroyed or placed under the control of the authorities. Only 11,600 cooperatives survived fascism, compared to the 20,000 that were operating in 1921 (Nejrotti 1986). The second period took place between the 1950s and 1960s. At this time, the economy was growing, centrist parties won the 1948 election, the Cold War era had set in and there was hostility toward Left parties. Cooperatives were generally small and were not as competitive as the private sector, which was booming. No major laws or public policy initiatives were passed during this period. These were the years of the 'economic miracle,' and there was little unemployment. The Scelba government (February 1954 to July 1955) intimidated Legacoop cooperatives by conducting unwarranted cooperative inspections (Castronovo 1987).

The third phase of hostility commenced in 1992, the year when the Tangentopoli investigations into political corruptions changed the political landscape. All previous major political parties transformed into other political parties and lost influence to a resurgent Liberal/Nationalist coalition led by Silvio Berlusconi. During this period, the State updated the Civil Code that permitted cooperatives to demutualize. The State also reduced tax concessions on profits and removed tax incentives for members' loans. Even though center-left governments have alternated in power with the center-right governments, the cooperative sector had by this time declared their political autonomy and had not regained its political influence, despite having Legacoop's ex-President as a government minister.[6]

3.4 Legacoop's System of Authority Up to 1992

Legacoop's system of authority enabled it to promote a vision for change and to persuade cooperatives to embrace it. This was possible because there were strong alignments and cohesion between political parties of the Left, but predominantly the Communist Party, Legacoop leaders, cooperative executives and cooperative members. This led to the development of a vision of the role cooperatives could perform in society, a strategy of alliances and the promotion of large cooperatives, financial structures and new sectors that we will discuss in the next section. What is important to understand is that the system of authority was one that enabled Legacoop to direct and coordinate the activities of its members, almost as if it were a holding company, but it did so without any ownership control through developing a common vision, common culture and interlocking directorships (Zan 1982; Ammirato 1996).

Legacoop's vision of the role of cooperatives in society was aligned with that of the political Left. In fact, after 1948, leadership positions were allocated along party lines with the Communists, who had the most members, receiving over 50 percent of the posts. The remaining positions would go to the Socialists and the Republicans. They saw cooperatives as enterprises that would contribute to democracy and socialism. When, in the 1960s, the Communists developed the strategy of an anti-monopoly alliance between workers, artisans and cooperatives, Legacoop fully supported it by promoting large cooperatives, national consortia and organizing cooperatives of retailers. In 1978, Legacoop saw the cooperative sector as the third sector of the economy and developed a national strategy of employment, expansion into southern Italy and dealing with the housing sector and youth unemployment problems (Fabbri 2011).

The national and local leaders who headed the national, local and territorial structures and consortia had political legitimacy and authority within society and within cooperatives as a result of their association with the parties that led the resistance movement. Many of these leaders and managers had participated in the resistance movement and, later, were supported by younger leaders who had been involved in political movements in the 1960s (Battilani and Zamagni 2011). Together they had good leadership skills, enjoyed people's trust and had common values, and this facilitated consensus building. This alignment of ideology, party membership and political experiences built consensus and facilitated the decision-making process.

The decision-making process was further facilitated by what Stefano Zan described as "a system of interlocking directorships" (Zan 1982) that coordinated decision-making within Legacoop. This was formed as some leaders were board members of a number of key decision-making bodies, such as the Central Association, the national sectoral associations, consortia and major cooperatives. So when a decision was taken by the Central Association, this interlocking directorship system model made sure that it would be consistently carried out throughout the organization's structures. These, in turn, made sure cooperatives would promote the same policies. This was not difficult, since there was also strong alignment between members, management and political parties. These factors ensured that Legacoop's strategic decisions were accepted and implemented (Zan 1982; Ammirato 1996).

The level of cohesiveness was further enhanced by the fact that Legacoop was able to provide executives with various career paths that further enhanced organizational cohesion. Executives could work in many places, commencing with the local federation and moving to the regional and then national structures. Equally, executives could find a path within a cooperative or a consortium and, later, within the national sectoral association. They could also find a role in a financial consortia, a financial company, a political party or a trade union (Viviani 2017).[7] This practice allowed executives who worked in different areas of the organizations to create linkages with other leaders, understand how the whole organization worked and view the organization holistically and strategically when making decisions. It also built cohesion within the leadership group and facilitated the decision-making process as well as succession planning, with people transferred from one position to another.

In addition to political cohesiveness, the interlocking directorship model and career opportunities, Legacoop leaders were able to provide leadership on how to achieve cooperative growth. It was Legacoop that promoted cooperative growth via the development of both large cooperatives and new cooperative sectors such as retail or financial services. These policies, which we will explore in the next section, were fully aligned with the strategy of creating an anti-monopoly alliance between small and medium-sized businesses that had matured in 1962 (Castronovo 1987).[8] Thus, the strategy for growth of the cooperative sector came mainly from a political vision rather than a business school.

3.5 Promoting Large Cooperatives, Economic Development and Crisis Management

All Central Associations in Italy have promoted the formation of new cooperatives and cooperative growth. All Central Associations promoted the development of consortia in agriculture, construction or social services to help small and medium-sized cooperatives compete in the market by reducing the cost of raw materials, providing access to machinery at low cost, bidding for public works or providing a wider range of services. All Central Associations provide financial and non-financial services.

Legacoop's journey provides a good understanding of the role that a Central Association can perform in promoting cooperative growth. Legacoop's alignment with the long-term strategies noted in the previous section led to its promotion of unique strategies. These include the development of large cooperatives (rather than small cooperatives), national consortia (rather than local ones), retail cooperatives supporting privately owned retailers (rather than only focusing on consumer cooperatives), financial structures in support of the whole cooperative sector and an organizational culture that rescued cooperatives in financial difficulties.

3.6 Developing Large Cooperatives

Legacoop has consistently promoted large cooperatives. During the post-war period, the Bologna Federation suggested that one cooperative for each area was to be formed rather than many small ones competing against one another (Viviani 2015). However, the process of developing large cooperatives took off from the 1960s and has continued to this day. Large cooperatives have been created through a process of organic growth, mergers with other cooperatives and via the acquisition of private enterprises. These larger cooperatives are better equipped to achieve economies of scale, diversify their activities, withstand economic downturns and internationalize their activities. This meant that retail cooperatives would open supermarkets and commercial centers rather than having a small shop. It also meant that manufacturing cooperatives would internationalize; construction cooperatives would build highways, tunnels and rail networks rather than local roads and apartments; and general maintenance cooperatives would be able to provide all the services needed by hospitals rather than just cleaning services. This strategy was successfully implemented and, by 1989, the largest 394 cooperatives (out of 12,889 cooperatives) were producing 54 percent of Legacoop's total turnover (Petralia 1988). In 2003, 98 cooperatives produced 68 percent of Legacoop's total turnover (Zamagni and Felice 2006).

3.7 National Consortia

Consortia have been formed since the 1880s and have been promoted by all Central Associations. Indeed, Confcooperative's initial policy of promoting small cooperatives led it to make consortia formation a key part of its economic strategy, as they were seen as the best way to keep cooperatives small while improving their market competitiveness. Legacoop has promoted the formation of consortia in all sectors of the economy, but the majority of consortia (and the largest) have been formed in the consumer, retail, agriculture, construction and, more recently, service sectors. Consortia provide common structures that enable cooperatives to conduct a variety of activities. Wholesale activities are prominent in the consumer and retail sectors. The common bidding for public contracts is prominent for construction cooperatives. The common marketing of activities is prominent in the retail and consumer sectors. The manufacturing and marketing of dairy products is a key feature in the agricultural sector. These consortia enable cooperatives to compete in the market by achieving economies of scale and enabling cooperatives to do what they could not do on their own. Over time, national consortia were created by merging provincial consortia, leading to the formation of Coop Italia servicing the consumer cooperatives, the Consorzio Nazionale Servizi servicing predominantly the service sector or the Consorzio Cooperative Construzioni (now renamed Integra) servicing the construction sector. The national consortia were able to operate and assist the cooperative sector on a national scale, achieve economies of scale and increase their bargaining power versus national suppliers and the market. They also provided a platform for large and small cooperatives to exchange knowledge and skills and to allow large cooperatives to expand into the national market. Legacoop had established 87 consortia by 1980 and 282 by 2013 (Zamagni and Felice 2006).

3.8 Conad: The Retail Cooperatives

A key decision that led to growth in the cooperative sector and diversification was the decision to establish retail cooperatives and later consortia that would coordinate the buying power and sales of privately owned retailers. These were shopkeepers who managed the local delicatessen or local butcher, some of whom were ex-farmers or migrants returning home. Another group comprised ex-managers of consumer cooperatives.[9] This policy was part of the broader strategy of creating an anti-monopoly alliance between working people and middle classes delineated in 1962. The key obstacle was the fact that Legacoop had already set up consumer cooperatives to serve consumers who did not support retailers who were, in fact, their competitors.

In fact, retailers were seen as those middle-persons who raised food prices and created inflation. Despite this adverse reaction, Legacoop's leadership convinced the consumer cooperatives and their members that retailers were now their allies and should be supported. Cooperatives, they argued, would enable retailers to modernize their outlets, protect them from large retailers and allow them to provide cheaper products. Once Legacoop leadership approved the establishment of the Cooperative National Retailers Association, it allocated staff from the consumer cooperative sector to help establish the retail consortium Conad. Coop Italia (the national consortium for consumer cooperatives) also became the supplier of goods for Conad members (Viviani and Dessi 2005). When Conad was set up in 1962, its role was "to defend themselves from the large capitalist producing companies and to improve the retail outlets in the interest of consumers" (Gombi 1990). The remarkable story here is that Legacoop leadership had successfully convinced the consumer sector to help establish a rival retail organization in the interest of the whole of the cooperative sector and Italian consumers. Conad today is quite successful, and it holds 12 percent of the national retail market and 20 percent of supermarket sales (Conad 2016).

3.9 Financial Structures

Legacoop leadership was also instrumental in developing Legacoop financial strategy and structures. More detail on the development of Legacoop's financial structures will be provided in Chapter 4. What follows is a brief discussion of how it established the financial consortia Fincooper and the insurance company Unipol to meet the movement's financial needs (Ammirato 1996; Zamagni and Felice 2006).

Fincooper was established in 1969 by 200 cooperatives. By 1990 it could count on 2,011 cooperative members and investors. Fincooper's principal role was to act as a vehicle through which the cooperative sector could maximize the use of their capital. It did this by providing better rates of return on their investment; facilitating access to bank loans at a lower interest rate; and providing financial services, including international transactions, bill paying facilities and investment advice. Most importantly, Fincooper invested in strategically important companies such as Banec (the cooperative bank), Finec (the cooperative merchant bank) and Unipol Insurance (Lega Nazionale delle Cooperative e Mutue 1990; Viviani 2013).

Legacoop established the Unipol Insurance Company in 1962 when 195 cooperatives, all but two from Emilia Romagna, raised 30 million euros and bought the insurance license from the Lancia.[10] The first years were difficult, and Unipol was only the 26th largest insurance company in Italy by early 1970. Unipol's success came following the development of its strategy to become the insurance company of working people and not only cooperatives. This paved the way for establishing new alliances, attracting finance and achieving economic growth. Unipol established commercial relations with an Austrian-based insurance company owned by the Russian cooperative sector and, most importantly, with the German trade union insurance group Volksfürsoge which became a major shareholder, acquiring 33 percent of its capital. The policy of alliances continued, and in 1972 the three Italian trade union confederations became shareholders. In 1974 the confederations of artisans, agricultural workers and retailers became shareholders, as did a number of local Italian banks and two mutual societies from France and Belgium in the 1990s (Macif and Provoyance Sociale). Unipol became very influential because, in addition to providing insurance and banking products, it funded cooperatives in crisis, funded the expansion of consumer cooperatives by building and owning their warehouses and commercial centers and owned real estate that housed cooperative and trade union offices (Zamagni 2016). Unipol Group has grown to become the second largest insurance group in Italy through the provision of insurance products for working people and the cooperative sector (Unipol Gruppo 2016).

It is important to emphasize that the decisions to establish Fincooper and Unipol came from the leadership team. Leaders were able to promote a vision and a course of action with support from the larger cooperatives from all sectors. It is also important to emphasize the innovative Unipol strategy based on alliances that resembles that of a political party rather than one devised at a business school.

3.10   Rescue Operations

Legacoop has also been able to coordinate the activities of its members to help rescue cooperatives in financial difficulties. A key example was the rescue operation performed in the mid-1970s on behalf of the consumer sectors from regions of Lombardy, Piedmont, Liguria and Marche-Romagna. They all faced financial difficulties for different reasons: too slow to modernize; financial losses; overspending in establishing new supermarkets; and, in the case of Lombardy, it was operating in a competitive market and was not well managed. Initially, the consumer cooperative sector had decided not to support those cooperatives. Informally, however, some agreed to save only those cooperatives that had a chance of success (Barberini 2009). Knowing that the failure of these large regional consumer cooperatives would have led to reputational damage for the whole sector and would have undermined the goal of becoming a national consumer movement, Legacoop's leadership persuaded consumer cooperatives to rescue all other cooperatives that were having difficulties. The debate was tense and compromises were made, but in the end, all cooperatives were rescued. The plan included Unipol Insurance together with cooperatives from Emilia Romagna to buy their assets to reduce debts. Coop Italia, the national consortium, was required to sell some of its assets and use its liquidity to provide loans. A decision was also made to transfer executives from Coop Italia and other well-managed consumer cooperatives to manage those cooperatives in difficulty. The consumer cooperatives from Emilia-Romagna funded a review of their operations, and its final recommendations, which included rigorous strategic plans, were subsequently implemented (Zamagni, Battilani and Casali 2004).

This example demonstrates the capacity of the leadership team to bring together large consumer cooperatives, Coop Italia and Unipol, to operate for the common good and the needs of the cooperative movement. These consumer cooperatives became profitable within a few years and are successfully operating today, having given the consumer sector a national dimension.

3.11 Toward a Unitary Movement

A defining feature of the Italian cooperative movement has been its pluralist nature, with cooperative movements affiliated to the Left (Red cooperatives), the Catholics (White cooperatives) and Republicans (Green cooperatives). This has enabled the movement to attract a wide range of people from all social classes. It has also led to distinctive features: the Red cooperatives excelled in establishing consumer, manufacturing and construction cooperatives, while the White have been prominent in agriculture and banking. The Red have always favored larger cooperatives, while the White, for most of their time, have privileged small to medium cooperatives. This has led to very different business models, as the chapter on entrepreneurship will show when comparing the Consorzio Gino Mattarelli and Cadiai, both exemplary experiences in the provision of social services.

The three major Central Associations have commenced a process that should lead to a unified movement. In 2011, they formed Alleanza delle Cooperative Italiane (Alleanza hereafter) for the purpose of organizing the transition. The divisions that led to initial splits from Legacoop are no longer in existence. For instance, the differences regarding having a class-based concept of the cooperative movement versus an inter-classist model favored by the Catholics, and the divisions caused by the Cold War and the respective political affiliation to the Italian Communist Party and the Christian Democratic Party, are no longer an issue. So the move toward unity seems a logical one and, in fact, at the economic level, the three

Central Associations have been working together for quite some time. Evidence of this includes:

- The joint signing of collective industrial relations agreements with the trade union confederations in the 1990s that apply to all of their members.
- Managing, along with the three major trade union confederations, the Cooperazione Finanza Impresa consortium, which funds WBOs and Fon.Coop, a training agency for cooperative workers.
- Establishing one national credit consortia, Cooperfidi Italia, out of nine small ones as well as health funds and health and safety companies (Alleanza delle Cooperative Italiane 2017).
- Allowing cooperatives to join more than one Central Association; jointly funding new cooperatives; jointly funding university courses and encouraging all consumer and retail cooperatives to purchase products through Legacoop's Coop Italia.

The potential for achieving economies of scale and synergies is enormous. Synergies could take place in every sector, leading to the formation of larger cooperatives. Service integration could lead to more qualified and professional service centers all over Italy. The synergies between banking and insurance offer much potential. The inter-sectoral cooperation between key sectors such as consumer-agriculture-transport-service cooperatives is one of many areas where growth could take place. The three cooperative development funds, if merged, could perform a very strategic role.

At the time of writing, the three organizations have not yet merged. The Alleanza has established sectoral committees and territorial committees, which include members of all three organizations, to discuss how further integration and mergers should take place. However, what is missing is a shared vision for the cooperative movement and a long-term political project. Chapter 10 on cooperative identity will elaborate further.

3.12 Concluding Remarks

The Central Associations have contributed to the growth of the Italian cooperative movement through many interrelated activities. The key activities can be summarized as follows:

- The Central Associations have come from different political persuasions, which have enabled them to influence the state, develop unique cooperative models and promote cooperatives on a national scale.
- They have provided the basis for a networked organization that offers a series of services and support structures; these help cooperatives throughout their lifecycle by providing management skills (via the provision of services and consortia) and finance (via their financial

support structures), which are needed to start, consolidate and grow cooperatives.

- The Central Associations bring together cooperatives from all sectors of the economy, facilitating inter-sectoral trade and enhancing the capacity of the cooperative sector to perform a prominent role in the national economy.
- Legacoop has managed to promote entirely new sectors, such as retail cooperatives and financial structures, which have enabled the cooperative sector to grow and diversify.
- The links to political parties influenced Legacoop's strategies, which led to the formation of large cooperatives, the retail sector and also Unipol's unique business strategy. Alignment with the Catholic Social Doctrine influenced Confcooperative's strategy to establish cooperative banks and agricultural cooperatives supported by consortia.
- The Central Associations' cohesiveness, along with support from their financial structures, allows them to perform rescue operations of cooperatives that are experiencing difficulties, as the case of consumer cooperatives has demonstrated.

The three Central Associations displayed a willingness to cooperate and find common ground even though they held different beliefs, visions of society and supported different political parties. This manifested itself not only in influencing the State to pass appropriate legislation but also in co-managing important financial consortia and other companies that benefited the whole cooperative sector.

The case study on Legacoop provided in this chapter demonstrated how vital its system of authority has been in setting a long-term strategy and in its implementation via a system of interlocking directorships, political appointees, cohesive ideology and cooperative business culture. These features have been weakening since the early 1980s, and by 1992 were no longer present. Large cooperative enterprises began to have more say, and they have been reducing the role of Legacoop to that of a traditional business association that no longer has the capacity it once had to coordinate its members' activities. This certainly has weakened what had been regarded as the leading Central Association of the cooperative sector.

The three Central Associations are now in the process of merging and have declared their political neutrality. This provides many opportunities for synergies, inter-sectoral trade, mergers and acquisitions, exchange of technology and know-how, better communication strategies and sectoral consolidation. However, they have distanced themselves from the political process, there is less cohesiveness between the leaders, management and cooperative members, and they have not yet defined a clear project or long-term goal that links the role of the state, the economy and society into a vision for the future. Chapter 10, on identity, will continue the discussion on the need to develop a long-term project. The next few chapters explore in more detail the financial structures, the consortia system, the rise of cooperative groups and the way new sectors have been created. The information and analysis that follows provides a better understanding of the relationship between the Central Associations and their members.

Notes

1. Please refer to Chapter 1, endnote 1, for an explanation on the reasons that the number of registered cooperatives is higher than the active cooperatives.
2. Please refer to the Introduction for the reason why Legacoop has been selected as a case study to complement the broader discussion.
3. Confcooperative has a national presence. The national congress appoints a CEO, an executive, the audit committee and the oversight body. It has 22 regional bodies, 37 provincial bodies and 11 interprovincial bodies. It operates nine sectoral associations: agriculture, housing, health, banking, consumer, fishing, culture/tourism, services and welfare (Confcooperative 2017).
4. In 1992, following a series of judicial investigations, the post-1945 political order collapsed. The Christian Democratic Party, which had ruled since 1945 in centrist and center-left coalitions, ceased to exist. The Socialist Party also disbanded. The Communists had changed course a few years before. In this context, Berlusconi led a center-right coalition into office. It was dubbed the Second Republic.
5. Chapter 4 discusses the cooperative sector's financial structures.
6. For instance, the center-left Renzi Government in 2016 announced a reform package for the cooperative banks without consulting the cooperative sector (Cooperazione Trentina 2016).
7. For instance, the highly competent and successful head of Unipol Group, Pierluigi Stefanini, headed the local Communist Party, Legacoop Bologna and the consumer cooperative Coop Adriatica, and now chairs the Unipol Group (Stefanini 2008).
8. The Italian Communist Party developed the policy of creating an anti-monopoly alliance between cooperatives, working people and small business.
9. Consumer cooperatives used to hire managers to run their stores. In the 1960s, they started to manage their own shops or supermarkets directly, and this led many of these store managers to open their own retail outlets and join Conad.
10. The Lancia automobile company was granted an insurance license that they never activated and subsequently sold its license to Legacoop, which led to the birth of Unipol.

References

Alleanza delle Cooperative Italiane. 2017. *L'Associazione*. 16 February. Accessed February 16, 2017. www.alleanzacooperative.it/l-associazione. Accessed October 24, 2017. www.alleanzacooperative.it/l-associazione.

Ammirato, Piero. 1996. *La Lega: The Making of a Successful Network of Cooperative Enterprises*. Aldershot: Dartmouth Publishing Company Limited.

Barberini, Ivano. 2009. *Come Vola il Calabrone*. Milano: Baldini Castoldi Calai Editore.

Battilani, Patrizia, and Vera Zamagni. 2011. *The Managerial Transformation of Italian Co-operative Enterprises 1946–2010*. Working Paper, Bologna: University of Bologna.

Cafaro, Pietro. 2008. *Una Cosa Sola*. Bologna: Il Mulino.

Castronovo, Valerio. 1987. "Dal Dopoguerra ad Oggi." In *Storia del Movimento Cooperativo in Italia, 1886–1986*, edited by Renato Zangheri, Giuseppe Galasso and Valerio Castonovo, 497–848. Turin: Giulio Einaudi Editore.

Conad. 2016. *Conad News*. 15 December. Accessed February 2, 2017. www.conad. it/conad/home/global/chi-siamo/news/2016/15-12-2016-conad-cresce-a-12-5-mil iardi-e-investe-785-milioni-nello-sviluppo.html.

Confcooperative. 2017. *Statuto della Confederazione Cooperative Italiane*. Confcooperative Website. Accessed February 13, 2018. http://www.confcooperative.it/ Portals/0/FileAssociazione/STATUTO-CONFCOOPERATIVE.pdf

Cooperazione Trentina. 2016. "Riforma BCC." *Cooperazione Trentina*, March: 4–11.

Earle, John. 1986. *The Italian Cooperative Movement: A Portrait of La Lega Nazionale delle Cooperative e Mutue*. London: Allen and Unwin.

Fabbri, Fabio. 2011. *L'Italia Cooperativa: Centocinquant'anni di Storia e di Memoria. 1861–2011*. Rome: Ediesse.

Galasso, Giuseppe. 1986. "Gli Anni della Grande Espansione e Crisis del Sistema." In *Storia del Movimento Cooperativo Italiano*, edited by Renato Zangheri, Giuseppe Galasso and Valerio Castronovo, 219–498. Torino: Giulio Einaudi Editore.

Gombi, Mario. 1990. "Cooperazione tra Dettaglianti: La Storia di un Successo." In *Emilia-Romagna Terra di Cooperazione*, edited by Angelo Varni, 252–254. Bologna: Edizioni Tecniche Associate.

Lanzalaco, Luca. 2007. "Business Interest Associations." In *The Oxford Handbook of Business History*, edited by Geoffrey Jones and Jonathan Zeitlin, 293–318. Oxford: Oxford University Press.

Legacoop. 2012. *La Governance di Legacoop*. Legacoop website. Accessed February 13, 2018. http://www.legacoop.coop/associazione2/wp-content/uploads/sites/ 7/2015/03/Governance.pdf.

———. 2014. *Statuto Legacoop Nazionale*. Rome, 18 December. Accessed February 18, 2017. www.legacoop.coop/associazione2/wp-content/uploads/sites/7/2015/03/ Statuto.pdf.

Legacoop Toscana. 2013. *Statuto della Lega Regionale Toscana Cooperative e Mutue*. Legacoop Toscana website. February 13, 2018. http://www.legacoopto scana.coop/wp-content/uploads/2017/04/F-Statuto-2017-LEGA-TOSCANA.pdf.

Lega Nazionale delle Cooperative e Mutue. 1990. *Il Sistema Finanziario della Lega delle Cooperative*. Bologna: Lega Nazionale delle Cooperative e Mutue.

Marzocchi, Franco. 2012. *A Brief History of Social Cooperation in Italy*. Forli: Aiccon.

Nejrotti, Mariella. 1986. "La Lunga Notte Fascista." *La Cooperazione*, October: 181–188.

Petralia, Rino. 1988. *Movimento Cooperativo: Prospettive e Problemi*. Rome: Lega Nazionale Cooperative e Mutue.

Stefanini, Pierluigi. 2008. *Le Sfide della Cooperazione*. Roma: Donzelli Editore.

Unipol Gruppo. 2016. *Presenti per Disegnare il Futuro*. Press Kit, Bologna: Unipol Gruppo.

Viviani, Mario. 2013. *Piccola Guida alla Cooperazione*. Soveria Mannelli: Rubbettino.

———. 2015. *Ricostruzione: La Lega delle Cooperative di Bologna (1945–1948)*. Bologna: CLUEB.

———. 2017. *Cinzio Zambelli*. Bologna: Centro Italiano di Documentazione sulla Cooperazione e l'Economia Sociale.

————, and Roberto Dessi. 2005. *Conad: prudenti capitani e bravi commercianti.* Bologna: Il Mulino.

Zamagni, Vera. 2016. *Come si è affermata la grande impresa cooperativa in Italia. Il ruolo strategico di Enea Mazzoli.* Bologna: Il Mulino.

————, Patrizia Battilani, and Antonio Casali. 2004. *La Cooperazione di Consumo in Italia.* Bologna: Il Mulino.

————, and Emanuele Felice. 2006. *Oltre il Secolo: la trasformazione del sistema cooperativo Legacoop alla fine del secondo millennio.* Bologna: Il Mulino.

Zan, Stefano. 1982. *La Cooperazione in Italia.* Bari: De Donato Editore.

Zangheri, Renato, Giuseppe Galasso, and Valerio Castronovo. 1987. *Storia del Movimento Cooperativo in Italia 1886–1986.* Torino: Giulio Einaudi Editore.

4 Financing Cooperatives
Members, Markets and Networks

Access to finance has historically been a key barrier to cooperative development and growth. Barriers may be caused by members having little capital to invest, lack of collateral to access bank loans, lower profits or lack of access to risk capital from external shareholders. The need for finance, however, varies according to a cooperative's characteristics, its place in the economy, its size and whether it operates in the local or international economy. Finance is less of an issue for small social cooperatives providing welfare services because their competitive advantage is human capital and most do not need external capital to finance their operations (European Commission 2014). Similarly, cooperative banks and consumer cooperatives, as a result of their large membership or customer base, can access a significant portion of their financial requirements from their members. Worker cooperatives in the manufacturing or construction industry, especially the large cooperatives that operate in the world market, require more external capital since members' capital and retained profits are not sufficient.

This chapter analyzes how the Italian cooperative sector is meeting the financial needs of cooperatives. The first section of this chapter explains the various methods used by cooperatives to raise finance. The second section examines how the State has supported cooperatives and the limitations of its actions. The third section discusses the financial frameworks developed by three Central Associations, including an in-depth analysis of Legacoop's financial network. The fourth section discusses the role performed by two financial consortia that service the whole of the cooperative sector, while the fifth section discusses the role of popular banks. The sixth section will summarize the key findings.

4.1 Cooperative Access to Finance

Cooperatives have historically accessed capital through a variety of means. As cooperatives have grown and expanded their markets, they have sought money from more sources, including the financial markets. The period up to 1983 saw cooperatives raise capital internally or via bank loans. After 1983, but especially after 1992, cooperatives have also sought external capital to raise funds. All cooperatives can now raise capital via issuing shares, retained profits, bank and member loans and capital markets or capital partners.

4.1.1 Traditional Means of Raising Finance: 1947–1983

The traditional path by which cooperatives access capital is via member investment through the purchasing of shares in the cooperative. The Basevi Law of 1947 did not encourage this form of investment. It limited the amount that could be invested,[1] and it limited returns to a maximum of 5 percent. It was not surprising, then, that by 1980 the average value of cooperative members' shares did not exceed 430 euros (Midoro 1984). This led to a change in the legislation in 1983 that increased the allowable level of remuneration to 2.5 percent above postal bonds (which provided higher returns in years with high inflation) and also increased the amount that could be invested to what is now 100,000 euros. This has led members to invest more money, varying from 800 to 42,000 euros each, depending on the type of cooperative.[2]

Retained profits are profits not distributed to remunerate shares or pay for worker rebates. Italian cooperatives prioritize long-term stability over short-term gains and, to this end, they have preferred the retention of profits over their distribution in the form of rebates or dividend payouts. The Law of 1977 further encouraged self-financing by declaring all profits deposited in the indivisible reserve fund as tax exempt. This provision lasted until 2004, when the new tax laws declared cooperatives must pay company tax on at least 40 percent of profits for worker cooperatives, 20 percent for agricultural cooperatives and 65 percent for consumer cooperatives. This new provision, however, has not deterred cooperatives from depositing profits in the reserve fund. A study of 361 mid-to-large cooperatives revealed that 88 percent of their profits were deposited into the reserve fund, thus confirming cooperatives' preference for long-term goals (Petrucci 2009).

Cooperatives also access capital through bank loans and members' loans. Between 1945 and the 1960s, cooperatives had difficulties obtaining bank loans because they lacked collateral. In fact, many cooperatives were only granted loans because they were Legacoop members, whom the banks trusted knowing that Legacoop would intervene if loans were not repaid (Viviani 2013). The Catholic-inspired cooperatives associated with Confcooperative found it easier because they could access loans from popular banks and rural banks. Legacoop cooperatives also had more difficulties because they were larger and needed more money than Confcooperative cooperatives, which were usually smaller (Mazzoli 2005). As cooperatives grew in size, assets and reputation, it became easier to get bank loans. For instance, the Cooperativa Muratori e Cementisti CMC has a revolving credit line worth 125 million euros with BNP Paribas and Unicredit. Cooperative start-ups and smaller cooperatives still have difficulties, but cooperative credit guarantee companies have been set up to facilitate access to credit.

Members have been allowed to provide loans to their cooperative in return for regular interest payments since 1971. They can lend up to 67,000 euros. All cooperatives can access member loans but, because of their 8.5 million members, the consumer cooperatives have been the most successful. In consumer cooperatives, loans are like bank deposits: members get a savings account with a cooperative credit card, which can be used to pay for their shopping. For instance, the Consumer Cooperative Coop Alleanza 3.0 has 2.7 million members, of whom 462,000 provided loans totaling 4.4 billion euros. This is a substantial amount that allows members to get a return on their investment and to financially support their cooperative, which receives capital to invest in new supermarkets, warehouses, research and marketing (Coop Adriatica 3.0 2016). The goal is for members to receive an interest rate higher than what they would receive from a bank and for the cooperative to pay less interest compared to loans received from a commercial bank.

4.1.2 Non-Traditional Means 1983–2016

The traditional ways of raising finance were no longer sufficient by the 1980s, especially for larger cooperatives trading or working internationally or engaged in competing with international companies. In support of cooperatives' needs, the legislation was altered in 1983 to allow cooperatives to own private companies and to list companies on the stock exchange. In 1992, cooperatives were also allowed to attract external shareholders.

The 1992 legislation introduced the investor-member, to enable cooperatives to attract external capital. Investor-members can be individuals, private companies and cooperative development funds or cooperative-owned financial companies. External shareholders have voting rights but cannot exceed one-third of the total votes. This provision has enabled cooperatives to attract external capital from cooperative-owned financial companies and cooperative development funds, but it has not attracted many external investors.[3] The fact that the value of external shares is not linked to property rights and that shares are not tradeable is a deterrent for external investors. This led the larger cooperatives to look for other alternatives to accessing finance.

The cooperative sector started to make full use of the 1983 provisions in the 1990s. This manifested in a number of ways. Cooperatives established holding companies that held majority shares in subsidiaries. This allowed them to access part of their capital needs from the market. They also invested in property development and in other strategic companies with private partners that allowed cooperatives to access new work and new markets. The significant cultural shift took place when cooperatives listed their subsidiaries or their majority-owned companies on the stock exchange. This allowed cooperatives to keep control and, at the same time, access capital by selling the remaining shares to private investors. Unipol Insurance Group was listed in 1986, followed by Sacmi-owned companies, Manutencoop Spa and Servizi Italia (two general maintenance cooperatives), and Immobiliare Grande Distribuzione, a listed property trust company majority owned by consumer cooperatives (Viviani 2013). In 2014, CMC took another route to raising capital by becoming the first cooperative in the world to issue international bonds worth 400 million euros tradeable at the Milan and Luxemburg stock exchanges (Cavallari 2017).

4.2 The Role of the State

The State has also supported cooperatives in accessing credit. It has already been noted that tax concessions helped cooperatives build up their indivisible reserves. It also provided cooperatives with bank loans through Cooperbanca, the cooperative branch of the Banca Nazionale Del Lavoro (BNL), and grants and loans through job creation and business development schemes.

The State-owned BNL was set up in 1913, and it was re-established after 1945. The cooperative sector wanted it to be a cooperative bank, but instead, BNL set up Cooperbanca as a specific cooperative branch within BNL. Cooperbanca initially made available 250,000 euros, which was gradually increased to 50 million euros by 1971. The cooperative sector welcomes these funds, but they were less than 1 percent of the total state funds available for investment.[4]

To counter rising unemployment, especially youth unemployment, and de-industrialization, the State promoted job creation schemes, making available grants and loans to businesses, including cooperatives. Key job creation schemes included the following:

- A youth specific job creation scheme was established in 1977. It provided financial support and public works contracts to young people forming cooperatives. It is estimated that from 1977–1979, 1,248 cooperatives were formed under this scheme, creating 16,000 jobs (Thornley 1981).
- The Marcora law program was established in 1986. It managed 125 million euros made available via two funds. The first fund was called Foncooper. It provided loans below market rate to cooperatives that either introduced new technology or restructured. The loans were repayable within eight to ten years. The maximum loans of up to 1 million euros were made available for restructuring and reconversions. Through this scheme, 273 cooperatives received funds from 1987–1991 (De Bertoli 1993).
- The second Marcora Law fund was called 'Special Fund.' It commenced in 1987, and it funded WBOs of private enterprises in crisis. It provided cooperatives with non-repayable grants equivalent to three years' wages, subject to employees investing 2,000 euros. Employees were also excluded from accessing unemployment benefits for three years. The Special Fund provided 86 million euros from 1987–2001 to 157 cooperatives, saving 6,000 jobs (Cooperazione Finanza Impresa 2017a).[5]

- The De Vito Law youth creation program commenced in 1986. It provided start-up capital and low interest loans for any business which mostly employed young people between 19 and 29 years of age. Through this scheme, 110 cooperatives were established (Franci 1992).

Cooperatives have welcomed State support, but it has not met the needs of cooperatives. Indeed, in 1991, the Ministry of Finance revealed that each year businesses and non-business entities received up to 40 billion euros in exemptions and grants, of which only 1.75 percent is attributable to cooperatives. Considering that in 1991 cooperatives employed 4 percent of the national workforce, they received less than their fair share (Chelli 1991).

State support was gradually reduced. Italy's public debt increased from 57 percent of GDP in 1975 to 95 percent in 1989. Globalization meant markets had become more competitive. Italy's strategy of currency devaluation combined with business support as a way to compete in a world market where people, goods, and finance were freer to move beyond national borders was no longer possible post-Maastricht Treaty.[6] This led to a reduction of public spending and privatization of State assets. Privatization commenced in 1992 and was completed by 2006 (Trento 2012; Battilani and Fauri 2014). The BNL bank was privatized in 1992 and publicly listed in 1996. In 2016, public debt rose to 135 percent of GDP (OECD 2017). Cooperatives no longer expected the State to finance their activities.

4.3 Confcooperative and the Trentino Cooperative Federations

All three major Central Associations and the Trentino Cooperative Federation (Trentino Federation) have developed their own financial structures to assist cooperatives. They all have their own cooperative development funds, access to banks or their member banks, finance companies providing risk capital and financial services and insurance companies providing life, health and house insurance. While there are similarities, there are also differences between the model developed by the Trentino Federation and Confcooperative, which have close ties with the Catholic-inspired cooperative banks, and Legacoop's financial network.[7]

4.3.1 Trentino Cooperative Federation

Trento is the capital of the autonomous province of Trento, which has a population of close to 500,000. There are 413 cooperatives employing 13,000 people. They form 1 percent of total firms but provide 8 percent of total employment. They are present in most sectors of the economy, but 40 percent of cooperatives operate in agriculture and 55 percent in financial services. The Trento area is regarded as a cooperative district where agricultural cooperatives control 90 percent of the market, cooperative banks 60 percent and consumer cooperatives 38 percent (OECD 2014).

The Trento area is a well-developed agricultural region, with a strong association with the Catholic Church. Local priests established local banks to provide loans and support for farmers (Wollemborg 2009). This is in line with the Catholic Social Doctrine, which promotes family-owned private property in the hope that it will lead to social stability and a redistribution of wealth (Trezzi 2011).

The Trentino Federation today includes both Catholic and Legacoop cooperatives and is affiliated with Confcooperative. It provides financial and non-financial services to its members. Its key financial companies have been set up since the 1980s. They include:

- Promocoop Trentina, established in 1992 to manage Trentino's cooperative development fund. In 2016, it had invested 23.5 million euros in over 40 cooperatives and consortia. It also receives funding from the Trento provincial government (Cooperazione Trentina 2017).
- Fincoop is a financial company providing risk capital. It is owned by 64 members, including the Trentino Federation, local consortia, cooperatives and the local cooperative banks. It has 12 million euros in capital (Dalpalu' 2015).
- Cooperfidi was set in 1980 to provide credit guarantee.
- Coopersviluppo (1996) is the development arm of the consumer sector. Members include consumer cooperatives, the Trentino Federation, local cooperative banks and Cooperfidi.
- Assicura brokers assist members in accessing insurance products. It is owned by the Trentino Federation, local cooperative banks, local retailers association and the cooperative sector of Friuli Venezia Giulia (OECD 2014).

The Trentino cooperatives sector is led by the Trentino Federation with support from the large provincial consortia and the local cooperative banks. The key investors are the Trentino Federation and the local cooperative bank network, with support from the large consortia and cooperatives. Assicura brokers have attracted investments outside of the cooperative sector and outside of the Trentino area. The cooperative principle of mutuality that is vital to the formation of cooperatives has also been extended to form cooperative-owned companies that service the whole of the Trentino cooperative sector (Ianes 2014; Dorigatti 2014).

4.3.2 Confcooperative

Confcooperative, in line with the Catholic Social Doctrine, has viewed cooperatives as organizations that could help both farmers access credit and sell their produce at a good price and assist working people and the middle class in purchasing their own home or buying cheaper food at consumer cooperatives. This model is not antagonistic to the capitalist system but is one that viewed cooperatives as improving the conditions of farmers and middle classes who were excluded by the capitalist system (Menzani 2007). Confcooperative's model also preferred the formation of small cooperatives. These are viewed as better suited to promoting internal democracy and participation, although this has not stopped the formation of large cooperatives.

This cooperative business model centered on small cooperatives supported by consortia. It allows cooperatives to achieve economies of scale while remaining small and farmers or artisans to withstand the competition of larger businesses. Small, local cooperatives did not need large sums of money and were able to access loans from cooperative banks and the State. The latter, after 1945, made available to the agricultural sector over 50 percent of the available finance. Agricultural cooperatives could also access the services provided by Federconsorzi, a publicly funded organization that supported Catholic cooperatives accessing machinery, fertilizers and raw materials (Castronovo 1987).

The Confederation provides a variety of financial services via a financial network comprising the Banche di Credito Cooperativo (BCCs), Fondosviluppo and Assimoco. More specifically:

- The cooperative development fund, Fondosviluppo, is co-managed with the BCCs. Since 1993, it has provided loans to 123 cooperatives valued at 327 million euros. It provides cooperatives with equity capital and has acted as a guarantor to social cooperatives. It claims that its investments helped create 26,000 jobs (Federcasse 2015).
- The insurance company Assimoco provides auto, business, and professional insurance. It is co-owned by Fondosviluppo, BCCs, Cooperative banks from the province of Bolzano, and a cooperative-owned German insurance company (Gruppo Assimoco 2013).
- Consorzio Gino Mattarella Finance is a small financial consortium with close to 400 members and over 20 million euros in capital and deposits. It mainly supports social cooperatives. In 2016, it provided 16 million euros to 166 cooperatives (CGM Finance 2016).
- The 337 cooperative banks provide loans, financial services or financial products from companies owned by ICCREA, the Istituto Centrale delle Casse Rurali ed Artigiane (Central Institute of Cooperative and Small Business Banks).

4.3.3 The Cooperative Banks

Cooperative banks were formed in 1883 and were then known as rural banks. The regulations required that 80 percent of their members be artisans, farmers or agricultural cooperatives. The 1993 reform transformed BCCs into modern banks by allowing all individuals and businesses residing in the area covered by the bank to become members. Table 4.1 provides further details (Cusa 2009). While this enabled BCCs to grow, they were

Table 4.1 Cooperative Banks' Legislative Requirements

1. A cooperative bank can be formed by 200 members. Each member must hold a minimum share value of 25 euros and a maximum of 100,000 euros (previously 50,000).
2. The cooperative bank members can include individuals and businesses who reside and operate with continuity in the geographic area covered by the bank.
3. The cooperative bank must engage prevalently with members. They must demonstrate:
   a) That at least 50% of bank loans need to be allocated to members
   b) That at least 95% of total loans and other type of investments need to be made to persons/businesses that reside in the territory covered by the bank.
4. Bank surpluses needs to be distributed as follows:
   a) 70% of surplus to be deposited to the banks indivisible reserves
   b) 3% is deposited to the cooperative development funds (Fondosviluppo)
   c) 7% is used for community activities
   d) The remaining funds can be used to pay dividends on members' shares and/or deposited in the reserve fund.

Governance

5. Each member is entitled to one vote.
6. The general assembly elects the Board and the collegio sindacale (review and audit committee). Members must hold at least two-thirds of the votes and elect at least two-thirds of Board members and of the Audit Committee members.
7. The Collegio dei Proibiviri committee reviews disputes between members and the bank.
8. The Bank of Italy oversees banking activities and Federcassa, the cooperative bank's association, reviews cooperative banks' compliance with cooperative principles.

Cooperative Oversight

9. Federcassa assesses compliance with cooperative principles by reviewing the extent to which cooperative banks:
   a) Are effectively trading with members
   b) Are providing a variety of services
   c) Are demonstrating that members are benefiting from trading with the bank (e.g. savings, special packages, dividends, rebates etc.)
   d) Mostly trade with members and not third parties
   e) Have improved their members' moral and cultural standing (financial planning, budgeting, cooperative culture etc.)
   f) Comply with code of ethics and International Cooperative Alliance's seven principles. To this end it has to demonstrate a commitment to cooperative development, inter-cooperative support and community development.

Source: Cusa, Emanuele. 2009. Lo Scopo Mutualistico delle Banche di Credito Cooperativo. Rome: Ecra.

still small compared with international banks, which had increased their presence in Italy from 38 in 1988 to 79 by 2007. In response, larger cooperative banks were created via mergers, and their number was reduced from 726 in 1988 to 337 in 2016 (Carretta and Boscia 2009; Federcasse 2016). They have also strengthened the role of ICCREA, which through its holding company provides financial services and financial products including a central payment system, financial and insurance products, portfolio management, securitization, in-pool operations and factoring and leasing services (ICCREA 2016).

The strategy to create larger cooperative banks allowed the cooperative banks to consolidate and grow. On average, each bank had 11 branches and 80 employees by 2012. Their market share in lending to families and businesses increased from 6 percent at the end of the 1990s to 9 percent for business and 8.5 percent for families by 2016. In Trento and Bolzano the market share is higher (53.6 percent and 40.4 percent respectively) (Catturani and Stefani 2014; Federcasse 2016). Despite this, the Government still deemed them too small and in 2016 conducted a review which led to a major recommendation requiring cooperatives with less than 200 million euros in assets to join a Cooperative Banking Group (CBG) and those with more than 200 million euros to transform into a public company. The CBG is to be 50 percent owned by cooperative members and has oversight over its members' governance arrangements (Cooperazione Trentina 2016).[8]

4.4 Legacoop's Financial Network

Legacoop cooperatives have historically relied on State-owned Cooperbanca or local banks to access loans. It was common for Legacoop or cooperative directors to have to provide collateral in order for cooperatives to access loans. Legacoop did attempt to establish cooperative banks and insurance companies, but the government did not approve its applications except, fortuitously, on one occasion when the Cooperative Bank of Ozzano, then named St. Christopher, was approved by the authorities, not realizing that it was linked to Legacoop (Mazzoli 2005).

From the 1970s onward, a new scenario emerged that required Legacoop to be more proactive. Cooperatives became very competitive and grew in size, with some starting to operate in global markets. Markets were becoming more competitive, and cooperatives needed more capital in order to grow and compete. At the same time, especially following the 1977 Law, cooperatives were accumulating cash reserves. Legacoop saw this as an opportunity to pool their savings and invest them strategically in order to facilitate cooperative growth.

4.4.1 *Legacoop's Initial Financial Strategy: 1969–1992*

Legacoop's initial strategy (1969–1992) centered on Fincooper, its financial consortium, and Unipol, its insurance company. Fincooper was to play a leading and coordinating role. In 1969, 200 Legacoop cooperatives established Fincooper. By 1990, 2011 members had invested 12 million euros in shares and deposited 400 million euros. Fincooper was a consortium and, as such, it accessed the same tax benefits as cooperatives and did not have to make any deposit with the central bank. This gave it a competitive advantage over banks.

Fincooper performed four key functions. First, it distributed funds within the cooperative sector by accepting funds from cooperatives that had cash reserves and lending them to cooperatives who needed a loan. The interest spread was high, so everyone could benefit.[9] In 1986 alone, it funded 440 cooperatives (Bettini 1986). Second, it acted as a guarantor with a number of banks, thus facilitating members' access to credit at a discounted rate (Sacconi 1986). Cooperatives accessed 45 million euros this way (Lega Nazionale delle Cooperative e Mutue 1987). Third, it provided financial services such as bill payment facilities, raising loans on the national and international market and assistance in foreign transactions and investment services (Sintesi del Sistema 1989). Fourth, it invested in strategic areas on behalf of the cooperative sector, including:

- Unipol group of companies (Fincooper owned 32 percent of total shares).
- Banec, the bank for the social economy, was established in 1987 to provide banking services to cooperatives. It was 90 percent controlled by the cooperative sector. Fincooper controlled 27 percent (Il Giornale della Banca 1990).
- Finec, a merchant bank established in 1987 to provide advice on investment, mergers and acquisitions, market analysis and restructuring. Legacoop companies owned 70 percent (Fincooper owned 33 percent). A State-owned bank, IMI, owned 30 percent (Collina 1988).
- The investment in 41 companies including leasing, factoring, real-estate and management companies (La Lega Nazionale delle Cooperative e Mutue 1990).

The most strategic investment was in the Unipol Insurance Group. It was formed in 1962 when 230 cooperatives bought an insurance license from the Lancia family. It commenced selling car insurance but soon developed other products to meet the needs of cooperatives that needed loans, leasing and factoring services and the needs of consumers who sought life and health insurance. Investments were also made in real estate and tourism. Unipol grew as a result of a successful strategy directed at working people and small businesses. It marketed itself as the insurance company for the world of labor. As a result, in 1973 it was able to attract the interest of the German trade union insurance group Volksfürsorge, which bought 30 percent of its shares. The three Italian trade union confederations and three national small business associations also joined, two of which were members of the Confcooperative (Zamagni 2015).

Unipol performed a significant role in the cooperative movement and the insurance market. It provided the market with a broader range of products that were more suitable for consumers. It reduced the cost of car insurance by an average of 11 percent. Cooperatives benefited from Unipol through lower insurance costs and by receiving dividend payments. They also benefited from Unipol's investments in real estate, warehouses, commercial centers, offices and assets previously owned by the cooperative sector and the trade union movement. Unipol's ex-vice president, Enea Mazzoli, noted that up until 1986, the majority of the 35 percent of investments that the law allowed to be spent on real estate were spent in the cooperative sector. In some cases, Unipol bought assets from cooperatives so they could repay their debts. In return, Unipol required cooperatives to invest 25 percent of the total investment in Unipol shares (Zamagni 2015). In the case of consumer cooperatives, having Unipol build and own new warehouses or new supermarkets created opportunities for expansion (Sacconi 1986). The business model suited all stakeholders.

Unipol's path to growth was organic and took place via acquisitions. To achieve growth via acquisitions, it needed external capital, and ultimately it went to the market to access capital. In 1986 it listed preferential shares and in 1990 ordinary shares on the stock market. By 1990, Unipol had become the sixth largest insurance company in Italy, with a market share of 3.6 percent (Varni 1990). It employed 1,300 staff directly and another 1,800 via agencies (Degli Esposti 1989).

Fincooper, Unipol, Banec and Finec were the backbone of Legacoop's financial strategy. In addition to these four key financial players, however, Legacoop could also count on dozens of cooperative-owned local financial companies (servicing one geographic area) and specialized financial companies servicing key sectors of the economy such as agriculture or retail or fishing. It also could count on 30 friendly local banks. Local financial companies serviced smaller rather than larger cooperatives. Some promoted new cooperatives, but most focused on providing loans and bridging finance and bank guarantees as well as on conducting market analysis, feasibility studies and investment analysis (Cuccurullo and Jacobelli 1988; La Lega Nazionale delle Cooperative e Mutue 1990).

This initial phase lasted until 1992, when a number of events and developments led to changes to Legacoop's financial network. Coopfond, the cooperative development fund, began operating in 1992, and as deposits grew so too did its role. Fincooper began to lose influence because Coopfond was now able to provide cooperatives with loans and investments. Also, interest margins were lower, and Fincooper began to have difficulties pleasing both depositors and borrowers. In 1999, Fincooper merged with the financial consortium Consorzio Cooperativo Finanziario per lo Sviluppo (CCFS). Unipol was now a listed company with external shareholders, and this placed constraints on activities directly supporting the cooperative sector (Viviani 2016; Zamagni 2015; Viviani 2013).

4.4.2 *Legacoop's Current Financial Strategy 1992–2017*

In the 1990s, Legacoop's financial network was restructured and consolidated. Its major financial players are Unipol Group, CCFS and Coopfond, supported by specialized companies such as Cooperare and Cooperfactor and a number of local financial companies. As shown in Figure 4.1,[10] it includes:

- Unipol Group in 1996 incorporated Banec and Finec, renaming them Unipol Banca and Unipol Merchant. It provides banking and insurance products for cooperatives, SMEs and families.
- CCFS is the national consortium supporting small and medium-sized cooperatives.
- Cooperare, mostly owned by Coopfond, invests in large cooperatives.
- Cooperfactor is a factoring company supporting cooperatives with cash flow problems.
- Local cooperative-owned financial companies invest in Legacoop financial companies, cooperatives and the local community.

4.4.3 Unipol Group

The Unipol Group has become the second largest insurance group in Italy through organic growth and acquisitions. Legacoop cooperatives control the majority of Unipol Group shares through their holding company, Finsoe.[11] It provides banking services and life, car, health, fire, house and travel insurance. It also owns substantial real estate, business hotels, tourist resorts and agricultural lands and supports Libera cooperatives (Unipol Gruppo 2016).[12] The consumer cooperatives are the major investors in Unipol whose insurance policies are sold to their 8 million members. Unipol also supports cultural activities organized by bookshops owned by the consumer sector.

The Unipol Group provides banking and investment banking services through Unipol Banca. Unipol Banca provides business and retail banking services. Its subsidiary, Unipol Merchant, provides long-term investment and investment advice on mergers and acquisition to the cooperative and private sectors (Unipol Banca 2014). A key involvement in support of the cooperative sector came in 1996 when Unipol Group invested 265 million euros to save and restructure 31 cooperatives (Zamagni and Felice 2006). As of December 2015, Unipol is Italy's second largest insurance group, with an income of 16.5 billion euros generating 579 million euros in profits. It employs 14,000 people (Unipol Gruppo 2016).

4.4.4 Consorzio Cooperativo Finanziario Per Lo Sviluppo

The CCFS is a financial consortium. In 2015, it had 1,061 cooperative members, including institutional investors like Coopfond. The board is democratically elected with a weighted voting system that allows investors of 500,000 euros or more to hold five votes. Salary differentials are set at 5:1,

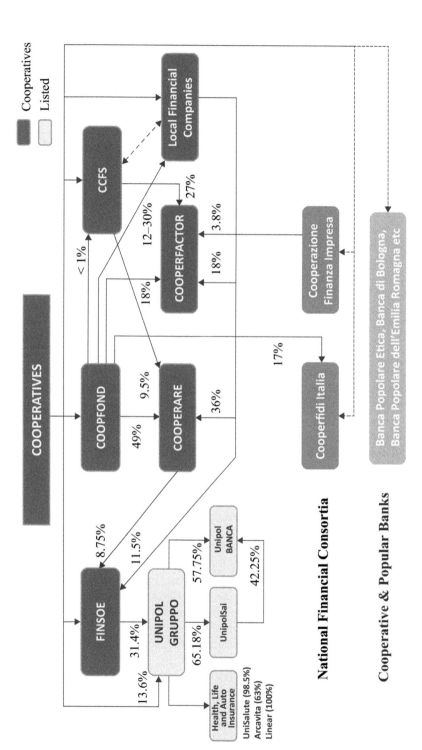

National Financial Consortia

Cooperative & Popular Banks

Figure 4.1 Legacoop Financial Network

emphasizing its egalitarian culture. CCFS provides the following financial services:

- Provision of loans. In 2015, it had provided loans to the value of 630 million euros to 202 cooperatives of which 143 received loans above 2 million euros.
- Guarantor. CCFS acts as a guarantor so that cooperatives can access credit via third parties. In 2015, 57 million euros were used to fund these activities.
- Provision of risk capital. In 2015, CCFS invested five million euros in 35 cooperatives and consortia and 63 million euros in more than 20 financial companies linked to the cooperative sector.
- Facilitates finance from third parties. CCFS enters into agreements with other banks as a loan guarantor or it co-invests in cooperatives with other institutions. It has co-invested in 48 cooperatives with Coopfond, but it has also worked with Unipol Banca, Banca Popolare of Emilia Romagna, Banca Popolare Etica and other local institutions. This approach allowed cooperatives to access an additional 100 million euros.

(CCFS 2015a; CCFS 2015b)

CCFS provides loans and risk capital to small and medium sized cooperatives and social cooperatives. It does this directly or in alliance with cooperative and non-cooperative partners. It is also an investor in strategic national cooperative companies like Cooperfidi Italia, Cooperare Spa and Cooperfactor and local companies that provide services to the local cooperative economy. CCFS investments are aligned with those of Coopfond, which over time has become Legacoop's key financial institution.

4.4.5 Coopfond: Legacoop's Cooperative Development Fund

Coopfond is Legacoop's cooperative development fund. It was established in 1992 and became operational in 1994. Its governance structure includes an executive board, an oversight committee and an audit committee. The Board comprises 17 members who represent all the key sectoral associations. The Legacoop President chairs the Board. The Board provides strategic direction, approves expenditure and develops policies and procedures. The Board appoints an executive director who is responsible for implementing the strategic directions. The strategic directions comply with the Law of 1992, which requires cooperative funds to be used for promotion of new cooperatives, support of existing cooperatives, promotion of innovation and investment in Southern Italy, and investing in companies owned by cooperatives and in educational programs and research activities.[13]

Coopfond resources come mainly from the 3 percent of profits deposited by cooperatives, loan repayments and equity withdrawals. As of 2015, Coopfond has received the cumulative sum of 438.5 million euros. The largest 100 cooperatives contribute up to 80 percent of the total deposits.

The region of Emilia Romagna deposits 56 percent of total deposits, but its cooperatives receive 43 percent of total investments. Further, the consumer and retail sectors contribute 43 percent of total deposits but receive 14 percent. It is clear that there is a redistribution of wealth from the large cooperatives to the small, since Coopfond mainly funds small to medium sized cooperatives; from Emilia Romagna to other regions (mainly the South); and from the consumer and retail sectors to other sectors (Coopfond 2015c; Soldi 2013).

Coopfond supports the growth of the cooperative sector nationally and internationally. The fund's priorities cover all cooperatives and Legacoop's strategic directions. The fund is a rotational fund with a grant component less than million euros per year. It promotes cooperatives that invest in Southern Italy, or that promote social inclusion or innovation. It supports existing cooperatives that develop new business activities and cooperatives experiencing financial difficulties by offering finance to encourage consolidation or restructuring. Coopfond also supports mergers and cooperative networking projects, globalization and international trade. It strategically invests in the cooperative sector's other financial companies (Coopfond 2015a; Coopfond 2015c).

Coopfond has developed rigorous investment policies and procedures to assess and evaluate funding proposals. It provides loans or investments in equity that are to be repaid and remunerated. For each short-to-medium term investment, Coopfond can invest up to 50 percent of the capital invested by cooperative members, but not exceeding 600,000 euros for loans and 750,000 euros for capital investments. Investments in cooperative-owned companies cannot exceed one-third of the total capital. The risk is shared with credit guarantee companies. Strategic investments loans can exceed these limits but must be less than 50 percent of the total capital. Each application will be assessed against a criterion that considers social merit, innovation, job creation, return on capital invested and financial risk (Coopfond 2015c; Laurini and Moreschi 2016).

Coopfond provides short-to-medium term investments and long-term stable-strategic investments. Since 1994 it has invested a total of 473.5 million euros in 760 investment projects involving 600 cooperatives. This included equity investments of 87 million euros, business loans of 286 million euros and other investments. Investments have been directed at new cooperatives and at existing cooperatives that have plans to grow, merge or enter international markets (Bulgarelli and Viviani 2006; Coopfond 2016; Laurini 2016).

Coopfond is investing over 200 million euros in long-term strategic investments. It invests in finance companies of national significance such as CCFS, Cooperfactor or Cooperfidi Italia, the national credit guarantee consortium. It also invests in local finance companies which support local economies, cooperative business networks and Legacoop strategic companies (Coopfond 2015b). Coopfond's biggest investment, however, is with Cooperare which funds large cooperatives that perform a strategic role for the cooperative sector.

4.4.6 Cooperare Spa

Cooperare is a Bologna-based finance company founded in 2008. Lega-coop cooperatives, CCFS and local financial companies own 96 percent of the company, of which Coopfond owns 47 percent. Three local banks own the remaining 4 percent (Cooperare 2015). Its role is to coordinate long-term strategic investments on behalf of Legacoop cooperatives and to provide medium-term loans or equity to large cooperatives and cooperative groups of companies involved in internationalization, innovation, acquisitions and mergers. It invests more than five million euros per project. In 2015, the total investments amounted to 354 million euros, of which 65 million were invested in companies and 288 million in long-term strategic investments. Its most significant long-term investment is with Finsoe, the holding company that controls Unipol Group. Cooperare has invested 203 million euros and holds 8.75 percent of Finsoe's stock (Finsoe 2016). Other key strategic investments have included:

- Unibon, a food processing joint venture between a cooperative and a privately owned company focusing on acquisition and global trade—47 million.
- Granarolo, a dairy company manufacturing and marketing products worldwide—9 million.
- Manutencoop, a national facility management company—20 million.
- Agrienergia, a joint venture with other cooperatives to produce electricity—2.8 million.
- Future SRL, a real estate company owned by cooperatives—3.4 million.
- CMC holding, a company, owned by the CMC construction group to make acquisitions in the United States and Mozambique—10 million.

(Cooperare 2016)

4.4.7 Cooperfactor: Overcoming Cash Flow Problems

Cooperfactor is a national company, the role of which is to provide factoring services to cooperatives dealing with the public sector. This company is wholly owned by cooperatives, consortia and cooperative-owned financial companies. Coopfond and CCFS own 45 percent of its shares. The key role of this company is to make available cash flow to companies that are owed money from public authorities. This improves cash flows and allows cooperatives to operate in the market without incurring debts to pay their staff, expenses and suppliers. Cooperfactor can advance up to 80 percent of the money owed for a fee, which covers administrative costs (Cooperfactor 2017). A survey of 200 cooperatives conducted by Legacoop in 2002 revealed that only 5 percent were paid within 60 to 90 days. This mainly affects social, construction or service cooperatives (Fabbri 2011).

4.4.8 *Local Financial Companies*

Legacoop can also count on six local financial companies owned by the cooperative sector that are mostly based in areas with a high cooperative density, such as Bologna, Florence, Modena and Reggio Emilia. They invest in local cooperatives, in Legacoop strategic financial companies such as Finsoe, Cooperfactor and Cooperare and in important local projects (FIBO of Bologna, for instance, is an investor of the Bologna Exhibition Centre). Coopfond is a major investor, owning between 12–30 percent of their total shares (Coopfond 2015b).

4.4.9 *Summary*

Legacoop's financial network is one centered on Coopfond, CCFS and Unipol Group of Companies, supported by local financial structures and various subsidiaries providing real estate, leasing, factoring and management services. Its key features include:

- Cooperatives from all economic sectors fund Coopfond and invest in CCFS, Cooperare, Cooperfactor, Finsoe and local financial institutions. This form of inter-sectoral cooperation is a unique feature of Legacoop and also the other major cooperative associations.
- Legacoop's financial network is decentralized. There are multiple centers of financial power, including Unipol Group, Coopfond and CCFS. The Legacoop board leads Coopfond, and it can perform a coordinating role in alignment with the Legacoop strategy. There are greater synergies between Coopfond, CCFS and local financial companies through cross-ownership and co-investing in key companies such as Cooperfactor or Cooperare. Unipol provides banking and insurance services with close links to the consumer sector.
- The large cooperatives from consumer, retail, manufacturing and service sectors are the key suppliers of capital. The top 100 cooperatives provide 80 percent of deposits to Coopfond and are the key investors in Finsoe, Unipol's major shareholder. Consumer cooperatives are the major shareholders in the Unipol Group through either Finsoe or direct investments.
- Legacoop's financial network supports cooperatives throughout their lifecycle. This includes support for start-ups and small cooperatives' access to loans; loans and equity for consolidation, growth and restructure; and loans or equity capital for large investments facilitating mergers or internationalization.
- Legacoop's financial companies are working with each other, other cooperative-friendly banks and national consortia to provide loan guarantees, loans and equity. This network also includes Banca Popolare Etica and other local banks operating in areas with a high cooperative

density. This approach has increased the pool of funding available, creates unity within the cooperative sector and broadens cooperative alliances outside the traditional cooperative sector.

- The funding and governance arrangements of the financial network encourage inter-sectoral cooperation and forms of solidarity. There is a distribution of wealth from the large to the smaller cooperatives, from the consumer and retail sector to other sectors and from Emilia Romagna to other regions.

4.5 National Financial Consortia

In addition to each Central Association's own financial network, there are two national financial consortia that service all Central Associations: Cooperfidi Italia and Cooperazione Finanza Impresa (CFI).

Cooperfidi Italia is a national financial consortium that offers credit guarantees and financial services. It was formed in 2009 following the merger of nine regional credit guarantee consortia. It has a membership of 3,500 cooperatives from all sectors of the economy. Each cooperative owns shares and has access to its financial services. Each cooperative pays a membership fee and is required to invest 1 percent of their loan. Members are spread throughout Italy, but over 50 percent reside in central Italy. The three major cooperative development funds have each invested 1.3 million euros (Cooperfidi 2016).

Cooperfidi Italia underwrites 50 percent of the loans, while lending institutions accept the remaining risk.[14] This allows cooperatives to access credit at a lower rate. Loans are available to cooperatives, their subsidiaries and companies that invest in cooperatives. Cooperatives may seek loans for liquidity, updating machinery or plants and other investments (Vannucci 2013). Most loans are short-term loans, but one-third are classified medium-to-long term and can extend to ten years (Cooperfidi 2014). Cooperfidi Italia deposits are placed in cooperative banks or with cooperative-friendly banks. The two most significant deposits are with Banca Prossima (18 percent) and Banca Popolare Etica (17 percent), both of which specialize in funding social cooperatives (Cooperfidi 2016). In 2016, Cooperfidi Italia guaranteed 489 loans to a value of 42.9 million euros, generating loans of 89.9 million euros (Confcooperative 2017).

The other national financial consortium is CFI. Its members include 270 cooperatives as well as the Ministry of Economic Development and Invitalia SPA, a state-owned public company that promotes economic development. It manages a rotational fund with 84 million euros in equity and 12 million in indivisible reserves. It was initially established to support WBOs. Since 2001, it has also invested in social cooperatives (Cooperazione Finanza Impresa 2015).

The fund has strict guidelines on eligibility and funding. CFI only invests in cooperatives that have more than nine members, employ fewer than 250 employees and have an annual turnover of fewer than 50 million euros. Each cooperative member is required to invest at least 4,000 euros (reduced to 1,000 euros for social cooperatives). Projects funded may include a new start-up or cooperatives that have plans to consolidate, grow or market repositioning (Cooperazione Finanza Impresa 2017c).

Funding guidelines and practices are designed to encourage investment from third parties and for cooperatives to repay investments within seven to ten years. CFI provides equity capital or loans. Equity investments cannot exceed twice the value of members' shares. It is expected that cooperatives buy back at least 75 percent of the shares within ten years. Loans are to be repaid within seven years at an agreed interest rate (Cooperazione Finanza Impresa 2017a). Investments are usually made in partnership with the cooperative funds, Cooperfidi, or with four other banks.[15] It is common for three or four partners to support the same project. This risk-sharing approach increases the available finance for each project. From 1986 to 2016, CFI invested a total of 205 million euros on 370 cooperatives that have created or saved 14,520 jobs. CFI currently holds investments in 108 cooperatives (Cooperazione Finanza Imprese 2017b).

4.6 Banche Popolari

Banche Popolari started as urban-based cooperative banks. First established in 1864, they quickly grew in popularity, with 736 formed by 1902. As a result of mergers and acquisitions, by 2016 there were 54 Banche Popolari in operation with over 1 million members, 48,000 employees, and over 5,000 branches. They hold a 25 percent market share in lending (Assopopolari 2016).

Today there are two types of Banche Popolari: those that hold more than 8 billion euros in assets, which are required to demutualize, and those that fall below this threshold. Those under the 8 billion euro threshold can operate throughout Italy, but they must limit shareholding to no more than 0.5 percent of total shares and operate under the principle of one-person-one-vote, and are required to place 10 percent of profits into the reserve. In contrast to cooperative banks, Banche Popolari assets are not indivisible (asset lock), and they are not subject to mutuality requirements (50 percent trading with members). They can also demutualize without any restrictions. Those that have assets above 8 billion euros have to convert into a public company. These have become listed companies, and their governance arrangements operate under the principle of one share equals one vote (Catturani and Cutcher 2015).

One example of a Banca Popolare that is listed on the stock exchange is Banca Popolare of Emilia Romagna (BPER Banca). BPER Banca is still a bank closely embedded with the local economy and is cooperative-friendly as it engages with Cooperare Spa, Cooperfidi Italia, CCFs and so on. Its sustainability report shows it promotes energy efficiency; provides microfinance;

promotes ethical investments; distributed over five million euros in community grants; and promotes enterprise welfare; almost all employees are permanent employees. While BPER Banca no longer operates democratically, it still is a socially responsible bank embedded in the local community (BPER Banca 2017).

Banca Popolare Etica was established in 1999 to help third sector organizations access credit. It operates as a cooperative bank. Each member is only entitled to one vote. The bank promotes the civil economy and, as such, funds cooperatives, not-for-profits and private enterprises from all sectors of the economy as long as they are deemed to be acting in the public interest. In 2017, the bank had over 40,000 shareholders and 60 million euros in capital equity. The bank holds deposits of 1.2 billion euros, and it has provided loans worth 950 million euros to over 9,000 enterprises (Banca Popolare Etica 2017).

The bank has a close relationship with the cooperative sector. Cooperative finance companies, cooperatives and consortia are shareholders (Coopfond 2017). Banca Popolare Etica has entered into agreements with CCFS, Cooperfidi Italia and cooperative banks. It has co-financed WBOs and social cooperatives with Coopfond and CFI. Co-investing allows Banca Popolare Etica to share the risk and access information about the market, industry sectors and cooperatives.[16] Banca Popolare Etica is performing a vital role in financing social cooperatives and WBOs.

4.7 Concluding Remarks: A Complex, Evolving and Diverse Financial Network

The cooperative sector has developed a complex financial support network that comprises a number of interrelated layers. The first layer comprises the legislative framework that enables cooperatives to attract and access capital at the enterprise level and provides various legal structures that allow cooperatives to access capital from the market. The second layer comprises the two national consortia, Cooperfidi Italia and CFI. These provide services to all cooperatives and are managed by the major Central Associations. The third layer comprises four sub-networks: the financial network managed by the three major Central Associations and Federazione Trentina. These focus on growing their own cooperative network comprised of cooperatives, consortia, cooperative banks and insurance and financial companies. The fourth layer comprises cooperative-friendly banks that are not affiliated with any Central Association but are embedded in local economies, such as popular banks—in particular, Banca Popolare Etica. The State comprises the fifth layer. It makes available funds from time to time and provides equity investments via Invitalia Spa in CFI or via the Trento local government in Promocoop. The sixth layer is international capital from the European cooperative and mutual sector, which has invested in Unipol, Cassa Centrale Banca of Trentino and the insurance company Assimoco.

In addition, there is a level of cross-ownership and co-investing taking place within the sub-networks. Popular banks have invested in Cooperare Spa. Legacoop cooperatives and their financial companies have invested in Banca Popolare Etica. Conventions have been signed between popular banks and CCFS, Coopfond and others, which provide access to credit for cooperatives at discounted rates. All cooperative development funds invest in Cooperfidi Italia. The cooperative development funds and Banca Popolare Etica have co-funded many WBOs. This is significant because it shows that political, ideological and different forms of ownership have not prevented cooperative associations and popular banks from finding common ground and working together.

The cooperative financial network has also developed three unique features that are of benefit to individual cooperatives and the whole of the cooperative sector. These are inter-sectoral cooperation and co-investing, taking a lifecycle approach to economic development and strategic investments. More specifically:

- Inter-sectoral cooperation. Cooperatives from all sectors of the economy and in all sizes invest in the various financial structures established by the cooperative movement. These include cooperative banks, financial consortia, local financial companies or cooperative development funds. This enables pooling resources together and funding cooperatives in need. As noted in Coopfond's case, it can redistribute funds from the cooperative-wealthy regions to other regions with a low cooperative density and from large cooperatives to smaller ones. This approach enables the cooperative sector to grow nationally, rejuvenate by promoting new cooperatives, remain cohesive and promote the principle of solidarity and community support.

- Lifecycle approach. The financial network offers cooperatives support throughout their lifecycle. Access to start-up capital is provided by the cooperative development funds, Cooperfidi Italia, CFI, CCFS, Banca Popolare Etica and cooperative banks. Equity capital and loans to grow and consolidate their business can be made available by the cooperative development funds as well as CCFS and CFI. Legacoop cooperatives that need restructuring can access funds from Coopfond and Unipol Merchant. The large cooperatives can access funds from the cooperative development funds and from Cooperare Spa, which focuses on large cooperatives wishing to enter new markets at home or internationally. Cooperatives also access capital on many occasions and in so doing can establish long-term relations with financial companies. This encourages cooperative entrepreneurship, growth and resilience, because funds are also available for cooperatives in economic difficulties that need to restructure or experience cash-flow problems.

- Strategic investments. Legacoop's management of its financial resources is strategic and is aligned with Legacoop's strategy to develop the sector

nationally, to promote economic diversification and to grow large cooperatives. Coopfond promotes cooperatives in Southern Italy to expand
the presence of cooperatives in that region. It also finances Cooperare
Spa, which invests in large cooperatives wishing to expand overseas.
It intervenes to rescue cooperatives in crisis. It has a strong focus on
WBOs to ensure that the cooperatives maintain a strong presence in
the manufacturing sector. All financial structures invest in Cooperfactor, which helps many small cooperatives access liquidity. All financial
structures and large cooperatives invest in Unipol Insurance Group,
which in turn has a very close business relationship with the consumer
sector and its 8 million consumer members. This approach promotes
growth in Italy and abroad, sectoral and geographic diversification and
cooperative resilience through rescue operations.

Both legislation and financial support structures have changed and developed over time to meet the needs of cooperatives and the cooperative movement. Innovations such as member loans; access to external capital while
preserving the majority of votes for members; and the establishment of holding companies subject to profits being placed in the indivisible reserves have
been very successful. Despite growing its financial offering, however, the
cooperative sector is still not able to meet the financial needs of large cooperatives, which have had to turn to the market. For instance, CMC raised
400 million euros via an international bond issue. Here lies the paradox: the
cooperative system relies on large cooperatives' financial contributions to the
cooperative development funds and their financial and insurance companies,
yet it cannot meet the financial needs of these large cooperatives. To this end,
it is vital for the cooperative movement to keep its inter-sectoral unity and
cohesiveness and continue to form alliances with cooperative-friendly banks,
insurance groups and financial companies in Italy and Europe in order to
attract long-term equity capital for all its members.

Notes

1. Five hundred lire is the nominal equivalent of less than one euro.
2. The amount invested varies: Camst requires members to pay 800 euros; Cadiai,
   1,800; CMC members have paid 42,000 euros.
3. External retail investors have mainly been ex-members, relatives and people
   close to the cooperative movement.
4. The total amount of funds available were equivalent to 16 billion euros (Castronovo 1987).
5. In 2001, the Marcora program was modified. Chapter 7 provides more details.
6. The Maastricht treaty parameters include keeping budget deficits to 3 percent of
   GDP and reducing public debt to 60 percent of GDP.
7. The third largest Central Association, Associazione Generale Cooperative Italiane, has its own bank (Banca AGCI), cooperative development fund (General-
   fond) and financial services company (Fin.Copra srl) (AGCI 2010).
8. The Cooperative Banking Groups are to be majority owned by cooperative
   banks and have the authority to provide leadership and coordination, invest

in each cooperative and intervene in governance arrangements, including the removal of directors.

9. The difference between interest paid and interest charged by banks was high. In 1976 Fincooper paid depositors 10 percent instead of the 8 percent paid by banks, and charged lower interests on loans than the 15 percent charged by banks. This allowed Fincooper to make a small gain to pay for administration costs (Castronovo 1987).

10. The data in Figure 4.1 was obtained from the annual reports of the Unipol Group, CCFS, Coopfond and Cooperare Spa, and from Cooperfactor's website.

11. Finsoe is the financial company of the social economy. It is fully owned by Legacoop cooperatives and it controlled 31.4 percent of Unipol Group's shares as of December 2017. The company will be split on 15 December 2017, with Unipol shares distributed to individual cooperatives (Finsoe 2017).

12. Libera establishes cooperatives or social businesses to manage land that the State has confiscated from organized crime.

13. Please refer to the Law: Nuove Norme in Materia in Societa' Cooperative, Legge 31 Gennaio 1992, Number 59.

14. As of 2015, credit guarantee agreements were entered with 47 financial institutions (Cooperfidi 2016a).

15. These banks include: Unipol Banca, ICCREA, Banca Popolare Etica and Banca Prossima (a subsidiary of Intesa San Paolo).

16. Banca Popolare Etica's bad loans are 2.76 percent compared with the national average of 10.4 percent (Banca Popolare Etica 2015).

References

AGCI. 2010. *Cresciamo Insieme Alle Nostre Imprese*. Information Booklet, Rome: AGCI Publications.

Assopopolari. 2016. *Dati Principali*. 31 December. Accessed November 3, 2017. www. assopopolari.it/banche-popolari/dati-principali/.

Banca Popolare Etica. 2015. Bilancio Integrato: Esercizio 2015. Banca Popolare Etica website. February 13, 2018. https://www.bancaetica.it/sites/bancaetica.it/files/web/la-banca/Chi-siamo/Assemblea%20dei%20soci/Assemblea%20dei%20soci%20 2016/ordine%20del%20giorno/bilancio%20integrato%202015_definitivo.pdf

———. 2017. *I Nostri Numeri*. 28 February. Accessed March 24, 2017. www. bancaetica.it/i-nostri-numeri.

Battilani, Patrizia, and Francesca Fauri. 2014. *L'Economia Italiana dal 1945 ad Oggi*. Bologna: Il Mulino.

Bernardini, Andrea. 2016. *L'Italia Che Ce La Fa'*. Rome: Cooperazione Finanza Impresa.

Bettini, Giorgio. 1986. "Una Rete fra Credito e Coop." *La Cooperazione Italiana*, October: 289–291.

BPER Banca. 2017. *Sustainability Report*. Sustainability Report, Modena: Banca Popolare dell'Emilia Romagna.

Bulgarelli, Marco, and Marco Viviani. 2006. *La Promozione Cooperativa: Coopfond tra Mercato e Solidarieta'*. Bologna: Il Mulino.

Carretta, Alessandro, and Vittorio Boscia. 2009. *Il Ruolo Economico delle Banche di Credito Cooperativo nel Sistema Finanziario*. Rome: Ecra.

Castronovo, Valerio. 1987. "Dal Dopoguerra ad Oggi." In *Storia del Movimento Cooperativo in Italia*, edited by Renato Zangheri, Giuseppe Galasso and Valerio Castronovo, 497–839. Turin: Giulio Einaudi Editore.

Catturani, Ivana, and Leanne Cutcher. 2015. "Financial Cooperatives in Australia and Italy." In *Cooperative Enterprises in Australia and Italy*, edited by Anthony Jensen, Greg Patmore and Ermanno Tortia, 37–57. Florence: Firenze University Press.

———, and Maria Lucia Stefani. 2014. "Il Credito Cooperativo." In *La Cooperazione Italiana Negli Anni della Crisi: Secondo Rapporto Euricse*, edited by Carlo Borzaga, 73–84. Trento: Euricse.

Cavallari, Maria. 2017. "Interview of Massimo Matteucci: Lascio soddifatto il lavoro che ho fatto." *La Betoneria*, March: 2.

CCFS. 2015a. *Bilancio Sociale*. Annual Social Report, Reggio Emilia: Consorzio Cooperativo Finanziario per lo Sviluppo.

———. 2015b. *Bilancio D'Esercizio*. Annual Financial Statements, Reggio Emilia: Consorzio Cooperativo Finanziario per lo Sviluppo.

CGM Finance. 2016. *Bilancio Sociale 2016*. Annual Report, Milan: CGM Finance.

Chelli, Virgilio. 1991. "Se lo Stato si Mette in Cooperativa." *La Cooperazione Italiana*, May: 4–7.

Collina, Piero. 1988. "Finec." In *Il Sistema Finanziario di Fronte All'Innovazione Finanziaria*, edited by Lega Nazionale delle Cooperative e Mutue, 70–73. Rome: Lega Nazionale delle Cooperative e Mutue.

Confcooperative. 2017. *Da Cooperfidi Piu' Credito alle Cooperative*. 21 January. Accessed February 24, 2017. www.confcooperative.it/LInformazione/Archivio/da-cooperfidi-pi249-credito-alle-cooperative.

Coop Adriatica 3.0. 2016. *Rapporto sullo Scambio Mutualistico e le Iniziative per le Comunita' 2015*. Annual Report, Bologna: Coop Adriatica 3.0.

Cooperare. 2015. *Relazioni e Bilancio al 30 Giugno 2015*. Annual Report, Bologna: Cooperare Spa.

———. 2016. *Investimenti in Portafoglio*. 30 December. Accessed March 21, 2017. www.cooperarespa.it/it/Gli_investimenti/Investimenti_in_portafoglio.

Cooperazione Finanza Impresa. 2015. *Il Lavoro Riparte dal lavoro*. Annual Report to the Board, Rome: Cooperazione Finanza Impresa.

———. 2017a. "CFI. Foglio Informativo." *Cooperazione Finanza Impresa*. January. Accessed March 23, 2017. www.cfi.it/public/wp-content/uploads/2017/02/CFI-foglio-informativo-modalità-di-intervento-rev-01-2017.pdf.

———. 2017b. "CFI in Cifre." *CFI—Chi Siamo*. January. Accessed March 23, 2017. www.cfi.it/public/chi-siamo/#cfi-in-cifre.

———. 2017c. *Foglio Informativo*. Rome, January.

Cooperazione Trentina. 2016. "Riforma BCC." *Cooperazione Trentina*, March: 4–11.

———. 2017. "Promocoop: Crescono le Partecipazioni." *Cooperazione Trentina*, June: 33–34.

Cooperfactor. 2017. "Elenco Soci." *Cooperfactor*. January. Accessed March 27, 2017. www.cooperfactor.it/cooperfactor/elenco-soci.

Cooperfidi. 2014. *Foglio Informativo garanzia*. 28 October. Accessed February 12, 2016. www.cooperfidiitalia.it/System/15935/48.%20%20Foglio%20Informativo%20Vers.%20%2009-2015%20-%20Generale.pdf.

———. 2016. *Bilancio 2015*. Annual Financial Report, Bologna: Cooperfidi Italia.

Coopfond. 2015a. *Regolamento e Condizioni Applicate ai Beneficiari del Fondo*. Policy Document, Rome: Coopfond.

———. 2015b. *Bilancio D'Esercizio 2014–2015*. Financial Statements, Rome: Coopfond.

————. 2015c. *Rendiconto Sociale: 2014–15.* Annual Sociale Report, Rome: Coopfond.

————. 2016. *Rendiconto Sociale 2014–2016.* Annual Report, Roma: Coopfond.

————. 2017. "Quattro Nuovi Interventi per L'Economis Sociale." *Coopfond.* 5 March. Accessed March 8 and 24, 2017. www.coopfond.it/coopfond-quattro-nuovi-interventi-per-far-crescere-leconomia-sociale/.

Cuccurullo, Raffaele, and Dora Jacobelli. 1988. "Finanza Locale e Settoriale." In *Il Sistema Lega di Fronte All'Innovazione Finanziaria,* edited by Lega Nazionale delle Cooperative e Mutue, 230–239. Firenze: Lega Nazionale delle Cooperative e Mutue.

Cusa, Emanuele. 2009. *Lo Scopo Mutualistico delle Banche di Credito Cooperativo.* Rome: Ecra.

Dalpalu', Renato. 2015. *Fincoop: Bilancio Positivo della Finanziaria della Cooperazione, un Milione di Utile.* 20 May. Accessed March 6, 2017. www.cooperazionetrentina.it/Ufficio-Stampa/Notizie/Fincoop-bilancio-positivo-della-Finanziaria-della-cooperazione-1-milione-di-utile.

De Bertoli, Renato. 1993. "Foncooper: Adequare la Normativa e le Risorse ai Bisogni Reali." *La Cooperazione,* Febbraio: 4–7.

Degli Esposti, Massimo. 1989. "Le Coop D'Europa Fondano Holding dell'Assicurazione." *Il Sole 24 Ore,* 18 November.

Dorigatti, Michele. 2014. "Il Modello Trentino Oggi." In *Guida Alla Cooperazione Trentina,* edited by Cooperazione Trentina, 87–106. Trento: Cooperazione Trentina.

European Commission. 2014. *A Map of Social Enterprises and Their Ecosystems in Europe: A Country Report: Italy.* Country Report, London: European Union.

Fabbri, Fabio. 2011. *L'Italia Cooperativa.* Roma: Ediesse.

Federcasse. 2015. *Bilancio di Coerenza del Credito Cooperativo.* Annual Report 2015, Roma: ECRA.

————. 2016. *Bilancio di Coerenza delle BCC.* Annual Report, Rome: Federcasse.

Finsoe. 2016. *Relazioni e Bilancio al 31 Dicembre 2015.* Annual Report, Bologna: Finsoe Spa.

————. 2017. *Firmato L'Atto di Scissione di Finsoe SPA.* Bologna: Finsoe, 15 December.

Franci, Gianfranco. 1992. "Il Vantaggio delle Cooperative non Partire Favorite." *La Cooperazione Italiana,* June–July: 52.

Gruppo Assimoco. 2013. *Company Profile.* Company Profile, Rome: Gruppo Assimoco.

Ianes, Alberto. 2014. "La Storia. La Cooperazione Trentina e Italiana. Un Modo Diverso di Leggere e Interpretare L'Economia e la Societa'." In *Guida Alla Cooperazione Trentina,* edited by Cooperazione Trentina, 55–86. Trento: Cooperazione Trentina.

ICCREA. 2016. *ICCREA Press Kit.* Information Booklet, Rome: Gruppo Bancario Iccrea.

Il Giornale della Banca. 1990. "Voglia di Mercato." *Unipol Press,* January: 16–17.

La Lega Nazionale delle Cooperative e Mutue. 1990. *Il Sistema Finanziario della Lega delle Cooperative.* Bologna: La Lega Nazionale delle Cooperative e Mutue.

Laurini, Luca. 2016. *Coopfond Spa: A Company Overview.* Bologna, 18 October.

————, and Barbara Moreschi. 2016. "La Rendicontazione Sociale di Coopfond." *Le Risorse per Finanziare la Ripresa.* Rome: Coopfond.

Lega Nazionale delle Cooperative e Mutue. 1987. *Lega.* Rome: Lega Nazionale delle Cooperative e Mutue.

Mazzoli, Enea. 2005. "Gli Sviluppi della Cooperazione Italiana dal Dopoguerra a Oggi Ripercorsi da un Protagonista." In *Verso Una Nuova Teoria della*

Cooperazione, edited by Enea Mazzoli and Stefano Zamagni, 57–95. Bologna: Il Mulino.

Menzani, Tito. 2007. *La Cooperazione In Emilia Romagna*. Bologna: Il Mulino.

Midoro, Renato. 1984. *Gli Strumenti per il Finanziamento delle Cooperative*. Roma: Editrice Cooperativa.

OECD. 2014. *The Cooperative Model of Trentino*. Paris: OECD.

———. 2017. *Italy Survey 2017*. Economic Survey, Brussels: OECD.

Petrucci, Paola. 2009. *La distribuzione degli avanzi di gestione e la Pratica del Ristorno nelle Imprese Cooperative*. Annual Economic Review of Cooperative Enterprises, Rome: Centro Studi Legacoop.

Sacconi, Stefano. 1986. "Da Quel Sogno del Vecchio Cassina." *La Cooperazione Italiana*, October: 274–281.

Sintesi del Sistema. 1989. "Fincooper: Strumento Finanziario della Lega." *Sintesi del Sistema*, March: 3.

Soldi, Aldo. 2013. *Linee Generali Di Coopfond: Incontro con I Partecipanti di Master di Secondo Livello sull'Impresa Cooperativa*. Rome: Coopfond.

Thornley, Jenny. 1981. *Workers' Cooperatives: Jobs and Dreams*. London: Heinemann Education Books.

Trento, Sandro. 2012. *Il Capitalismo Italiano*. Bologna: Il Mulino.

Trezzi, Luigi. 2011. *Il Movimento e L'Organizzazzione Cooperativa*. Accessed January 1, 2017. www.treccani.it/enciclopedia/il-movimento-e-l-organizzazione-cooperativa_ (Cristiani-d'Italia).

Unipol Banca. 2014. *Informativa: Gruppo Bancario Unipol Spa*. Annual Report, Bologna: Unipol Banca.

Unipol Gruppo. 2016. *Presenti per disegnare il Futuro*. Press Kit, Bologna: Unipol Gruppo.

Vannucci, Ferruccio. 2013. *I Consorzi Fidi e le Garanzie per il Credito alle Cooperative*. Stakeholder Update, Bologna: Cooperfidi.

Varni, Angelo. 1990. "Unipol: La Compagnia d'Assicurazioni del Mondo del Lavoro." In *Emilia Romagna Terra di Cooperazione*, edited by Angelo Varni, 427. Bologna: Eta.

Viviani, Mario. 2013. *Piccola Guida alla Cooperazione*. Soveria Mannelli: Rubbettino.

———. 2016. *Cinzio Zambelli: Prassi di un Dirigente Cooperativo*. Bologna: Il Mulino.

Wollemborg, Leone. 2009. "La Banca che Ridesta Negli Animi Avviliti la Speranza." In *Banche Con L'Anima*, edited by Sergio Gatti, 3–7. Rome: ECRA.

Zamagni, Vera. 2015. *Come si e' Affermata la Grande Impresa Cooperativa in Italia: Il Ruolo Strategico di Enea Mazzoli*. Bologna: Il Mulino.

———, and Emanuele Felice. 2006. *Oltre il Secolo*. Bologna: Il Mulino.

5   Consortia Network
Economies of Scale and National Expansion

The previous chapter noted how the financial network, including financial consortia, had supported cooperatives by facilitating access to credit, loans, equity capital, factoring services and other financial services. This chapter assesses how non-financial consortia help cooperatives compete in the market. It provides an overview of consortia in Italy, the regulatory environment, typology of consortia, their functions, how they have evolved and the impact they have on the cooperative sector. It will highlight the experiences of Coop Italia, the Trento Winegrowers Cooperative (CAVIT), the National Services Consortium (CNS) and Consortium for Construction Cooperatives (CCC) to assess how their approaches have improved cooperative competitiveness and encouraged inter-sectoral trade. The key question here is to understand how consortia help cooperatives compete in the market and the extent to which they can meet the needs of the small, medium-sized and large cooperatives competing in world markets.

5.1 What Is a Consortium?

A consortium is a business association of cooperatives established to improve their market position. These consortia operate as a cooperative, and they are required to comply with cooperative laws. Laws regulating consortia have been enacted since 1909. New laws have been passed ever since to accommodate cooperative needs in a changing public and private market. Today consortia can legally be formed for the purposes of:

- Bidding for public works.
- Promoting a common activity (acquisition of raw material or machinery).
- Manufacturing and marketing of products on behalf of their cooperative members.
- Forming welfare consortia, provided that 70 percent of members be social cooperatives.
- Forming consortia, which can include a minority of non-cooperative members.

- Forming consortia as cooperative societies, which can invest in private companies as a minority or majority shareholder, and establishing a holding company to manage its investments in investor-owned or private companies.
- Promoting consortia as a 'joint group of companies' where a cooperative is given the authority to lead and coordinate the activities of other members. The lead cooperative's role and goals are stipulated in a contract signed by all participants. This legal form provides cooperatives with an opportunity to operate as a holding company without the head of this group having any controlling interest in other cooperatives. It offers a way for cooperatives to operate as a group of enterprises without losing their cooperative form (Bonfante 2011).

5.2 Consortia: Functions, Benefits and Development

Just as individuals form a cooperative so that they can achieve goals that they would be unable to achieve on their own, so too cooperatives form consortia to achieve goals that they cannot achieve on their own. Consortia allow cooperatives to achieve economies of scale, are present in all sectors of the economy and attract cooperatives of all sizes. The most commonly used consortia are established for:

- The acquisition of raw materials, fertilizers or machinery, as is the case for agricultural cooperatives, or food and non-food items, as is the case for consumer cooperatives. The primary aim here is to access quality goods in a timely fashion at a lower than market prices.
- The manufacturing and marketing products on behalf of their members. These consortia could be used by agricultural cooperatives to sell their dairy products or wine or to allow consumer cooperatives to market their own label products or to engage with suppliers. The consortia allow cooperatives to manufacture and sell their products by combining capital, know-how and marketing skills with other members.
- The bidding for public works, welfare services and commercial contracts. These may be of interest to construction, welfare and service cooperatives. Consortia allow small cooperatives to join large cooperatives to win contracts that they would be unable to win on their own. This also enables them to access new markets, acquire new skills and grow their business.

Consortia have grown in number, diversity and size. A study conducted in 2011 identifies a total of 2005 consortia operating in Italy (Linguiti 2014). The study reveals that consortia produced 21 percent of the cooperative sector's total production. The study also reveals differences in geographic locations, size and turnover. Key findings include:

- Consortia operate throughout Italy, with the North accounting for 45 percent, the Center 27 percent and the South 28 percent.
- Consortia operate in all sectors of the economy but are mostly present in the service (38.5 percent) and welfare sectors (22.6 percent), reflecting the demand for these services and the policy of outsourcing practiced by both the State and large private enterprises.
- Sixty-four consortia with a turnover of more than 50 million euros produce 75.1 percent of the total turnover. This indicates that the larger consortia are more competitive than the smaller ones.
- Forty-two consortia produced consolidated annual reports. These reports revealed that controlled companies produced 23 percent of their turnover and were responsible for 50 percent of their employment.

Table 5.1 provides more detail on the sectoral distribution of consortia and the size of consortia.

Table 5.1 Number and Turnover of Consortia, 2011

Total Number of Consortia

Sector	Number of Consortia	Percentage
Agriculture/Food	304	15.2
Construction	159	7.9
Industry	17	0.8
Housing	205	10.2
Retail	63	3.1
Social Welfare	452	22.6
Services	771	38.5
Other	34	1.7
Total	**2005**	**100**

Turnover of Consortia

Turnover (Million Euros)	Number of Consortia	Turnover (Million Euros)	Percentage of Turnover
Up to 1 m	998	214	1.0
1–5 m	395	962	4.8
5–10 m	129	922	4.5
10–50 m	148	2955	14.6
50–100 m	29	2083	10.3
100 m to 1 billion euros	32	9322	46.0
more than 1 billion euros	3	3810	18.8
Total	**1734**	**20268**	**100**

Source: Linguiti, Francesco. 2014. "I Consorzi tra Societa' Cooperative." In *La Cooperazione Italiana Negli Anni della Crisi: Secondo Rapporto Euricse*, by Carlo Borzaga, 53–72. Trento: Euricse

5.3 Consortia Typology

As already indicated, consortia differ in functions, size, geographic reach and legal structure. Another way to understand the functions and operations of consortia is to analyze the level of economic integration between consortia and cooperatives. This approach provides a further understanding of the relationship between cooperatives, consortia and the market and the significance of the consortium model to the cooperative sector.

Cooperatives have broadly established three types of consortia: horizontal sectoral consortia, which provide professional and support services; vertical sectoral consortia, which display a high level of economic integration with their members; and multi-sector consortia, which provide an integrated set of services to public and private clients (Menzani and Zamagni 2010). A brief explanation of each typology is given next, followed by four consortia case studies that will provide more detailed information on how these consortia work.

The first consortia are horizontal consortia. These are mainly present in the building, agriculture, services, welfare and banking sectors. Their purpose is to provide cooperatives with business services at a lower price or to enable cooperatives to achieve economies of scale to reduce the price and cost of various business inputs. These may provide professional services such as legal, accounting, tax and consultancy services. They help agricultural cooperatives access raw materials, fertilizers and machinery at lower costs or building cooperatives access raw materials and building fixtures at lower prices. Welfare cooperatives set them up to access legal, accounting and tax services. In this relationship, the cooperatives make use of these services, but it continues to maintain a direct relationship with its customers and clients.

Some consortia provide a higher level of business services by bidding for public or large private contracts on behalf of their members. This way the consortia can win a cleaning contract or building contract or the right to provide child care services in a city or town. In these instances, the consortia develop a direct relationship with the market. It is the consortia, not the cooperative, that engages with clients. This is the first step toward a higher level of integration, and it is the direct result of small and medium-sized cooperatives not having the capability, experience or resources to bid for these contracts on their own and using the consortia to engage with the market.

The second consortia are vertical sectoral consortia. These consortia can operate at a national or regional scale and within an economic sector such as retail or agriculture. These consortia promote integration throughout the whole supply chain and are crucial for the economic activity of their cooperative members.

The third consortia are multi-sector consortia. These consortia associate large and small cooperatives from different sectors of the economy. They evolved in the 1980s in response to private enterprises and the state administration outsourcing non-core business functions. These clients demanded that one business provide a variety of services in one or a number of locations (ports, hospitals, offices and so on). The sectoral or horizontal consortia were not suitable, so the multi-sector national consortia were formed with a broader membership that included cooperatives from the construction, industry, services, catering and welfare sectors. Multi-sector consortia are accountable to their client and guarantee the quality and completion of each job. To this end, these consortia support their members in getting quality accreditations, management training and reviewing their operations to promote sound financial management, compliance with the law and alignment with cooperative principles. They provide a blend of support services and consultancy services and bid for public and private contracts on their behalf. These consortia engage with the market on behalf of their members but are not as economically integrated as the vertical sectoral consortia. Cooperatives do not produce all of their turnovers through jobs acquired via the multi-sector consortia. This is especially the case with large cooperatives whose turnover is as large as the consortium and which often win contracts on their own.

5.4 Consortia Case Studies

To get a better understanding of how consortia operate and help their members compete in the market, the four consortia from the consumer, agricultural, service and construction sectors will be reviewed. Case studies of these large consortia will provide insights into their level of economic integration with their members and the overall benefits they offer their cooperative members.

5.4.1 Coop Italia: A National Consortium Servicing the Consumer Sector

Coop Italia is the national consortium formed in 1968 to coordinate purchasing, marketing and logistics on behalf of the consumer sector. Until 1968, the consumer sector consisted of the Italian Alliance of Consumer Cooperatives (AICC), the role of which was to reach agreements with suppliers and increase the range of products available to the cooperative sector and some 31 provincial consortia that managed warehousing and logistics on a local scale. In 1956, this business model serviced over 3,300 cooperatives, which managed 7,000 retail outlets.

This system was very fragmented, and the Legacoop National Association of Consumer Cooperatives and AICC decided to form Coop Italia as a national consortium with broader coordinating powers. This new approach would better equip the consumer sector to deal with a changing market that was ripe for modernization. Indeed, consumers were considered ready to embrace self-service supermarkets as they had done in Europe and the

United States. The decision to form Coop Italia was part of a broader strategy to modernize the consumer sector by establishing larger cooperatives through mergers and to replace small shops with modern supermarkets (Zamagni, Battilani and Casali 2004). Coop Italia was formed by merging the activities of AICC and by incorporating 31 provincial consortia. Its role was to negotiate national agreements with suppliers and to modernize warehouses and logistics to cut costs, lower food prices and improve services. To this end, warehouse centers were reduced to 11, costs were reduced and cooperative purchases from Coop Italia increased from 10 percent to 46 percent of total sales (Casali 2000).

Under the initial governance arrangements, however, Coop Italia internalized all the financial risks because it was solely responsible for payments to suppliers. When some large consumer cooperatives from Lombardy, Piedmont and Liguria delayed payments, and eventually could not pay, Coop Italia faced financial difficulties and the debts incurred had to be paid by all other cooperative members. The troubled cooperatives, as explained in Chapter 3, received financial and management assistance and eventually turned around their fortunes, but the business model needed to change, and Coop Italia was restructured (Barberini 2009; Tassinari 2015).

A new business model was implemented in 1979. Coop Italia no longer bought and sold goods but simply negotiated contractual arrangements with suppliers on behalf of members. This made cooperatives directly responsible for paying for purchased goods. Cooperatives were also responsible for managing their warehouses. These changes made each cooperative accountable for their actions so the demise of one would no longer have a major impact on the cooperative network. Under these new arrangements, Coop Italia became a marketing center for the consumer sector. Its new role included negotiating collective agreements with suppliers, promoting and managing the quality of cooperative brand products and conducting market research (Barberini 2009).

In performing its role, Coop Italia has had to consider the consumer sector's mission, changes in consumer needs in a changing society and the needs of cooperative members. Over time, consumers were not only interested in being able to purchase quality goods at lower prices but also in being part of an organization that considered the environment, promoted well-being and actively promoted human rights.[1] Coop Italia began developing cooperative brand products that reflected consumer needs and cooperative values. Key achievements have included:

- Lower prices for consumers. On average cooperative price rises are 1 percent lower than the national consumer price index rises and their brand products are 30 percent cheaper than similar products.
- Lower prices for over-the-counter pharmaceutical products. On average, these are 25 percent cheaper than equivalent products.

- Product quality and safety. Coop Italia conducted 3.3 million product checks in 2015 in cooperative-owned and accredited laboratories and over 1,600 on-site inspections.
- Promoting the local economy by purchasing 90 percent of products from local suppliers.
- Promoting inter-cooperative trade by engaging with cooperative suppliers of fruit and vegetables, small goods, dairy products, wine, other food and house/cleaning products.
- Promoting European cooperation by being a member of Coopernic, a central purchasing consortium servicing European cooperatives.
- Promoting human and environmental rights by requiring all its 508 suppliers and close to 1,000 sub-contractors to attest and subscribe to its human rights charter. Inspections are conducted by Coop Italia and independent parties.
- Promoting compliance with the law. Cooperatives have sold 70 percent of all products sold by Libera Terra, an association that manages land confiscated from organized crime.
- Promoting international solidarity by purchasing products from developing countries via its Solidal label and selling 40 percent of all Fairtrade products sold in Italy (Coop Italia 2016).

Coop Italia is now the largest retail distributor in Italy, with 18.7 percent of the market servicing 93 cooperatives with 8.5 million members, employing 54,000 people and producing a turnover of 12.3 billion euros. It has promoted a common brand through a centralized marketing role, a wide range of products supplied at competitive prices and cooperative labeled products that reflect cooperative values. However, the success of the consumer sector is also attributable to the long-term strategy and values delineated by the national sectoral association and the role performed by the largest seven cooperatives, which produce 90 percent of the total turnover. The large cooperatives have developed modern supermarkets, efficient warehousing and logistics. They have also developed consumer products for gas, electricity and telephone bills and have set up bookshops, travel services, pharmacies and gas stations (Coop Italia 2016; Coop Adriatica 3.0 2015).

Coop Italia can be characterized as a vertically integrated consortium, the activities of which are in alignment with the consumer association mission and values charter and cooperative needs. Coop Italia provides products at low prices, markets the whole sector and manages suppliers of cooperative brand products. It promotes cooperative principles such as inter-cooperative trade and support for the local and world community. It promotes a unifying vision and services equally available to and accessed by all cooperatives. There is a clear demarcation between the marketing role of Coop Italia and that of cooperatives, which manage their businesses and engage with the market. This is a key reason for this enduring and successful business model.

5.4.2 CAVIT (Trento Winegrowers Cooperative)

CAVIT was established in 1950 by grape growers in the province of Trento to help improve their farming methods and the quality of their products. Today CAVIT is a consortium representing ten cooperatives with a combined membership of 4,500 grape growers producing 70 percent of Trentino's wine. Grape growers established cooperatives to get a better price for their produce by negotiating with wine producers as a group rather than individually. Soon, cooperatives bottled and sold their own wine to increase growers' income further. The next development phase was to establish consortia to perform a technical, marketing and quality oversight role to further improve their market position (Cooperazione Trentina 2014; CAVIT 2014).

CAVIT's function is fully integrated with growers and their cooperatives. It oversees farming methods, winemaking and bottling and is responsible for marketing and sales. It performs three key functions:

- Initially, CAVIT provided technical expertise to farmers so they could plant and manage vines suitable for the soil and climate of the area. It then promoted good practice standards to reduce the use of pesticides and to produce organic products. To this end, it conducted applied research, in cooperation with local institutes, to identify higher quality vines suitable for the area's soil and climate.
- Its second function is product quality oversight. CAVIT controls the whole supply chain from the planting of vines to harvesting and winemaking through to the bottling process to ensure consistent quality. It has established policies, processes and procedures to ensure that all growers and cooperatives comply with agreed standards and protocols. This reassures the public that the quality and labeling of wines is authentic.
- Its third function is marketing. CAVIT exports 80 percent of all wines to 50 countries, of which 98 percent are produced by its members (OECD 2014; CAVIT 2016).

CAVIT has become an investor on behalf of its members. It wholly owns a wine company in Germany that produces sparkling wine at the cost of 2.5 million euros. It has invested 815,000 euros in cooperative members, a number of local cooperative banks and a credit guarantee company. Six cooperatives have received 96 percent of this investment pool, further strengthening the links and integration with its members. The third type of investment, 1.1 million euros, was invested in six companies associated with the Trentino Federation (CAVIT 2016).

CAVIT operates as a traditional cooperative with a tripartite governance structure. Cooperative members elect the board of directors and the audit committee at the annual general assembly. It complies with the principles of mutuality as 98 percent of its sales are produced by its members.

In 2016, its members had invested 6 million euros in shares, and the consortium had accumulated 72 million euros in net assets. Its turnover for 2016 was 171.5 million euros. Net profits amounted to 5 million and were re-invested according to cooperative law: 3 percent of profits were deposited with Promocoop and 30 percent to the indivisible reserve fund, with the remaining 67 percent also deposited in the reserve fund. Re-investment of profits has improved CAVIT's capitalization to the point that in 2016 it did not have any bank loans. It employs 199 persons, of whom 84 percent are employed full time (CAVIT 2016).

CAVIT is a wholly vertically integrated consortium. It acts and operates like a single business, yet it is comprised of ten cooperatives that bottle wine and coordinate 4,500 grape growers. Each of these three components is interrelated. CAVIT leads and coordinates the network by providing technical, marketing and quality support at each phase of the supply chain. It gives direction and advice on what to produce (grape selection), how to produce it (farming techniques) and winemaking practices. CAVIT engages with the market and is responsible for marketing and sales. It operates as one large company, but it is not actually one because each cooperative and each grower are separate legal entities and are free to leave. CAVIT has also shown an ability to diversify its services to members and to provide financial assistance to cooperative members and the Trentino Federation. Its re-investment of profits indicates that CAVIT and its members have a long-term business focus.

5.4.3 CNS (Consorzio Nazionale Servizi)

Legacoop's National Services Sectoral Association established the CNS in 1977 to promote cooperatives from the services sector on a national scale. At first, 11 cooperatives joined, including Manutencoop, one of the largest cooperatives. It steadily grew to 175 members in 1995, with 202 members in 2015. The CNS initially focused on winning cleaning, catering, waste management and maintenance contracts, but gradually it added facilities management, logistics, energy maintenance, reception/security services and welfare services into its areas of expertise. CNS moved into new sectors because it wanted to capture a new evolving market fueled by private companies outsourcing non-core activities, the public sector outsourcing government services and both wanting to deal with one client that could provide a variety of services in multiple locations. This is what led CNS to become a multi-sector national consortium (CNS Board 2016; Felice 2010).

The consortium's primary role has been to win government and private sector contracts and distribute work to its members. CNS has a competitive advantage because it can provide services to clients with offices or facilities in multiple locations (for example, ports or railways) and can guarantee compliance with agreements. CNS enables small and medium-sized cooperatives to achieve economies of scale, access markets that they would not have been able to access on their own, access the know-how of the larger cooperatives and become more professional. The larger cooperatives benefited because CNS allowed them to access new markets and to operate in all regions of Italy.

To be successful, CNS realized that it required all cooperatives members to be financially viable, quality accredited, more professional and client-focused. To this end, CNS provided the following services and support:

- Technical, planning and financial management support.
- Management training courses in cooperation with the Legacoop National Services Association, academia and consultants.
- Professional assistance to members to facilitate accreditation to international standards: ISO 9001 (quality), ISO 14001 (environment) and SA 8000 (social responsibility reporting).
- Consultancy services dealing with cooperative restructuring, mergers and specialization.
- Financial assistance by acting as a guarantor, providing loans and risk capital to cooperative members and facilitating factoring services via Cooperfactor.
- Cooperative oversight, in cooperation with Legacoop's National Services Association, to ensure financial stability, adequate levels of debt and compliance with cooperative principles.

CNS, like CAVIT, has become an investor on behalf of its members. CNS has accumulated over 58 million euros in assets, plus 4 million in members' shares. It has made investments in three key areas: strategic investments, support of cooperative members and support of the cooperative sector. More specifically, it:

- Invested in eight strategic companies the sum of 864,000 euros.
- Invested 4.6 million euros in cooperatives, consortia or companies associated with Legacoop, of which most were invested in the consortium Consorzio Formula Ambiente, in Cooperfactor, and with CCFS.
- Provided loans totaling 9.5 million euros to 11 companies, of which 6.8 million was lent to Cooperfactor.
- Purchased 16 million euros in bonds, of which 15 million were invested in Unipol bonds (Consorzio Nazionale Servizi 2016b).

CNS has become very successful. It has managed to increase its turnover from 2.3 million euros in 1977, to 128 million in 1995, to 621 million in 2012. The contracts won have been shared among its members. CNS claims that the consortium provides up to 10 percent of its cooperative members' combined total turnover. In distributing work, it considers economic performance, financial health, business plan, debt, cash flow, assets and compliance with the law and cooperative principles. As a result, the distribution of work between large and small cooperatives varies. In 2006, CNS distributed 73 percent of its work to smaller cooperatives. In the same year, 34 percent of CNS members received more than 50 percent of their total turnover from CNS contracts (Consorzio Nazionale Servizi 2006). In 2009, 74 percent of total contracts were allocated to 30 cooperatives (Consorzio Nazionale Servizi 2009).

The consortium has adopted a cooperative legal structure. It is a democratic organization, albeit with larger cooperatives having up to five votes. CNS adopts the dualistic governance model where the general assembly elects a board that in turn appoints a management team. The Board also appoints an audit committee and board sub-committees (Consorzio Nazionale Servizi 2017). It raises funds via member shares, external investors (mainly Coopfond) and retains a 2 percent commission on the amount of work allocated to members (Felice 2010). Profits are distributed according to cooperative rules, and almost all are deposited in indivisible reserves (Consorzio Nazionale Servizi 2016a).

The CNS model has also shown some limitations. One limitation is the difficulty in achieving a consistent level of quality among its members. It has attempted to do this via promoting international standards accreditation, but the uptake from members has not been consistent. CNS's own reviews have found areas of non-compliance, and some have been fined for not meeting contractual obligations (Consorzio Nazionale Servizi 2009). Another limitation is the inherent conflicts between large and small cooperatives, with the former openly competing for work against CNS and expanding their activities to other parts of Italy where other cooperative members operate. Sometime synergies can be found between cooperatives with complementary skills. Other times conflicts are mediated via promoting mergers and specialization. Winning more contracts helps to manage this issue, but it re-emerges in times of economic crisis when there are fewer contracts to be distributed. So a fine balance needs to be found between meeting the needs of large cooperatives because they have the finance, know-how and credibility and the smaller cooperatives who want to survive, grow and be allocated work from their local areas.

CNS's activities may also pose a financial and reputational risk to cooperative members. CNS encountered financial problems in the 1990s when a cooperative could not repay a 1.6 million euro debt it owed CNS. In response, CNS raised capital from its members to cover the loss, but in the process, 37 cooperatives left the consortia (Felice 2010). In 2016, CNS and one of its members, Manutencoop, were fined 110 million euros for collusive behavior by the anti-trust authority. CNS was left with only 1.8 million in assets, and to recapitalize the business it raised 12 million euros from the large cooperatives and Coopfond. On both occasions, CNS replaced its board and management (CNS Board 2016).

CNS is a national inter-sectoral consortium servicing cooperatives with complementary services in order to offer clients a complete package. It has managed to change its strategy, operates in many market segments, attracts cooperatives and regularly win contracts for its members. CNS manages an environment where cooperation and competition co-exist.

Small and medium-sized cooperatives benefit by accessing markets, know-how and technical and business skills but resent the fact that large cooperatives from other regions operate within their local area in competition with them. Large cooperatives benefit from CNS's capacity to facilitate their expansion into other regions of Italy, but they only get a small portion of their work via CNS, and it is not enough to meet their needs and aspirations. In 2014, for instance, CNS's turnover was 720 million euros, but it was less than Manutencoop's 974 million euros and almost on par with Coopservice's 660 million euros (CNS Board 2015; Gazzetta di Reggio 2015; Manutencoop 2015). As a result, it is not unusual to see the large cooperatives compete with CNS for the same public works. CNS performs a valuable role in developing cooperatives, but once they reach a certain size they become more autonomous, and CNS's value to them diminishes.

5.4.4 CCC (Consorzio Cooperative Costruzioni)

CCC is a Legacoop national consortium that operates in the building, infrastructure, civil engineering and industrial works. It was initially formed by eight cooperatives from Bologna in 1911 to bid for public works. In response to Legacoop's strategy of developing large cooperatives and a national movement, CCC became a regional consortium by incorporating a number of consortia from Emilia Romagna. By the 1990s it had become a national consortium with offices throughout Italy. In 1998, it incorporated Acam, the national procurement consortium for the construction industry, adding procurement to its core works division. In 2007, it became a cooperative society, which allowed it to set up a holding company or buy shares in private companies (Consorzio Cooperative Costruzioni 2011). It has averaged 200 cooperative members.

CCC has, since 2007, adopted the 'dualistic' governance model, which includes the general assembly election of a Board that in turn appoints a management team. The Board appoints, directs and monitors the performance of management. The Board also appoints the oversight committee. The general assembly appoints the external auditors, approves the budget, decides how profits should be distributed and approves the Board's remuneration. It has adopted a weighted voting system that allows one member to have a maximum of five votes. Votes are distributed according to how many shares they own: one vote for those members who own shares worth less than 10,000 euros and up to five votes for those who own shares worth more than 300,000 euros. External shareholders must invest a minimum of 500,000 euros. While the larger cooperatives individually have more shares, their voting power is limited. In 2010, for instance, the largest 12 cooperatives invested 65 percent of the capital but had only 16 percent of the votes (Consorzio Cooperative Costruzioni 2011).

The primary role of CCC is to win public and private contracts on behalf of their members in public works such as infrastructure, civil engineering and residential and commercial building. In support of this function, it provides a procurement service, technical expertise, project management and strategic planning services, and facilitates access to finance by providing loans or by acting as a guarantor. The competitive advantage of CCC is that it offers clients a one-stop-shop when dealing with the cooperative sector, guarantees the quality of work and also guarantees completion should a cooperative cease to operate or if it cannot meet contractual obligations. CCC provides further advantages because it has been able to forge alliances with the private sector and has won many contracts when bidding in partnership with private companies. It has formed many ad-hoc companies to manage public works in alliance with private partners. It has also partnered investment banks in projects requiring project financing that require the bid winner to build-own-operate-transfer public works. CCC has been quite successful, regularly winning contracts worth 1 billion euros each year and making regular yearly profits of between 350,000 euros and 2.5 million euros. In compliance with its mutuality obligations, 92 percent of contracts won were allocated to cooperative members in 2006, declining to 73 percent in 2014 (Consorzio Cooperative Costruzioni 2003; Consorzio Cooperative Costruzioni 2006; Consorzio Cooperative Costruzioni 2014).

The procurement division has also been very active. It offers cooperative members the opportunity to buy raw building materials, building fixtures and energy products from over 1,000 approved suppliers at a discounted price. The suppliers are cooperatives and private providers. The business model is one where CCC reaches agreement with suppliers so that members can buy items at a discount while receiving a commission. The suppliers have access to a large market because CCC members' combined turnover is estimated at 5 billion euros, which is much higher than CCC's average turnover of 1 billion euros. Cooperatives have regularly purchased over 1 billion euros' worth of items via CCC's procurement services. Of these, between 9 and 11 percent of items were purchased from other cooperative enterprises, thus promoting inter-sectoral trade among cooperatives.[2]

In the 1990s, cooperatives paid more attention to financial affairs. Globalization increased competition in all sectors and cooperatives needed external capital so they could continue to grow their business. CCC was no exception and used its position and accumulated reserves and equity to make investments on behalf of members and the cooperative movement. Investments were made in controlled companies, related companies and companies supporting the cooperative sector. In 2002, 54 million euros were invested in 120 companies, but by 2010 CCC had invested 131 million euros in 136 companies. CCC made key investments in:

- 12 controlled companies providing consultancy, engineering, financial management and procurement services.
- 28 property development companies in partnership with other cooperatives and the private sector.

- 96 cooperatives or companies associated with the cooperative sector including Unipol, Cooperfactor and CCFS (Consorzio Cooperative Costruzioni 2003; Consorzio Cooperative Costruzioni 2011).

CCC funded itself in a number of ways. Member shares are the traditional way to raise funds. CCC required members to invest at least 3,000 euros. The amounts invested grew steadily, and by 2006 members had invested a total amount of 5.8 million euros, rising to 17.64 million euros in 2014. CCC has self-funded its operations by retaining 30 percent of profits. Also, it charges a commission fee as a percentage of work distributed and as a percentage of purchases made via its procurement division. This amount can vary, but it is usually less than two percent. As an investor, CCC also received dividends from its investments, bank deposits and bonds in Unipol and other financial companies. In 2010, for instance, investment returns amounted to 781,000 euros, while interest earnings equaled 1.34 million euros. In the same year, CCC had assets worth 100 million euros (Consorzio Cooperative Costruzioni 2011; Consorzio Cooperative Costruzioni 2014; Consorzio Cooperative Costruzioni 2016).

CCC developed into a complex network of cooperative enterprises from the construction, industry and engineering sectors. It evolved to support its members and Legacoop's financial structures. It centralized many risks: CCC was responsible for completing works if a cooperative ceased to exist and for paying creditors for those cooperatives for which it acted as a guarantor. It invested in many real estate companies to offset the declining amount of public sector works, which decreased by 23 percent in 2012 and 44 percent in 2013.

The prolonged economic crisis following the 2008 GFC tested CCC's business model. Construction cooperatives have had difficulties since the 1990s (Fabbri 2011), but in 2012, many had filed for bankruptcy, and 34 had made agreements with their creditors hoping to avoid bankruptcy. Where cooperatives could not complete allocated work, CCC stepped in to re-allocate work to other cooperatives, but it made a loss as a result. The real estate investments also faced difficulties in a poor residential market. Less work and fewer procurement sales meant fewer fees. A low growth economy also meant fewer dividends. In 2013, CCC suffered a loss of 20.8 million euros, followed by another loss in 2015. It attempted to manage the situation by reducing costs by as much as 34 percent and by selling assets, but this was not deemed sufficient to continue with its current business model (Fabbri 2011; Consorzio Cooperative Costruzioni 2013; Consorzio Cooperative Costruzioni 2014; Consorzio Cooperative Costruzioni 2016).

In 2016, CCC and Legacoop decided to restructure the consortium. A new consortium, Consorzio Integra, was formed to take over CCC's works division, while CCC would continue to manage the procurement function, financial investments and real estate companies. Integra was formed by 100 cooperatives who invested over 18 million euros. Legacoop financial structures invested 22 million euros. The financial structures include Cooperare, Coopfond and a number of Legacoop local financial companies from Emilia-Romagna (Cooperare 2016). Just like Coop Italia and CNS, CCC had a crisis to manage. Once again, the leadership group was removed and replaced, and once again Legacoop cooperatives and the movement got together to solve the problem, allowing the consortia to start again.

5.5 Concluding Remarks

Consortia have made an important contribution to cooperative growth, innovation and resilience. The four case studies demonstrate the number of benefits that they bring, including lower costs of raw materials or inputs, access to management and technical skills, access to financial support and access to new and diversified markets. There are also risks involved with being part of consortia, as cooperatives may face financial and reputational risks should the consortia business model fail.

Consortia's business models are different. CAVIT's provides comprehensive support and oversight of the wine network and engages directly with the market on members' behalf. Coop Italia performs a central role within the consumer network by engaging with suppliers and managing cooperative brand products. However, its cooperative members are the ones engaging with the market. CNS and CCC also engage with the market, but so too do their cooperative members, at times in competition, because they provide only a small share of their members' total turnover.

The consortia business model needs to be fit-for-purpose and in a position to manage and allocate risks adequately. Three consortia that centralized risks had difficulties. Coop Italia took responsibility for paying suppliers on behalf of cooperatives; CCC took responsibility for completing work on behalf of their members; and CNS provided loans to a cooperative that could not repay it. Risks can also emerge as a result of non-compliance or risky investments. Coop Italia has demonstrated that a simpler structure with clear lines of responsibility between it and the cooperative members has worked well. CCC has also recently simplified its structure by dividing the works function from the procurement and investment function. It would seem that a less risky proposition for consortia is to avoid becoming a one-stop-shop for cooperative needs and instead to focus on where they can add value by avoiding non-core business functions such as finance and by not absorbing risks that should be borne by cooperative enterprises.

The way Legacoop managed the crisis faced by Coop Italia, CCC and CNS demonstrates a strong, resilient culture that permeates the movement. Each time, the Central Association, Coopfond, Legacoop-linked financial companies and large cooperatives came together to solve the problem. The consortia concept is not questioned, but their business models and risk allocation have been reviewed. Each time, the crisis was solved by developing a new business model, along with new capital and a new board and management team. This allowed the consortia to survive and continue to serve its members.

All the consortia have shown that they can innovate in order to compete in the market and to meet their members' needs. CAVIT has extended its role in global marketing and sales in addition to finding new ways to improving farming methods and product quality. Coop Italia has extended its own label products into new areas, such as pharmaceuticals and organic products, and controls the whole-of-product supply chain to ensure suppliers comply with human rights. CCC has changed from a consortium focused on winning traditional public works to a general contractor and a promoter of project finance with private partners and private equity firms. Meanwhile, CNS has continuously added market segments to its offerings, including becoming a one-stop-shop for clients by offering services in multiple locations.

All four cooperatives have demonstrated a high level of integration with the cooperative movement. CAVIT invested in cooperatives and a number of financial companies associated with the Trentino Federation. Coop Italia purchases food and non-food products from other cooperatives that are then sold in supermarkets.[3] CCC promotes inter-cooperative trade by getting its members to purchase building materials from other cooperatives, usually amounting to 10 percent of total sales. CNS and CCC have invested in all key strategic Legacoop financial companies, such as Unipol, CCFS, Coopercredito and local financial companies. They annually deposit 3 percent of their profits into the respective cooperative development funds (Coopfond and Promocoop). CNS and CCC also pay generous membership fees to Legacoop, which have regularly amounted to 500,000 euros.[4]

The benefits provided by the consortia model do flow to small and large cooperatives, but some have demonstrated limitations in meeting the needs of large cooperatives. The vertically integrated consortia like CAVIT and Coop Italia can meet the expectations of both large and small cooperatives. CAVIT provides the same services to all its members, and it sells almost all of their members' produce. Producers are all small, and cooperatives do not have the ambition to operate on their own. Homogenous needs, similar sizes and reliance on CAVIT services means that conflicts are managed. Coop Italia makes available its agreements and products to all cooperatives, large and small. They operate in different market segments and different geographic areas. Large consumer cooperatives have expanded in Southern Italy where there were no local consumer cooperatives. As a result, large and small consumer cooperatives co-exist and benefit from Coop Italia's services. CCC and CNS are not able to provide their members with all the work they need. CNS provides 10 percent of its members' total turnover.[5] CCC also provides a small percentage of their total turnover. This is not unusual considering that one of its members, CMC, has a similar turnover to CCC (Cooperativa, Muratori Cementisti Ravenna 2015; Consorzio Cooperative Costruzioni 2015).[6] Cooperatives in these multi-sector consortia cooperate and compete with each other and their consortia. Small cooperatives benefit by accessing new work in new market segments as a result of working alongside the large cooperatives. The large cooperatives benefit by accessing new geographical territories. The large cooperatives cannot rely on the consortia for growth because the consortia have to distribute work to all members, so they are more autonomous and have formed cooperative-led business groups to improve their market position and competitiveness. The reasons behind the formation of cooperative groups, their operations, benefits and risks will be discussed in next chapter.

Notes

1. As their total expenditure on food decreased from 40 percent 1970 to 17 percent in 2014, consumers developed new preferences.
2. Please refer to the Annual Bilancio di Sostenibilita: www.ccc-acam.it/menu_later ale/bilancio.php, accessed on 29 April 2017.
3. Consumer cooperatives sell fruit and vegetables, dairy products, processed foods, wine, coffee and kitchen and household products produced by other cooperatives.
4. CNS annual reports indicate that it has regularly paid membership fees of 500,000 euros, while CCCs from 2007–2010 paid more than 700,000 euros per year in membership fees.
5. The smaller cooperatives from the Center and South of Italy received 35 percent and 45 percent of their total turnover respectively (Menzani 2010).
6. The cooperative CMC had a turnover of 1.1 billion euros in 2014, more than CCC's turnover of 1 billion euros (Consorzio Cooperative Costruzioni 2015; Cooperativa, Muratori Cementisti 2015).

References

Barberini, Ivano. 2009. *Come Vola il Calabrone.* Milano: Baldini Castoldi Calai Editore.
Bonfante, Guido. 2011. *Manuale di Diritto Cooperativo.* Bologna: Zanichelli.
Casali, Antonio. 2000. *Per Una Storia di Coop Italia: Mario Cesari (1926–1968).* Bologna: Il Mulino.
CAVIT. 2014. *Press Kit.* Company Information, Trento: Cavit.
———. 2016. *Bilancio 2015–2016.* Annual Report, Trento: Cavit.
CNS Board. 2015. *Relazione sulla Gestione al Bilancio Chiuso 31 Dicembre 2014.* Annual Report, Bologna: Consorzio Nazionale Servizi.
———. 2016. *Relazione Sulla Gestione al Bilancio Chiuso al 31 Dicembre 2015.* Annual Report, Bologna: Consorzio Nazionale Servizi.
Consorzio Cooperative Costruzioni. 2003. *Bilancio Consolidato 2002.* Annual Report, Bologna: Consorzio Cooperative Costruzioni.
———. 2006. *Bilancio Consuntivo.* Annual Report, Bologna: Consorzio Cooperative Costruzioni.
———. 2011. *Bilancio di Sostenibilita' 2010.* Annual Report, Bologna: Consorzio Cooperative Costruzioni.
———. 2013. *Bilancio Consolidato 2012.* Annual Report, Bologna: Consorzio Cooperative Costruzioni.
———. 2014. *Bilancio Consolidato 2013.* Annual Report, Bologna: Consorzio Cooperative Costruzioni.

————. 2015. *Bilancio Consuntivo 2014*. Annual Report, Bologna: Consorzio Cooperative Costruzioni.

————. 2016. *Bilancio Consolidato 2015*. Annual Report, Bologna: Consorzio Cooperative Costruzioni.

Consorzio Nazionale Servizi. 2006. *Bilancio di Responsabilita' Sociale*. Bologna: Consorzio Nazionale Servizi.

————. 2009. *Bilancio di Sostenibilita' Sociale*. Bologna: Consorzio Nazionale Servizi.

————. 2016a. *Statuto*. Accessed May 2, 2017. www.cnsonline.it/wp-content/uploads/36785Statuto-aggiornato-CNS.pdf.

————. 2016b. *Bilancio D'Esercizio*. Bologna: Consorzio Nazionale Servizi.

————. 2017. *Statuto*. Bologna: Consorzio Nazionale Servizi, 3 December.

Coop Adriatica 3.0. 2015. *Report di Sostenibilita' Sociale*. Annual Report, Bologna: Coop Adriatica 3.0.

Cooperare. 2016. *Relazione e Bilancio al 30 Giugno 2016*. Annual Report, Bologna: Cooperare Spa.

Cooperativa, Muratori Cementisti Ravenna. 2015. *Bilancio Sociale 2014*. Annual Report, Ravenna: Cooperativa, Muratori Cementisti Ravenna.

Cooperazione Trentina. 2014. *Guida alla Cooperazione Trentina*. Trento: Cooperazione Trentina.

Coop Italia. 2016. *Rapporto Sociale 2015*. Annual Report, Bologna: Coop Italia.

Fabbri, Fabio. 2011. *L'Italia Cooperativa: Centocinquant'anni di Storia e di memoria. 1861–2011*. Rome: Ediesse.

Felice, Emanuele. 2010. "The Strategies and Development of CNS." In *Cooperation Network Service*, edited by Patrizia Battilani and Giuliana Bertagnoni, 65–117. Lancaster: Crucible Books.

Gazzetta di Reggio. 2015. *Coopservice Brilla nel 2014, Utili e Ricavi in Crescita*. Gazzetta di Reggio, 27 June. Accessed on February, 14, 2018. http://gazzettadireggio.gelocal.it/reggio/cronaca/2015/06/27/news/coopservice-brilla-nel-2014-piu-utili-e-ricavi-1.11689917?refresh_ce

Linguiti, Francesco. 2014. "I Consorzi tra Societa' Cooperative." In *La Cooperazione Italiana Negli Anni della Crisi: Secondo Rapporto Euricse*, edited by Carlo Borzaga, 73–84. Trento: Euricse.

Manutencoop. 2015. *Comunicato Stampa*. Manutencoop. Bologna, 25 March.

Menzani, Tito. 2010. "For Good and for Bad: Aspects and Problems of the CNS Cooperative Network." In *Cooperation Network Service*, edited by Patrizia Battilani and Giuliana Bertagnoni, 118–176. Lancaster: Crucible Books.

————, and Vera Zamagni. 2010. "Cooperative Networks in the Italian Economy." *Enterprise & Society*, Volume 11, Number 1, 98–127.

OECD. 2014. *The Cooperative Model in Trentino*. Case Study, Paris: OECD.

Tassinari. 2015. *Noi, Le Coop Rosse. Tra Supermercati e Riforme Mancate*. Soveria Mannelli: Rubbettino Editore.

Zamagni, Vera, Patrizia Battilani, and Antonio Casali. 2004. *La Cooperazione di Consumo in Italia*. Bologna: Il Mulino.

6 The Rise of Cooperative Groups
A New Cooperative Model?

Since the 1960s, Legacoop cooperatives have believed that by growing into large enterprises they would be able to compete in the market and meet their mutual obligations to their members. They grew organically, via mergers and through becoming active members of a consortium and the broader cooperative network. Where cooperatives did not have critical mass, or where they did have but cooperatives did not wish to merge, this growth path was no longer viable. As noted in Chapter 5, growing through being an active member of a consortium was also no longer a viable option for many large cooperatives. As globalization intensified in the 1980s, the large diversified cooperatives needed to develop more capabilities, increase their know-how and access risk capital to meet their investment requirements. To this end, they formed cooperative groups of companies ('cooperative groups' hereafter) so they could grow, diversify, resist competition and make the most of the opportunities that a global market offered.

A cooperative group is a business group, led by a cooperative that wholly or partially owns a set of legally independent subsidiaries. This business model allows for a strategic use of governance, legal and operational arrangements that enable cooperatives to compete in the market while maintaining their cooperative legal status. This chapter is divided into six parts. The first section introduces different forms of business groups. The second focuses on the importance of cooperative groups to the Italian cooperative sector. The third section explains the context that led cooperatives to establish cooperative groups. The fourth section discusses the key economic benefits derived from cooperative groups. The fifth section examines how five cooperatives have developed into cooperative groups. The sixth section assesses the benefits and risks associated with the cooperative group model.

6.1 Business Groups as a Unique Way to Compete in the Market

The formation of business groups is one of four major organizational models that businesses adopt to compete in the market. These groups reflect a country's economic development and cultural characteristics that have developed over time. Each model holds unique competitive advantages. They compete on scale, scope, flexibility and speed (Fruin 2007). These models are:

- Modern firms: these firms internalize needed resources and capabilities. These are large multi-business and multi-divisional firms best represented by large North American companies. These companies control their strategy, administration and the whole productive process (Coplan and Takashi 2010).
- Business groups: these are firms that work together by common ownership and control. The key feature is that of a holding company or parent company fully or partially owning legally independent subsidiaries. The latter is controlled and directed via equity holding, interlocking directorships, aligned strategies and intra-group transactions (Coplan and Takashi 2010).
- Industrial districts: this refers to firms working together on the basis of location, shared culture and shared resources, including research and development, know-how and access to marketing, legal, accounting and consultancy services. These are supported by government policies, business associations, local banks and educational institutions. Their distinct feature is that firms cooperate and compete at the same time, and through this approach small specialized firms can achieve economies of scale while remaining small and flexible (Zeitlin 2007).[1]
- Inter-firm networks: firms of various sizes and specialties work together on the basis of shared information, frequent interactions, complementary services, common values and mutual benefits. These are independent firms that can freely join and leave the network. The Japanese vertically integrated *Keiretsu* system, such as that practiced by Toyota, which relies on thousands of suppliers to provide parts to manufacture its cars, is also seen as an inter-firm network (Fruin 2007).

The Italian cooperative network is one that overall competes as a network of cooperative enterprises, as the previous chapters and studies have already highlighted (Ammirato 1996; Menzani and Zamagni 2010). The five large cooperative groups of enterprises that will be reviewed later, however, will demonstrate that they take advantage of one or more of the four models identified. Usually, these cooperatives started growing via the inter-firm network model and developed by also taking advantage of the business group and the modern firm's models. One cooperative is also entrenched within the local ceramic industrial district.

6.2 The Significance of Cooperative Business Groups

The study of cooperative business groups is significant because they make a substantial contribution to the cooperative sector and the local economy, and they also provide an opportunity to assess the extent to which cooperatives can grow. In other words, can cooperatives grow as large as capitalist enterprises or are they resigned to perform a marginal role in the economy? Their key significance can be summarized as follows:

- They generate a high level of turnover. The largest 250 cooperatives (those with a turnover of 50 million euros or more) account for less than 1 percent of the total cooperatives but produce 61.8 percent of the cooperative sector's total turnover.[2] This reflects both Legacoop and Confcooperative's networks. In 2003, Legacoop's 98 largest cooperatives already produced 68 percent of Legacoop's total turnover (Zamagni and Felice 2006). Confcooperative's largest 1.9 percent of cooperatives produced 57 percent of their total turnover (Confcooperative 2016).
- They make investments in the cooperative sector. It is estimated that by 2003, Legacoop's 98 largest cooperatives had invested 2.8 billion euros in various companies plus another 3.3 billion euros in Unipol (Zamagni and Felice 2006). Also, Legacoop's largest 100 cooperatives contribute up to 80 percent of Coopfond's total deposits (Coopfond 2017).
- They have a high level of employment. The largest 250 cooperatives employ 21.1 percent of the cooperative sector's total employment.[3]
- Large cooperatives are more likely to compete globally. A Unioncamere study on Emilia Romagna noted that 239 cooperatives exported their products and services. Of these, the largest five cooperatives are responsible for 65 percent of total exports (Caselli 2016).
- Large cooperatives are more likely to withstand and survive a global financial crisis.[4]

6.3 The Context That Led to the Formation of Cooperative Groups

There are some key reasons why, by the mid-1990s, cooperatives had established cooperative groups. The first reason is that cooperatives operate with a long-term vision incorporating economic and social goals. Legacoop promoted large cooperatives so they could compete in an economy dominated by large companies. In support of this, it encouraged cooperatives to merge and form large national cooperatives. Legacoop promoted wider pay differentials to attract private sector managers to improve their professionalism and competitiveness (Battilani 2010). Confcooperative, while always supportive of small cooperatives, also responded to market pressures and developed large cooperative groups whose numbers now equal those of Legacoop. The strategy succeeded, and by 2011, 14.8 percent of all enterprises in Italy that employed more than 500 employees were cooperatives. Compare this with only 3.6 percent in 1971 (Alleanza Cooperative Italiane 2017).

Second, cooperatives and their members also came to understand that only by growing and achieving economies of scale would they be able to meet the needs of members. This led the consumer movement to grow so they could provide quality food at lower costs. The construction, manufacturing and service cooperatives grew in order to provide long-term employment for their members. Agricultural cooperatives also grew so that they could provide steady prices for the produce of their members, while cooperative banks grew so that they could offer loans and services at competitive prices. Growth was linked to the principles of mutuality and long-term planning and this suited members and management (Zevi 2005b).

The third reason why cooperatives had established cooperative groups, Alberto Zevi argues, is that tax policies facilitated asset growth, which in turn facilitated access to credit and cooperative growth. For instance, the 1977 tax policies allowed cooperatives to re-invest profits into the indivisible reserve fund tax-free, while rebates to members were deemed to be taxable. This encouraged cooperatives to re-invest almost all of their profits into the indivisible reserve fund, focusing on long-term benefits rather than short-term gains. A study conducted in 2004 revealed that 83 percent of all profits were placed in the indivisible reserve fund (Petrucci 2005). This practice allowed cooperatives to accumulate assets that facilitated access to credit because indivisible assets could be used as collateral. The ability to attract members' loans since 1971 and external capital since 1992 further facilitated access to credit and external capital. This allowed cooperatives to grow, but despite this, large cooperatives still found themselves reliant on bank loans for investment purposes. By the 1990s large cooperatives began to consider the formation of a cooperative group as the best way to meet their financial needs because its legal structure allowed them to attract equity capital (Zevi 2005a; Zevi 2005b; Zamagni and Felice 2006).

Fourth, the large cooperatives realized that continuing to grow organically, via mergers and via the consortia system, would limit their capacity to grow. Growing organically is less risky but it is slow, and cooperatives risked missing out on market opportunities. Growing via mergers suited those cooperatives that were operating in the consumer, agricultural, construction or service sectors, where cooperatives had achieved a critical mass but did not suit those operating in the manufacturing sector. In any case, not all cooperatives wanted to merge. As Chapter 5 noted, consortia are required to distribute work to all members, so programming growth via reliance on a consortium no longer suited the large cooperatives in the construction or services industry. Cooperatives, therefore, began to consider growing through joint ventures with private partners or via the acquisition of private enterprises (Bitossi and Simion 2008).

Fifth, the key event that gave the cooperative sector confidence to be more daring, to experiment, and to access external capital was the 1986 listing of the Unipol shares. Unipol has demonstrated a capacity to grow and pursue insurance policies that benefited working people and small business, open general medical practices that provided low-cost medical services and support cooperatives experiencing difficulties. It publishes an annual report demonstrating its social responsibility credentials to all key stakeholders. Unipol demonstrated that a large listed company could provide services in alignment with cooperative values (Zamagni 2015).

By the 1990s, then, cooperatives were ready to form cooperative groups. They had become large companies with access to credit and the confidence to engage with the financial markets and private partners. Mario Viviani, a notable co-operator and scholar, said that at this point cooperatives began to ask how far they could grow. What market position should they occupy: a leadership position or a marginalized position? If cooperatives wanted to become leading enterprises, they needed more capital. To this end, the formation of cooperative groups became the logical next step. Questions on how to promote democracy within cooperative groups and the role of external investors were also raised and debated. In the end, Legacoop cooperatives decided to form cooperative groups and deal with issues as they arise (Viviani 2016).[5]

6.4 The Economic Benefits of Cooperative Groups

There are a number of economic factors that led cooperatives to form cooperative groups as their preferred business model. These included: internationalization; the formation of joint ventures; separately managing non-core activities; acquisitions; accessing external capital; better management of risks and resources; and market positioning.

6.4.1 Internationalization

Those cooperatives that began to export or operate in international markets at first resorted to creating trading, sales and after-sales services companies overseas. These were either wholly owned or in partnership with a local partner who could speak the local language, was familiar with legal requirements and understood the local culture (Legacoop 2002). Today cooperatives own companies based overseas that manufacture on site, manage major construction works, produce dairy products and manage catering services. All of these investments provide cooperatives with access to new markets, new products, know-how and local knowledge.

6.4.2 Joint Ventures

Joint ventures include ad hoc project-based companies. The first joint ventures took place in the construction industry, where cooperatives partnered with large private businesses to bid for large public works that they could not have won on their own. These included building and managing a large public hospital or co-building a subway line. In these cases, different firms complete a project component. Joint ventures also include public-private partnerships, such as those entered into by Camst with local government to provide catering services to local schools. These joint ventures provided finance, know-how and capabilities that facilitated access to new markets and new services.

6.4.3 Separating Non-Core Activities

Over time, cooperatives invested in other cooperative-owned companies; in property trusts that owned offices and commercial centers and promoted housing developments; and also in local companies that they had rescued as part of their commitment to the local economy. Cooperatives decided that non-core activities would be best managed as independent companies that could be further developed or sold off. Managing them via a separate independent structure improved accountability and was seen as a better way to identify costs and profits (Bitossi and Simion 2008).

6.4.4 Acquisition of Private Companies

Acquisition of private companies provides the opportunity to grow at a faster pace. Total or part acquisition of private companies have allowed cooperatives to diversify their products. For example, Sacmi diversified from ceramics to packaging, food and automation. Acquisition has also allowed companies to access new markets or control the whole supply chain. For example, CMC purchased a number of construction companies in the United States, while Granarolo controls the whole supply chain from raw materials to manufacturing to sales. Acquisitions can strengthen a cooperative's position in the national market, as was the case when Cooperativa Adriatica bought the Veneto-based Full Supermarkets.

6.4.5 Accessing Capital by Listing Spin-Off Companies

Cooperatives have used the stock exchange and private investors to access risk capital. Two consumer cooperatives are the majority shareholders of Immobiliare Grande Distribuzione (IGD), a listed property trust company. Coop Adriatica owns 40 percent of a 2.2 billion euro company, while Unicoop Firenze and external shareholders own the rest (Coop Adriatica 2016). Cooperservice controls 59 percent of the listed company Servizi Italia via its subsidiary Aurium Spa. The company is worth 122 million euros and provides wash-hire and linen and surgical instrument sterilization services for hospitals (Servizi Italia 2017). These cooperatives have been able to access external capital while still maintaining control of their subsidiary.

6.4.6 Governance: Risk Management and Accountabilities

The cooperative group formation where a cooperative wholly or partially owns subsidiaries directly or via a holding company reduces risks and improves accountability. It has been argued that having separate companies reduces the financial risk because if a company fails, the loss is limited to the amount invested in that company. Considering that some cooperatives own many subsidiaries, having each governed by a separate board is deemed to be a better way to manage and monitor their performance. The formation of separate subsidiaries is a good risk management approach to entering a new market, launching a new product or diversifying into a new non-core business activity. The formation of subsidiaries as public companies is unavoidable when cooperatives enter into a partnership with private investors or capitalist companies, as this legal form allows investors to have their voting powers aligned to their property rights (the value of shares equal the value of assets). This would not be possible if they invested in a cooperative or consortia.

6.4.7 Market Positioning

A significant reason for the development of groups of companies by cooperatives is the desire to operate in a high-value market segment. This was the case with Manutencoop, a general contractor that in 2004 spun off its divisions into subsidiaries of its holding company, Manutencoop Facilities Management (MFM). Manutencoop Cooperative owns 67 percent of MFM, with the remaining shares owned by private equity companies as well as Unipol and Cooperare[6]. Manutencoop was already employing more than 11,000 employees at the time, but it wanted to grow to provide public and private clients with a set of integrated services on a national scale. These are the services that global competitors were offering, so Manutencoop repositioned itself to compete against them. It was the decision to become an industry leader that led Manutencoop to establish MFN, attract external capital and establish a group of companies. The alternative was risking marginalization (Manutencoop 2014; Manutencoop 2017a).

6.5 Cooperative Groups Development Models

This section examines how five cooperatives from different sectors of the economy have developed into cooperative groups. It explores whether they have grown, either within the cooperative sector or more independently. It examines the reasons for developing a group structure and how it has facilitated growth. Whether subsidiaries have been incorporated into the original cooperative business structure or maintained as legally independent businesses will also be reviewed. This provides some insights into cooperative behaviors and relations they hold with the Legacoop network and the rest of the market. The five cooperatives are Coop Adriatica, Camst, Granarolo, Sacmi and Cooperativa Muratori e Cementisti.[7]

6.5.1 Coop Adriatica

Coop Adriatica is a consumer cooperative headquartered in Bologna. It is a member of the national consortium Coop Italia. It commenced operation in 1945 as the Consumer Cooperative for the People of Bologna, operating 17 small retail outlets and employing 207 people. It began operating as Coop Bologna, but as it expanded it changed its name to Coop Emilia-Veneto, and Coop Adriatica to reflect its geographic expansion. By 2015, the latter had evolved into a cooperative group with over 2 billion euros in revenue and 9,500 employees. Its development into a cooperative group can be summarized as follows:

- The first phase, 1945–1980, included incorporations, mergers and expansion into the Veneto region. Coop Adriatica incorporated smaller cooperatives, and in 1968 it merged with ten cooperatives to form Coop Bologna, which managed 197 outlets. In 1975, Coop Adriatica merged with a cooperative from the Veneto region and became known as Coop Emilia-Veneto.
- The second stage, 1980–2003, included acquisitions, mergers and the formation of public companies in partnership with other cooperatives. In 1987, Coop Adriatica bought the Stargill Group, which owned the Full Supermarket chain in Veneto, in a joint partnership with Coop Estense, another consumer cooperative from Emilia Romagna. In 1991, it formed a public company with three other consumer cooperatives from Emilia Romagna to develop supermarkets along the Adriatic Coast. In 1995, it merged with the cooperative Coop Romagna-Marche to form Coop Adriatica (Zamagni, Battilani and Casali 2004). In 2003 it joined other consumer cooperatives to form three public companies designed to promote cooperative supermarkets in Sicily, Rome and the South. The mergers and acquisitions allowed it to achieve economies of scale and expand into other regions. Establishing public companies with other cooperatives allowed Coop Adriatica to access capital and share the financial and reputational risk associated with opening supermarkets in other regions.
- The third phase, 2004–2015, is characterized by the listing of IGD and the provision of additional non-food services. Coop Adriatica and Unicoop Tirreno listed their real estate assets under IGD. This property trust owns and manages 25 commercial and retail centers in Italy and 14 in Romania. This listing allowed the two cooperatives to access external finance while retaining a controlling share of the company (IGD 2017). Coop Adriatica diversified its services and products. It purchased or established companies in the non-core areas of travel, health and well-being, electricity and gas, books shops, health insurance and other related activities.

  Coop Adriatica had indeed become a cooperative group with a broad investment portfolio that includes ten controlled companies and 34 other companies, including major investments in the cooperative sector, the largest of which is Finsoe, Unipol's major shareholder (Coop Adriatica 2016a).
- In 2016, Coop Adriatica merged with two other large consumer cooperatives from the region of Emilia Romagna, Coop Consumatori Nord-Est and Coop Estense, to form Coop Alleanza 3.0. It operates in all the

regions along the Adriatic coast from Friuli to Puglia. It has 2.7 million members, 383 supermarkets, 4.3 billion in sales, and a combined 383 million euros in investments (Coop Adriatica 2016b). This merger is to achieve further economies of scale as well as economies of scope by consolidating their holdings and memberships.

The key feature of Coop Adriatica's development into a group of companies is that it has been planned in alignment with Legacoop's consumer association's national strategy and partnership with other consumer cooperatives. The consumer sectoral association promoted the development of large enterprises to compete against Italian and European supermarket chains. It also supported cooperatives' expansion into other regions. Its recent strategy is to develop three large consumer groups: one in the North, one along the Tyrrhenian coast and Coop Alleanza 3.0 to manage cooperatives along the Adriatic coast.

Coop Adriatica was also able to grow via the cooperative sector because consumer cooperatives had critical mass in Emilia Romagna but did not have a major presence in nearby regions. This allowed Emilian consumer cooperatives to grow and then to expand into other regions through mergers and acquisitions of private companies, and then via public companies before subsequently merging again into Coop Alleanza 3.0. As stated, the cooperatives that formed Coop Alleanza 3.0 had jointly invested in a number of companies, so they knew each other well, had developed similar investment policies and were all members of Legacoop's sectoral association and Coop Italia. Being from Emilia-Romagna, all displayed a cooperative culture that facilitated the final merger.

Consumer cooperatives have met their financial needs via its large membership. Coop Adriatica's 256,000 members provided 2.2 billion euros in loans. These can be withdrawn at notice, but in reality are long-term loans because members rarely withdraw their deposits. Therefore, this money has been used for long-term investments and contributed to Coop Adriatica being able to self-finance its operations through retained profits, member shares and member loans. It has achieved a leadership position through this self-financing model. The listing of IGD, however, allowed Coop Adriatica access to external capital by listing its property assets on the stock exchange. Leading a company with the potential to acquire more commercial properties would provide Coop Adriatica with the opportunity to open new supermarkets.

Coop Adriatica has incorporated all supermarket acquisitions into the cooperative, but it has kept non-core business as separate subsidiaries. The head cooperative contributes 97.5 percent of the group's total turnover, indicating that almost all of the growth is via the cooperative's core food and retail business.

6.5.2 Camst: A Catering Cooperative Group

Camst is a catering company that was formed in 1945. Throughout the 1950s and 1960s, it managed the buffet at the Bologna railway station and a number of fast food outlets. Following the non-renewal of the lease for the buffet in 1967, Camst focused on diversifying its operations and began to provide catering services for schools, companies, hospitals, business events and exhibitions. In the 1980s, it employed 1,000 people. In 2015, the Camst Group had 12,638 employees (Camst 2016).

Camst at first grew organically within the province of Bologna. The opportunity to develop into a national cooperative came in 1989, when Legacoop's sectoral association changed its policy from one that favored regionally based cooperatives to one that promoted a few large nationally based cooperatives operating in the catering sector. This new strategy was regarded as more suitable to compete against large companies from Italy and Europe. It paved the way for Camst to become a national company (Battilani 2002).

Camst embraced Legacoop's strategy and embarked on a policy of territorial expansion and product diversification. Key events included:

- Phase one, 1945–1985: organic growth. Camst initially managed coffeeshops/fast food restaurants, but soon branched out into managing restaurants and providing catering services for companies, schools, hospitals and the University of Bologna. By 1985, Camst employed over 3,000 people (Lolli 2002).
- Phase two, 1986–1993: growing via cooperative mergers and regional expansion. Camst merged with five cooperatives from Tuscany, Liguria, Marche and Friuli. This enabled it to achieve economies of scale and a presence in four other regions. It also established two joint ventures with local private entrepreneurs specializing in catering for business events and exhibitions.
- Phase three, 1993—present: growth via acquisitions of private companies and joint ventures. Camst purchased more than ten private companies operating in the regions of Emilia-Romagna, Lombardy and Veneto and one operating in Germany. Camst also established joint ventures with a number of local governments in Emilia-Romagna and in partnership with a private company in the city of Turin to provide catering services to schools. It recently formed two joint ventures with cooperatives focusing on overseas markets (Camst 2016).

The current Camst group comprises a finance company, which invests Camst's liquidity, and 13 other companies. Of these, two are joint ventures with private sector focus on events and exhibitions; six are cooperative-local government joint ventures focusing on catering for schools; two are joint ventures with two other cooperatives that focus on catering and international trade; two more are wholly owned companies operating in catering and cleaning services; and one is a wholly owned catering company operating in Germany.

Camst's development into a cooperative group of companies is in full alignment with Legacoop's strategy. It has benefited from the strategy of creating two large national catering groups because it could grow via merging with other cooperatives from other regions. This allowed Camst to become a large enterprise and to have the confidence to develop joint ventures with private and local government partners and acquire private companies. These enabled it to expand into other regions, diversify its product offering and achieve economies of scale and scope.

The second feature is that it gradually incorporated the subsidiaries into the cooperative structure, providing new employees the opportunity to become cooperative members. For instance, in 2015 the cooperative employed 10,633 persons, all of whom were permanent employees, while its subsidiaries employed 2,054. The policies of acquisitions and partnerships are aligned with the company's strategy for growth but are not designed to diminish the open door principle and democratic management.

Camst has continued to maintain close ties with the Legacoop network. It is a member of Karabak, a consortium of five cooperatives that builds, owns and operates child care centers on behalf of the City of Bologna. It is also a member of the consortia CNS, Integra and CCFS. It collaborates or provides catering and cleaning services to 24 social cooperatives, and 84 cooperatives are part of its supply chains (Camst 2016; Cadiai 2017; Consorzio Nazionale Servizi 2017).

6.5.3 Granlatte-Granarolo: A Dairy Cooperative Group

Granlatte-Granarolo is a consortium based in Bologna. It commenced operations as the consortium of Bologna dairy producers. It aimed to purchase raw milk from members and either process it, bottle it and sell it directly under its Granarolo brand or to re-sell the milk to other dairy companies. It operated until the 1980s on a not-for-profit basis. It was the view of Legacoop that this model was no longer viable and, in response to the 1973 EEC directive promoting a free market for dairy products, it encouraged Granarolo to become more entrepreneurial. The Maastricht Treaty of 1992 and the Italian government's decision to privatize local government-owned milk companies provided Granarolo with the opportunity to become a national company (Felice 2004).

Granarolo grew steadily into a group of companies with a national and international presence. By 2015, it had become a diversified group of companies, the largest milk producer in Italy and one of its largest cheese and yogurt producers. Its turnover amounted to 1.078 billion euros. It employed 2,489 people and provided income to a further 20,000 persons as a result of its activities. It made 18 million euros in profits (Granarolo 2016a). Granlatte-Granarolo's growth path consists of four distinct phases:

- Phase one, 1957–1971: organic growth within the municipality of Bologna. Granarolo produced both fresh and long-life milk and used the channels offered by the cooperative sector and the political left to market its products. However, during this time most of its raw milk was sold to other dairy companies. In 1971, it generated a turnover of 3 million euros (Battilani 2004b).

- Phase two, 1972–1985: Granarolo became a regional leader. The consortium grew via a number of mergers and small acquisitions. It merged with ten cooperatives, of which Felsinea was the most prominent, and purchased ten small companies from Emilia Romagna. As a result, the name was changed to Consortium of Milk Producers from Emilia-Romagna (CERPL). At this time, CERPL was operating on a not-for-profit basis and did not generate much capital. The investment money came from members' shares, members' loans and mostly bank loans. As a result of mergers and small acquisitions, the turnover reached 128 million euros in 1983 (Battilani 2004a).
- Phase three, 1986–1991: Granarolo became a profit-making enterprise. In the late 1980s, it acquired six dairy companies, some of which operated in Southern Italy. The failure to purchase two large companies, one of which was a cooperative, however, led Granarolo to change the way it operated. First, it became a for-profit cooperative. Second, it generated capital by paying members 20 percent of purchases at the end of the year rather than paying them the full price at the end of each month. Third, members were asked to invest more, resulting in members' capital rising from 11 to 30 million euros.
- Phase four, 1992–2012: saw the formation of a holding company and a strong national presence. The previous changes did not provide sufficient capital to meet the cooperative's aspirations, so in 1992 it established a holding company, Granarolo Spa, to attract external capital. More specifically, the CERPL was renamed as Granlatte. It would coordinate milk production and manufacturing as well as being the majority shareholder of Granarolo Spa. Granlatte currently has 623 members. Granarolo Spa's role was to attract external capital to facilitate acquisitions of dairy and related companies (transport and logistics) and to establish new companies. The dairy companies would purchase milk from Granlatte. In 1997, a state-owned investment company, Invest Italia, purchased 20 percent of its shares.[8]

    In the same year, the Banca di Bologna granted Granarolo a 50 million euro line of credit. This allowed Granarolo to expand via acquisitions, diversify its product range and become a national company. It bought 12 dairy companies producing parmesan cheese, goat's milk and yogurt and fresh pasta. The largest acquisition was the Milan Dairy Company, which was valued at 60 million euros. Granarolo Spa now wholly or partially owns nine subsidiaries all over Italy. Its turnover increased to 845 million euros by 2011 (Granarolo 2016b; Battilani 2004a).
- Phase five, 2013–present: Granarolo became an international company. Granarolo Spa established Granarolo International holding, of which 75 percent is owned by Granarolo Spa and 25 percent by Cooperare Spa. Granarolo International holding has a capital of 50 million euros.

Its role is to purchase dairy companies overseas that either produce or distribute dairy products. As of 2015, it had controlling interest in seven companies operating in Europe, Britain, South America and New Zealand, plus a commercial office in China. It owns six dairy plants and 20 percent of its turnover is now generated overseas (Calzolari 2015).

Granarolo's growth strategy is aligned with Legacoop's vision for the cooperative sector and its promotion of large cooperatives. Its early organic growth came about as a result of its links with the cooperative sector and the political left, which provided a market for its products sold in the province of Bologna. It then grew via merging with other dairy cooperatives to become a regional consortium. However, Granarolo could not grow via the cooperative sector anymore because the common values and vision that had previously allowed cooperatives to merge had weakened by the 1990s. Growth through acquisition, relying on internal funding or bank or member loans, was also not an option because it was costly and not sufficient. As a result, the Granlatte cooperative established Granarolo Spa and Granarolo International to access external capital.

Granarolo Spa is governed as a traditional public company. Granlatte is the majority shareholder and has appointed seven of the nine board members. Granlatte's Chair is also the Chair of Granarolo Spa. The Board appoints a CEO who in turn manages direct reports from various divisions or subsidiaries.

The Granlatte cooperative operates a dual structure whereby it is the major shareholder of Granarolo Spa, which owns or partly owns nine subsidiaries managed as conventional firms. Granarolo Spa's turnover of 1.078 billion euros dwarfs Granlatte's turnover of 236 million. The mutual obligations to members, however, are still being met because Granlatte sells 95 percent of its milk to Granarolo Spa, with the rest sold to third parties. As such, it sells all of its members' produce. The principles of mutuality are met because the dividends paid by Granarolo Spa to the cooperative Granlatte are distributed according to Italian cooperative law, which limits return on members' capital and requires remaining profits to be deposited into the indivisible reserve fund.

Granarolo has kept its ties with the Legacoop cooperative network. As noted, it has entered into a partnership with Cooperare Spa, which is its key investor in its international holding company. It sells its milk through the Coop and Conad Supermarkets throughout Italy. It is a key investor with Banco di Bologna cooperative bank and FIBO, the cooperative-owned investment company based in Bologna. In France, it purchases milk from French dairy cooperatives.

6.5.4 Sacmi: A World Leading Manufacturing Cooperative

Sacmi was founded in 1919 by nine mechanics. It started by securing a loan from the local cooperative bank and leased an empty gymnasium hall from the Socialist local government. Sacmi initially repaired machinery that produced tiles or that washed agricultural produce on behalf of two cooperatives. They also repaired machinery for the railway and hospitals. Following the end of the Second World War, La Ceramica Cooperative asked Sacmi to build new machine presses for the ceramics industry. Another local business requested that Sacmi manufacture machines for producing metal caps as those made in America were too expensive. In 1949, Sacmi employed 84 workers, of whom 32 were members. In 2015, Sacmi generated 1.34 billion euros and employed 4,180 people. It controlled 75 firms with exports comprising 85 percent of all sales (Sacmi 2017; Sacmi 2016).

The growth of Sacmi took place gradually and was not reliant on the cooperative sector. While Imola cooperatives engaged Sacmi to manufacture machinery for them, there were few of them. Further, Sacmi could not grow via mergers with other cooperatives because it was the only one operating in this sector. Sacmi grew organically until 1960, focusing on the Italian market and the ceramics industry, which was responsible for 67 percent of sales. To grow, it developed a strategy to diversify its products and markets which ultimately led it to become a global company offering a one-stop-shop for product lines. Key phases included:

- First phase, 1960–1980: focus on the ceramic industry and opening overseas offices. During this period Sacmi became a major shareholder in a company from Sassuolo that produced presses for ceramic tiles, later renamed Sacmi Molds and Dies. It established a subsidiary in Milan, Sacmi Impianti, to export Sacmi products, offer after sale service to its clients and open offices in Spain and Brazil. Sacmi Impianti built plants overseas and reduced Sacmi's financial risks (Benati and Mazzoli 2009).
- Second phase, 1980–2000: overseas expansion and diversification. Sacmi began to establish offices overseas to commercialize its products, offer after-sales service and engage with local partners who knew local customs, language and business practices. Offices were established in Germany, Portugal, Mexico and Singapore. Key acquisitions allowed Sacmi to access new product lines. These included: an Imola company with expertise in packaging agricultural products; another that manufactured ceramic sanitary and homeware products; another that manufactured machinery for food packaging; and two German companies producing homewares and industrial ovens.
- Third phase, 2000–2015: diversification, integration of subsidiaries, overseas plants and expansion. Sacmi is now present in 89 locations overseas, including manufacturing plants in nine countries. Key acquisitions have included: two companies that manufactured machines to produce chocolate and ice cream; Cosmec, a company that focused on automated brick handling solutions; and another German company that produced ceramic based crockery, refractory and carbon-based products. These acquisitions enabled Sacmi to diversify into the food industry and bricks production and strengthen its foothold within the ceramic industry.

Sacmi now controls 75 firms, which have been consolidated into four areas: ceramics, closure and containers, packaging and food. Each area can offer clients a one-stop-shop that includes the complete design, manufacture and sale of machines and complete plants, with an after-sales service for all of these areas. Further diversification occurs within each sector. For instance, Sacmi designs and builds plants to manufacture tiles as well as sanitary products, whiteware, heavy bricks (roofing tiles), refractory products and metal powders (Sacmi 2016).

The Sacmi group is a diversified, globally competitive company. Local cooperatives initially supported it, but the real linkage is with the local economy and the tile-producing industrial district of Sassuolo. It was local business people who gave Sacmi the idea of selling agricultural machinery and machinery to produce bottle caps. Most of Sacmi's acquisitions were also made within the region of Emilia Romagna, allowing it to access know-how, diversify and reach scale and scope. Today Sacmi spends 724 million euros on 2,000 suppliers, of which 509 million is spent on suppliers from Imola and Emilia-Romagna (Sacmi 2015).

The reason for forming a cooperative group does not appear to be driven by the need to access risk capital. Indeed, Sacmi owns outright its key subsidiaries, and where it has entered a joint venture the investments are not significant compared with its assets. The key reason for forming a group was to access know-how from partners involved in sales offices in other countries; access know-how to be able to design and build complete plants; increase market share by buying out competitors; diversify into other areas; manage financial risks via having independent subsidiaries; and have a more flexible structure, as it is easier to sell subsidiaries or parts of a subsidiary. These operations were financed from company profits, members' investments and a number of bank loans. Sacmi also deals with many foreign banks and insurance companies, mainly to facilitate clients' access to credit to buy their products (Benati and Mazzoli 2009; Bassani 2000).

Sacmi is growing more via its subsidiaries than the cooperative headquarters. The Sacmi group employed 4,180 persons in 2015, of which over 2,800 are employed in Italy. Of these, 1,084 are employed by Sacmi headquarters. Unlike the cooperative Camst, Sacmi has not incorporated these wholly owned businesses into Sacmi cooperative or turned them into a cooperative. Indeed, out of 1,084 employees, only 385 are members (Sacmi 2015). The cooperative holds a view that it is better to have fewer, dedicated members fully embracing the cooperative values, than having a large membership that can make democratic management unworkable (Hancock 2007).

6.5.5 Cooperativa Muratori e Cementisti: A Globally Competitive Construction Cooperative

Cooperativa Muratori and Cementisti, CMC, was established in Ravenna in 1901. Initial jobs included building a local bridge and managing the drainage system on behalf of a local government. It was involved in rebuilding

Southern towns hit by the earthquake of 1908. It survived under Fascist administration, and in 1945, 668 members re-established it as a democratically managed cooperative. From its very beginning, CMC was a large cooperative and worked in other Italian regions. It gradually diversified its product offerings to become a leading construction enterprise in Italy with an extensive overseas presence (Zamagni 2011). In 2016, CMC's turnover amounted to over 1 billion euros, and it employed 7,300 persons (CMC 2016b). Key stages of its growth path include:

- Phase one, 1945–1969: organic growth. CMC becomes a national company focusing on large public works. After 1945, CMC initially focused on building apartments but soon started to diversify into large public works such as silos, freeways, port infrastructure and tunneling. Public infrastructure soon constituted most of CMC's work, and by the early 1960s, it already employed over 3,000 people (Earle 1987; Cavallari 2017).
- Phase two, 1970s onwards: CMC develops into a diversified group of companies through acquisitions and partnerships. Key acquisitions included: Dam Projects, which specialized in water desalination plants; three companies operating in waste management and sewerage treatment; and another company specializing in prefabricated materials. It became a shareholder of many project-based companies with other cooperatives and private enterprises that closed once the projects were completed.
- Phase three, 1975–2016: CMC becomes an international company via partnerships with the private and cooperative sectors. CMC had unsuccessfully tried to win projects overseas. Its breakthrough came when Cogefar, a private company, offered it the opportunity to build silos in Iran. In the 1970s, Legacoop developed good relations with governments in Somalia, Tunisia and Mozambique and won many public contracts on behalf of the cooperative sector. CMC in partnership with the private sector and other Legacoop cooperatives build silos, dams, purification plans and roads. The largest work was the Mozambique Dam in 1981, which was worth 115 million dollars (Zamagni 2011). CMC later expanded into Asia and in 2011 into the United States. Today, 54 percent of CMC's turnover is produced overseas (CMC 2016a).

CMC today is a diversified, international cooperative group. Its main areas include transport, water and irrigation works, ecology and the environment, water control and marine works. It controls a company producing building material, another producing prefabricated material, a real estate property development company and an overseas investment company focusing on purchasing American companies, as well as companies in Asia, Mozambique and other parts of Africa. It wholly or partially owns 54 companies and also has 72 million euros invested in close to 80 companies, many of which belong to the cooperative sector (CMC 2016b).

CMC's growth pattern includes organic growth supported by partnerships and acquisitions. CMC did incorporate a couple of cooperatives in the 1970s and was a member of the consortium CCC, but initially grew by winning work on its own in Romagna and other parts of Italy. CMC was always a large cooperative, so it could be argued that it preceded Legacoop's policy of creating large cooperatives. In the 1970s, it demonstrated a degree of strategic autonomy from Legacoop because it was the first construction cooperative to form partnerships with private firms. At the same time, it also partnered Legacoop cooperatives in Italy and abroad. Through acquisitions, it acquired know-how and presence in new business segments. The recent US acquisitions have enabled CMC to enter a new market.

The companies that have been acquired or formed as public companies or limited companies have not been converted into cooperatives. Those which are project-based and of short duration fold as soon as the project is completed. In relation to its subsidiaries, CMC applies its code of conduct which states that employees need to be paid according to contractual agreements and encouraged to participate (CMC 2014).

Capital for acquisitions came from retained profits, members' shares (16.4 million euros), bank loans (341 million euros) and external capital (9 million). Cooperare has invested 10 million euros in CMC overseas holding company. In 2014, CMC issued bonds valued at 300 million euros, the first cooperative to do so. Bank loans and bonds seem to be the key source of capital along with the creation of public companies, which allow it to attract external capital or co-invest with other partners (CMC 2016a; Cavallari 2017).

CMC has developed a sizeable overseas employment component and more flexible organizational structures. CMC in 2015 employed 7,317 persons, of which 5,976 were employed overseas. Of these, 1,441 were employed in Italy, of whom 389 were cooperative members. Membership is lower than 50 percent of the total workforce, so CMC has lost its status of a prevalently mutual cooperative (CMC 2016b). Its high overseas workforce can partly explain this, and perhaps, too, its cautious approach to the appointment of new members. CMC stated that it employed 456 permanent staff in 2016. This is low compared to the 2,859 permanent staff employed in 1985. These figures point to CMC developing a more flexible structure suited the nature of its contract-based work.

CMC has maintained close ties with the cooperative sector. Despite having the possibility to demutualize since it is no longer a prevalent mutual cooperative, its members have decided against it. It is joint owner of a company with Cooperare and continues to work in partnership with other cooperatives. It is a member of the consortia CNS, CCC and Integra. It is a key investor in Legacoop companies and financial structures.

6.6 Concluding Remarks

Cooperatives have formed groups of companies to improve their competitiveness so they might better serve their members. The cooperative-focused growth model—consisting of organic growth, merging with other cooperatives to reach economies of scale and cooperating within the consortia system to improve their competitiveness—was quite successful. It has allowed cooperatives to grow into large enterprises and become national leaders of their sectors, whether retail, agriculture, construction, catering or service industries. The pressures from globalization and cooperatives' own beliefs about their place in the economy, leadership ambitions or capabilities highlighted limits to this growth model. The moment cooperatives could no longer grow within the cooperative sector (whether lack of cooperatives to merge or to partner with), they looked toward the private sector to form partnerships and joint-ventures. The inability of the cooperative model to attract sufficient external capital meant that it had to be found using non-cooperative models.

The move toward a cooperative group's model occurred gradually. Construction cooperatives established joint ventures with the private sector so they could access public works. Sacmi established offices overseas with local partners to access know-how and local knowledge. Acquisitions of private enterprises allowed CMC, Sacmi, Granarolo and Camst to get market share, access to know-how, access to new products and new markets. Cooperatives then established holding companies to manage and purchase other companies in full or in partnership with other investors. These have attracted external capital directly to the holding company or in the subsidiaries, which have further helped cooperatives to diversify, access new markets and manage risks. Moreover, just like Unipol, Coop Adriatica has listed a company on the stock exchange, accessing capital from retail and institutional investors.

There is no doubt that growth via the development of cooperative groups has added another dimension to the cooperative sector. The formation of holding companies and a listing of companies is quite an innovative approach for cooperatives to access capital while remaining a cooperative. This cooperative form has facilitated access to global markets and, as Chapter 8 will affirm, it has also made large cooperatives more resilient to the GFC. The model, however, has led to a number of structural and operational changes that challenge cooperative identity. Key developments include:

- An entrenched dual structure whereby cooperatives own subsidiaries that are managed as privately owned businesses. While the profits received from these subsidiaries are distributed according to cooperative law, it is a new way of operating. It adopts a governance structure whereby the cooperative is democratically managed and the subsidiaries are not. It is also more complex than this, as it becomes more difficult for members to understand and to make decisions for the whole group.
- Low membership levels with global cooperatives. The membership of Sacmi and CMC is less than 50 percent of the total workforce, and they have lost their prevalently mutual cooperative status. This development raises questions as to whether or not they are violating the open door principle. It also highlights the difficulty in transforming subsidiaries

into cooperatives, especially if they are based overseas. Lack of under-standing of cooperative culture, language barriers, differences in coop-erative legal status and the fixed-term nature of employment are all barriers to exporting the cooperative model overseas.

• Use of conventional private businesses to provide services to members. Consumer cooperatives have established businesses to provide new ser-vices to members but have not provided these services via cooperatives or, as Camst has done, transformed these companies into cooperatives. It is indeed quicker to establish conventional businesses. It may be difficult to start cooperatives or convert these businesses into cooperatives. Convert-ing them into cooperatives, however, would give more people the oppor-tunity to become co-operators and to practice economic democracy.

The questions raised about cooperative identity will be the subject of fur-ther discussions in Chapter 9 on cooperative principles and social responsi-bility and Chapter 10 on cooperative identity.

The formation of cooperative groups of companies has not distanced these cooperatives from the cooperative network. They still support Lega-coop; they are members of national consortia and ad hoc consortia; they invest in companies owned by the cooperative sector; and they engage with other cooperatives where possible and support the cooperative development fund. There is evidence of inter-cooperative trading between Camst, CMC, Coop Adriatica and Granarolo with other cooperatives. As noted, Cooper-are is also a key investor with Granarolo and CMC. Therefore, while coop-eratives have formed groups, they are also still embedded in the Legacoop network model based on inter-firm collaboration, inter-sectoral relation-ships, the consortia system and the financial structures. Also, the consumer cooperatives sell products from all cooperatives, so they truly network with the whole cooperative movement.

Sacmi and CMC have also demonstrated how embedded they are with the local economic community through their supplier's network. They engage with local businesses, creating long-term relationships and distributing wealth throughout the region of Emilia-Romagna. Sacmi is also embedded in the ceramic industrial district of Sassuolo, to which it provides turn-key installations for the production of ceramic tiles. It would seem that some cooperatives are competing against multinational companies by adopting aspects of the business group, inter-firm networking and, in Sacmi's case, the industrial district's model as well.

Notes

1. For a comprehensive study of industrial districts please refer to: (Beccattini, Bel-landi and De Propris 2009). Beccattini is regarded as the foremost scholar on industrial districts.
2. The top 250 cooperatives produced 71.9 billion euros (Alleanza delle Coopera-tive Italiane 2016). The total turnover for the cooperative sector was 116.343

billion in 2014 (not including banking and insurance) (Alleanza delle Cooperative Italiane 2015).
3. The top 250 cooperatives employed 276,430 persons. In 2011, the cooperative sector employed 1.310 million people (Fondazione Censis 2012)
4. Chapter 8 discusses how cooperatives managed the GFC.
5. Mario Viviani began to work for Legacoop Ferrara. He became CEO of CCC and of the consultancy firm Smaer. He teaches at the University of Bologna and is a consultant to Unipol.
6. In October 2017, however, Manutencoop cooperative bought back the shares held by external investors and now owns 100 percent of Manutencoop Facilities Management. See Manutencoop 2017a.
7. Other large cooperative groups that are members of either Legacoop, Confcooperative or the Trentino Federation include: the consumer cooperatives Coop Alleanza 3.0 (revenue exceeding 4 billion euros); Unicoop Firenze (2.3 billion euros); the agricultural consortia Agricola Tre-Valli (3 billion euros); Conserve Italia (644 million euros); Apofruit Italia (232 million euros); Coprob (202 million euros); the wine consortia: Cantine Riunite (201 million euros); Mezzacorona (174 million euros); the retail consortia Conad North East (2.17 billion euros); Conad Tirreno (1.6 billion euros); the social consortia Gesco (1.4 billion euros); the construction cooperative CMB of Carpi (570 million euros); the service sector cooperatives Manutencoop (957 million euros); and Cooperservice (754 million euros).
8. These shares are now owned by Intesa San Paolo.

References

Alleanza Cooperative Italiane. 2017. *Cooperative Enterprises in Italy: Percentages per Employment Cohort 1971–2011*. Cooperative Census, Rome: Unpublished.

Alleanza delle Cooperative Italiane. 2015. *Il Movimento Cooperativo in Italia 2008–2014*. Note e Commenti, Rome: Alleanza delle Cooperative Italiane.

———. 2016. *Le Grandi Cooperative Italiane*. Osservatorio Grandi Imprese, Rome: Alleanza delle Cooperative Italiane.

Ammirato, Piero. 1996. *La Lega: The Making of a Successful Cooperative Network*. Aldershot: Dartmouth Publishing Company Limited.

Bassani, Aureliano. 2000. *It All Began With Nine Mechanics: Eighty Years of Growth and Development*. Imola: La Mandrangora.

Battilani, Patrizia. 2002. "La Creazione di una Impresa Moderna 1985–2000." In *Camst: Ristorazione e Socialita'*, edited by Vera Zamagni, 115–170. Bologna: Il Mulino.

———. 2004a. "Il Gruppo Granarolo e le Sfide del Mercato." In *Una Storia di Qualita': Il Gruppo Granarolo tra Valori Etici e Logiche di Mercato*, edited by Giuliana Bertagnoni, 129–206. Bologna: Il Mulino.

———. 2004b. "La Risposta della Cooperazione alla Poverta': la Nascita del Cbpl-Granarolo e della Felsinea Latte." In *Una Storia di Qualita': il Gruppo Granarolo fra Valori Etici e Logiche di Mercato*, edited by Giuliana Bertagnoni, 93–128. Bologna: Il Mulino.

———. 2010. "Towards a Service Society." In *Cooperation Network Service*, edited by Patrizia Battilani and Giuliana Bertagnoni, 8–64. Lancaster: Crucible Books.

Beccattini, Giacomo, Marco Bellandi, and Lisa De Propris. 2009. *A Handbook of Industrial Districts*. Cheltenham: Edward Elgar.

Benati, Benito, and Marco Mazzoli. 2009. *Partecipazione, Ricerca, Innovazione*. Imola: La Mandrangora.

Bitossi, Serena, and Marco Simion. 2008. "Gli Strumenti della Crescita per le Cooperative dal Consorzio al Gruppo: La Realta' Toscana." In *I Gruppi Cooperativi:*

Strategie, Risultati, Criticita' delle Cooperative Holding, edited by Serena Bitossi, 153–198. Bologna: Il Mulino.

Cadiai. 2017. *Consorzi*. May 2017. Accessed May 31, 2017. www.cadiai.it/consorzi.

Calzolari, Gianpiero. 2015. *Relazione al Consiglio di Amministrazione 2015*. Chair's Report to Shareholders, Bologna: Granlatte.

Camst. 2016. *Bilancio di Sostenibilita' 2015*. Annual Sustainability Report, Bologna: Camst.

Caselli, Guido. 2016. *Osservatorio della Cooperazione in Emilia-Romagna*. Annual Report, Bologna: Unioncamere Emilia-Romagna.

Cavallari, Mara. 2017. "Lascio Soddisfatto il Lavoro." *La Betoneria*, March: 3–4.

CMC. 2014. *Codice Etico*. Ravenna: Cooperativa Muratori e Cementisti, May.

———. 2016a. *Rapporto Sociale 2015*. Annual Report, Ravenna: CMC.

———. 2016b. *Consolidated Financial Report*. Annual Consolidated Financial Report, Ravenna: CMC.

Confcooperative. 2016. *Bilancio di Sostenibilita'*. Annual Sustainability Report, Rome: Confcooperative.

Consorzio Nazionale Servizi. 2017. *Le Imprese Socie*. 22 June. Accessed June 2017. www.cnsonline.it/le-imprese-socie/.

Coop Adriatica. 2016a. *Bilancio 2015*. Annual Financial Report, Bologna: Coop Adriatica.

———. 2016b. *Bilancio di Sostenibilita' 2015*. Annual Report, Bologna: Coop Adriatica.

Coopfond. 2017. *Rendicontazione Sociale 2014–2016*. Annual Report, Rome: Coopfond.

Coplan, Asli M., and Hikino Takashi. 2010. "Foundations of Business Groups." In *The Oxford Handbook of Business Groups*, edited by Asli Coplan, Hikino Takashi and James Lincoln, 15–66. Oxford: Oxford University Press.

Earle, John. 1987. *Un Ritratto della Lega*. Rome: Editrice Cooperativa.

Felice, Emanuele. 2004. "Il Settore-Caseario in Italia dal Dopoguerra al Duemila." In *Una Storia di Qualita'*, edited by Giuliana Bertagnoni, 25–92. Bologna: il Mulino.

Fondazione Censis. 2012. *Primo Rapporto sulla Cooperazione in Italia: Sintesi*. Report on the Cooperative Sector, Rome: Alleanza delle Cooperative Italiane.

Fruin, Mark. 2007. "Business Groups and Inter-firm Networks." In *The Oxford Handbook of Business History*, edited by Geoffrey Jones and Jonathon Zeitlin, 244–267. Oxford: Oxford University Press.

Granarolo. 2016a. *Bilancio Sociale 2015*. Annual Social Report, Bologna: Granarolo Spa.

———. 2016b. *Sustainability Report 2015*. Annual Sustainability Report, Bologna: Granarolo.

Hancock, Matt. 2007. *Compete to Cooperate: The Cooperative District of Imola*. Imola: Bacchilega Editore.

IGD. 2017. *Roadshow Presentation*. Quarterly Report to Shareholders, Bologna: IDG.

Legacoop. 2002. *Potenzialita' e vincoli degli Investimenti Cooperativi all'Estero con Particolare Riguardo ai Paesi Oggetto di Ampliamento della Comunita' Europea*. Business Report, Rome: Legacoop Centro Studi.

Lolli, Silvia. 2002. "L'espanzione nella Ristorazione di Massa e il Risanamento." In *Camst: Ristorazione e Socialita'*, edited by Vera Zamagni, 73–114. Bologna: Il Mulino.

Manutencoop. 2014. *Bilancio Consolidato 2013*. Annual Consolidated Report, Bologna: Manutencoop.

———. 2017a. *Le Societa' del Gruppo Manutencoop*. Bologna, 12 June.

———. 2017b, Comunicato Stampa:CMF finalizza l'acquisto del 33,2% del capitale della società dagli Azionisti di Minoranza. Accessed February, 14. http://www.manutencoop.coop/uploads/MFMCMFClosingOperazioneAzionistiMinoranza.pdf

Menzani, Tito, and Vera Zamagni. 2010. "Cooperative Networks in the Italian Economy." *Enterprise and Society*, Volume 11, Number 1, 98–127.

Petrucci, Paola. 2005. "L'Istanza Mutualistica: Considerazioni in Merito alla Formazione di Gruppi Cooperativi." In *Processi di Sviluppo e Integrazione: I Gruppi Cooperativi*, edited by Alberto Zevi, 35–54. Rome: Legacoop Centrostudi.

Sacmi. 2015. *Bilancio di Sostenibilita'*. Annual Sustainability Report, Imola: Sacmi.

———. 2016. *Annual Report 2015*. Annual Report, Imola: Sacmi.

———. 2017. *The History of the Company*. June. Accessed June 6, 2017. www. sacmi.it/en-US/About-us/The-History-of-the-Company.aspx?ido=10837&idc= 899&ln=en-US.

Servizi Italia. 2017. *Star Conference Milano 2017*. Shareholder Presentation, Reggio Emilia: Servizi Italia.

Viviani, Mario, interview by Piero Ammirato. 2016. *Cooperative Groups*, 28 June.

Zamagni, Vera. 2011. *Da Ravenna al Mondo*. Bologna: Il Mulino.

———. 2015. *Come si e' Affermata la Grande Impresa Cooperativa in Italia*. Bologna: Il Mulino.

———, Patrizia Battilani, and Antonio Casali. 2004. *La Cooperazione di Consumo in Italia*. Bologna: Il Mulino.

———, and Emanuele Felice. 2006. *Oltre il Secolo: Le trasformazioni del Sistema Cooperativo Legacoop alla Fine del Secondo Millennio*. Bologna: Il Mulino.

Zeitlin, Jonathon. 2007. "Industrial Districts and Regional Clusters." In *The Oxford Handbook of Business History*, edited by Geoffrey Jones and Jonathon Zeitlin, 219–243. Oxford: Oxford University Press.

Zevi, Alberto. 2005a. "Il Finanziamento delle Cooperative." In *Verso Una Nuova Teoria Economica della Cooperazione*, edited by Enea Mazzoli and Stefano Zamagni, 293–332. Bologna: Il Mulino.

———. 2005b. "Motivazione alla Crescita, Una Scelta Consapevole, ma Grande Differenzazione." In *Processi di Sviluppo e Integrazione: I Gruppi Cooperativi*, edited by Alberto Zevi, 7–24. Rome: Centrostudi Legacoop.

7 Entrepreneurship
Start-Ups, Worker-Buyouts and Social Cooperatives

The growth and relevance of cooperative movements are reliant on their capability to systemically regenerate by starting new cooperatives, growing existing cooperatives and extending their presence in new sectors of the economy. It requires a capacity among individuals and cooperatives to continually understand people's needs, assess market opportunities and threats and collectively take financial risks. As the structure of our economies change—for example, from agriculture to manufacturing and service— cooperatives must continually adapt and demonstrate their relevance and value to members and their communities.

The previous chapter on cooperative groups has already noted the entrepreneurial capabilities of large cooperatives. These capabilities were manifested via strategies of diversification of products, services and markets; via mergers, acquisitions and joint-ventures; and through the ownership of listed companies and the creation of holding companies. This chapter explains how the Italian cooperative sector has managed to promote and sustain entrepreneurship focusing on the creation of new cooperatives and the promotion of new cooperatives sectors. First, it discusses the activities that promote cooperative awareness and education. Second, it discusses the formation of new cooperatives. Third, it examines the approach taken to facilitate WBOs. Fourth, it discusses new cooperative sectors, focusing on social cooperatives. The final section introduces community cooperatives that provide services to small villages.

7.1 Promoting Cooperative Awareness and Education

The future of the cooperative sector needs the next generation to understand the principles of cooperation and to want to work within or to start new cooperatives. The mainstream media's coverage of cooperatives is limited, but when it does report on cooperatives, it reports on their strong economic performance, growth in the cooperative sector or stories about cooperative failures. Cooperative principles and values and their benefits to society are rarely covered. To this end, the Central Associations have been engaging with schools and universities to promote cooperative history, their principles and their values. Key initiatives have included:

- Legacoop and Confcooperative, in association with a number of cooperatives and Bologna high schools, have developed the program: 'Copyright—Invent a Cooperative.' It involves high school students who, with the help of a tutor, develop ideas that could be promoted via a cooperative. Students develop a feasibility study, a business plan and a strategic plan. Prizes are offered to winning students. Over the past nine years 1,000 students across 53 classes within 17 high schools have been involved (Bologna Today 2016).
- Legacoop's Bellacopia program from Reggio Emilia organizes programs with high schools and universities. University students attend seminars to learn about cooperative ideals, law and operations. They attend workshops and form multidisciplinary groups to develop cooperative ideas. In 2015, 85 third-year students attended this course at the University of Modena-Reggio-Emilia (Reggio-Sera 2015).
- The Trentino Federation has been promoting cooperative values at schools for many years. Students can form a cooperative to manage a school activity. This allows students not only to learn about cooperative values but practice democratic decision-making. The program explains the importance of the cooperative sector to the local economy; includes visits to local cooperatives; and also trains the teachers on cooperative principles and practices. Six hundred students took part in 2016 (Cooperazione Trentina 2016).
- Since 2001, young people aged 18–28 can choose to work in a social cooperative instead of completing their compulsory civil service for 12 months. They need to work at least 30 hours per week and are paid a minimum salary of 433 euros per month (Legacoop 2017). Thousands of young people have been given opportunities to work in a cooperative and learn about cooperative values and democratic practices (Confcooperative 2017).

In 1996, The University of Bologna offered for the first time a Master's in Cooperative Economics (MUEC). The Italian cooperative sector has never had its own university or higher education institute, so this was a significant milestone. Prior to 2002, Legacoop used to organize private cooperative courses that taught cooperative history, values, the cooperative enterprise and the cooperative movement. These courses were taught by leaders of cooperatives, consortia or the Central Associations. Since 2002, cooperative courses funded by the cooperative development funds are taught at the universities of Bologna, Trento, Rome, Florence, Parma and Catania. The University of Bologna Business School also offers an Executive Master's in Business Administration focusing on cooperatives. The University of Trento and Legacoop local and regional associations organize short programs that focus on key aspects of cooperation, business management and legal compliance. These courses are funded by Coopfond to reduce costs for students. The consumer cooperatives have established their own school in Florence where they train staff and organize seminars and conferences.

7.2 Promoting New Cooperatives

From 2009 to 2015, there were more than 7,000 new cooperatives registered each year (Alleanza delle Cooperative Italiane 2016). Those cooperatives that are members of the Central Associations have access to a variety of services, funding and networking opportunities. To illustrate this point, the following sections discuss how Central Associations have been promoting new cooperatives.

7.2.1 Promotion Via Inter-Cooperative Solidarity and Local Cooperative Offices

The first approach to cooperative promotion was one based on inter-cooperative support and solidarity. When a group of people wanted to start a cooperative, an established cooperative leader would be assigned the task of helping the new cooperative in the start-up phase and learn from their experience. Considering that until the late 1960s cooperatives operated in local economies, and the culture of solidarity was strong, this system worked at the time with the cooperative of one city helping another from a nearby city or town (Bulgarelli 2006).

Another approach is one where a cooperative contacts the local cooperative branch for support. All Central Associations, through their own staff or their own specialist consulting companies, provide information on the legal and organizational aspects of cooperative and non-financial services such as legal, accounting, tax and industrial relations. They also assist cooperatives with developing a business plan, ongoing support and access to capital. All Central Associations may provide funding directly or via cooperative banks or the other financial structures of the cooperative sector in alliance with other local banks (Legacoop Emilia Romagna 2017; Cooperazione Trentina 2017b; Confederazione Cooperative Italiane 2017).

7.2.2 Cooperative Development Funds: Greater Financial Certainty and a Formalized Approach

Cooperative development funds have undoubtedly been a great source of funding for new and existing cooperatives and consortia. All Central Associations have their own funds, which they manage on behalf of new cooperatives and existing members. Key funds include the following:

- Promocoop is the fund managed by the Trentino Federation. It has received a total of 52.7 million euros as of 2016. It uses these funds to provide grants, guarantee loans from third parties, provide loans directly and invest equity capital with cooperatives and consortia. In 2016, its current investments totaled 23.5 million euros. Promocoop invested 10 million euros in over 40 cooperatives, consortia and cooperative-owned financial companies. Equity investments of 13.5 million euros are made via the Fondo Partecipativo fund, which was established in 2011 and is co-funded with the Trentino local government (Promocoop 2014; Cooperazione Trentina 2017a).

- Fondosviluppo is managed by Confcooperative. Fondosviluppo works closely with the cooperative banking sector, which provides 60 percent of its funds. Since 1993, it has made available 396 million euros to 147 cooperatives and cooperative companies. Sixty million euros of these funds were invested as equity capital (BCC-Federcasse 2016).

- Coopfond is the most significant fund and is managed by Legacoop. It provides short-to-medium term investments and long-term stable-strategic investments. Since 1994 it has invested a total of 473.5 million euros in 760 investment projects involving 600 cooperatives. Investments are directed at new cooperatives and at existing cooperatives that have plans to grow, to merge or to enter international markets (Coopfond 2016).

The establishment of Coopfond heralded a new approach for Legacoop because credit was now available to start new cooperatives.[1] Today, once the Legacoop office is satisfied that people wanting to form a cooperative understand its principles and values, it assists them with legal, accounting and management services. It provides assistance to develop a business plan so that the project can attract financial support. Once this is done and the cooperative is registered and joins the Association, Legacoop then provides further assistance by linking the new cooperative with its financial network. For instance: Cooperfidi can act as a guarantor to another bank. CCFS could provide part of the loan. Coopfond can provide a loan or make an equity investment. Coopfond, however, has been the real catalyst for Legacoop cooperatives entrepreneurship because members know that funds are available for new cooperatives.

Coopfond has developed rigorous investment policies and procedures to assess and evaluate funding proposals. It provides loans or equity investments. For each short-to-medium term investment, Coopfond invests up to 50 percent of the total capital raised by the cooperative but cannot exceed 600,000 euros for loans and 750,000 euros for capital investments. Investments in cooperative-owned companies cannot exceed one-third of the total capital. The risk is shared with credit guarantee consortia. Strategic investments loans can exceed these limits but must be less than 70 percent of the total capital (Coopfond 2016).

Each application is assessed against criteria (Coopfond 2016) considers social merit, innovation, job creation, return on capital invested and financial risk. The review process includes compatibility with the fund's objective; evaluation of the business idea; assessment of the business plan; and a presentation to Coopfond's Board seeking approval. Once approved, the investment is monitored to ensure the cooperative implements the agreed plan. It is estimated that Coopfond has assisted in the formation of over 260 cooperatives. Key investments include:

- Sixty new cooperatives located in Southern Italy to encourage cooperative development and create employment;
- Fifty new cooperatives are operating in new markets, including aquaculture, sports business, health treatment, marine engineering, building and operating healthcare facilities.
- Fifty-seven cooperatives established via WBOs of enterprises in crisis from 2008 to 2016, including cooperatives producing beer, glass, kitchens, leather, and tiles, publishing, health, cinematography, retail and agriculture.
  (Bulgarelli and Viviani 2006; Coopfond 2015; Coopfond 2017; L. Laurini 2016; Laurini and Moreschi 2016)

7.2.3 Cooperative Start-Ups: Transforming Ideas Into Cooperatives

In 2015, the cooperative sector launched two very interesting and successful cooperative start-up programs. Coopfond launched Coopstartup, a program that promotes new cooperatives in new markets by encouraging young people to transform ideas into cooperatives. Coopstartup works with local Legacoop offices, cooperatives, regional governments, universities and incubators to promote start-ups by offering a mixture of educational, management and financial support. Competitions are organized throughout Italy. Each program consists of three phases:

- Phase one: pre-start-up. Participants provide project ideas for review and are required to complete a four-module online training course including developing a business idea, team building, understanding cooperative legal requirements and cooperative governance and developing a business plan.
- Phase two: start-up. Shortlisting is announced, and participants receive face-to-face training (Coopfond 2016) culminates in fine-tuning their business idea and developing a business plan. Business plans are reviewed, and winners are chosen. Winners receive a start-up capital grant of 15,000 euros provided by Coopfond (5,000 euros) and partners (5–10,000 euros), usually a cooperative or regional government. Coopfond can also invest a further 50,000 euros if required.
- Phase three: post-start-up. Coopfond, local Legacoop offices and partners provide support for a further 36 months by making available at a set fee[2] management support, which includes: marketing, financial management, communication, human resources and so on. Coopfond may also offer loans or equity if warranted and Banca Popolare Etica, in agreement with Coopfond, can also offer micro-credit loans of up to 25,000 euros (Coopstartup 2017; Coopstartup 2016; Coopstartup 2015).

Coopstartup has funded 30 new cooperatives and provided 119 groups with formal training. It has engaged with 84 partners. Through its public program presentations, it has communicated the principles of cooperation to over 3,000 people. It has thus not only formed new innovative cooperatives in a variety of sectors throughout Italy,[3] but it also raised awareness of cooperatives' principles and values (Coopstartup 2017).

Confcooperative launched the program CoopUP. It has established 16 incubators in different cities, each managed by a coordinator ('junior angel'). Junior angels inform participants about the cooperative legal and organizational structure and help them develop ideas and put them into contact with existing cooperatives and the financial structures from the cooperative sector to access funds. In two years, 300 ideas have been reviewed and supported, leading to the formation of 40 new cooperatives. These represent a variety of sectors, including culture, social services, tourism, food and the environment (Confcooperative 2016).

7.3 Worker-Buyouts

WBOs refer to privately owned firms that have been converted into cooperatives. This conversion usually takes place when a firm is experiencing financial difficulties or when owners without a successor sell the business to its employees. It is estimated that in Europe there are over 1,000 cooperatives formed from employee buyouts. In Europe, most WBOs have occurred in Italy, France and Spain (CECOP 2013). Argentina is another country where they have been popular. There is a great appeal for WBOs because they prevent further de-industrialization, maintain local employment and promote a collective entrepreneurial culture rather than a culture reliant on State welfare.

7.3.1 The Marcora Legislative Framework

The Italian experience with WBOs commenced with the passing of the Marcora Law in 1985, named after the minister who proposed it, Giovanni Marcora. It was approved at a time when Italy began to experience high unemployment, high inflation and a rising public debt.[4] A process of de-industrialization was taking place that has continued to this day, with Italian manufacturing businesses closing or de-localizing to other countries. The Marcora Law was enacted to halt or limit this process by allowing workers to use their unemployment benefits to buy out the business that employed them (De Micheli, Imbruglia and Misiani 2017).

The first Marcora Law came into operation in 1986. It consisted of two programs that managed funds worth 125 million euros. The first program, called Foncooper, funded cooperatives that promoted innovation and introduced technology.[5] The second program, called the 'Special Fund,' funded employee buyouts. This section focuses on the Special Fund as it promotes new enterprises.

The Special Fund was managed by CFI, a company co-managed by the three Central Associations and the three trade union confederations. The former provided personnel to manage the company. It operated under the following criteria:

- Only workers with access to the special scheme for temporary laid-off workers were eligible to access this program.[6]
- Workers were to invest at least 2,000 euros, of which half was paid up-front.
- CFI provided grants of up to three times the equity capital invested by members. Members used their wages paid under the special scheme for temporary laid-off workers, on the condition that they could not access unemployment benefits for three years.
- Cooperative-owned companies could invest as much as 25 percent of members' own capital.
- CFI had the right to nominate a board member and an audit committee member.
- CFI provided consultancy and monitoring services, including support for developing a business plan.

(Zevi and De Bernardinis 2016;
La Cooperazione Italiana 1989)

The Marcora Law was welcomed but needed improvement. The lack of adequate funds and its focus on short-term solutions did not meet the needs of the cooperative sector. It was criticized for focusing on financial relief rather than on cooperative support structures (Gherardi 1987). Legacoop wanted the fund to enable all employees to buy out any small business and public firms that were being privatized. There were long delays of 18 to 20 months before funds were transferred to cooperatives. Despite these shortfalls, the Marcora Law was deemed to be a good, innovative law that needed improvement (De Bertoli 1993; Zevi 1993).

This initial scheme operated until 1996. That year the European Community raised concerns about the program's anti-competitive nature. After five years of deliberations, during which time the Special Fund was prevented from operating, it concluded that non-repayable grants were a form of State aid and that this constituted anti-competitive behavior. The Marcora Program was deemed illegal under European law and could not continue. In any case, from 1986 to 2001, CFI supported 157 WBOs that employed 6,000 people (Zevi and De Bernardinis 2016).

In 2001, the Marcora Law was modified in compliance with EEC directions. CFI was now required to either invest equity capital or provide loans but could no longer provide grants. It had a broader mandate, and the legal nature of CFI—at this point renamed as Cooperazione Finanza Impresa—changed to that of a financial consortium. It has a membership of 306 cooperatives and one major institutional investor in the Ministry of Economic Development via its finance company, Invitalia. CFI currently holds 84 million euros in members' equity and 12 million euros of accumulated assets (Cooperazione Finanza Impresa 2017a). Key features of the new arrangements included:

- Support for all small and medium-sized worker[7] and social cooperatives, with priority given to WBOs.
- A requirement that members invest at least 4,000 euros (50 percent up front). Members of social cooperatives are required to invest a minimum of 1,000 euros.
- CFI can invest an amount equal to that invested by worker-members, offer loans at market rate, act as a guarantor and re-invest with the same cooperative. Loans and investments have to be repaid within ten years. CFI receives dividends on its equity capital investments.
- The Ministry of Industry can nominate a CFI board member and an audit committee member.
- Since 2014, all employees have the right of first refusal should they seek to buy out companies in crisis or that are undergoing liquidation or bankrupt procedures. Previously only workers that could access the special scheme for temporary laid-off workers had this right.

(Zanotti 2011; Compagnia Finanza Impresa 2003; Vieta, Depedri and Carrano 2017)

7.3.2 A Collaborative Approach to Establishing and Supporting WBOs[8]

The promotion of WBOs post-2001 occurred under a more mature and facilitating environment. The three cooperative development funds were by this point established and were able to co-fund new cooperatives in cooperation with CFI. Cooperfidi Italia could provide guarantees to third parties, thus providing another avenue for accessing capital. Unipol Banca, Banca Popolare Etica, cooperative banks, local banks and cooperative-owned local finance companies also provided loans and equity capital. By now, CFI and the cooperative movement had accumulated 15 years of experience and know-how, and this was reflected in the venture capital-like processes put in place and the management and financial support services that were available.[9]

There are a number of steps that need to be taken before a WBO can be approved and funded. The first step for employees is to find out that the WBO alternative exists. Workers are generally not aware of the WBO scheme, but they may manage to find out about it in a variety of ways. A Union representative may be aware of the Marcora Program. The Central Associations may intervene once they find out that a local company is experiencing financial difficulties. The local mayor may suggest contacting the local branch of a Central Association. A local mayor concerned about de-industrialization may propose a WBO in cooperation with the unions and the Central Associations. A local consultancy firm may inform workers about the Marcora Program and introduce them to a Central Association.[10]

The second step involves a preliminary analysis to establish whether there is a possibility of transforming an ailing company into a cooperative. At this stage, the local branch of the Central Associations, the cooperative development funds and CFI conduct the initial analysis, identifying strengths and potential barriers. It includes: assessing their leadership skills; ensuring that the previous owner is no longer involved; assessing the level of group cohesiveness and worker capabilities; reviewing the causes of the crisis, its costs and capital requirements; and assessing whether there is a possibility of recuperating the company.

The third step involves developing a business plan, raising funding and establishing a new cooperative. During this stage CFI, cooperative development funds and local associations support workers in developing a business plan. Cooperative development funds may provide a small grant to develop a business plan. It is a pre-requisite that the plan and the financial forecasting should include: only motivated employees willing to invest; a flexible cost structure; realistic business goals; and financial forecasts. It is also a requirement for the new cooperative not to carry over any debt from the previous business and that workers are willing to become worker-entrepreneurs, because they would be required to make sacrifices, possibly work longer hours and potentially reduce their pay in the early years.

At this stage, finance is made available. CFI and cooperative funds usually match the amount invested by workers through their unemployment insurance benefits and their termination payments.[11] Cooperative funds may come with caveats designed to promote cooperative values, financial prudence and a flexible cost structure. Legacoop required Greslab not involve the old owner in the cooperative; keep salary differentials at a ratio of 3:1; hold 20 percent of salary as variable salary; and increase the working week to 40 hours, replacing the historical 35-hour week (De Micheli, Imbruglia and Misiani 2017).

The final step is continuous monitoring and the provision of services. This is important because new WBOs may also encounter difficulties from suppliers who may expect to be paid in cash, from clients who pay late and in winning future clients. Monitoring and review take place in many ways. Central Associations review cooperatives' compliance with the law every two years. CFI, cooperative funds and the Central Associations can nominate board members and review financial statements regularly. They also attend cooperatives' annual general meetings. Cooperatives welcome this stakeholder engagement because they feel they are part of a wider network of cooperatives. This phase could lead to re-financing if the cooperative needs it.[12]

7.3.3 Jobs, Survival Rates and Geographic Distribution

Euricse-based researchers recently conducted a comprehensive study on WBOs in Italy, based on a database from 1979 to 2014, and made a number of key findings. These are:

- There were 257 WBOs established between 1979 and 2014. Almost all were formed from private enterprises in crisis. They saved 9,500 jobs. Legacoop cooperatives accounted for 59 percent of all WBOs.[13]

- WBOs were established throughout Italy: 43 percent in the North, 45 percent in the Center and 13 percent in the South.
- WBOs have been formed in times of high unemployment and de-industrialization. Sixty-five percent of converted firms operated in the manufacturing sector. They were mostly formed from labor-intensive manufacturing firms operating in Central and North East Italy, where workers had non-transferable skills to other sectors, making it difficult to find jobs.
- Sixty-eight percent employ 10–49 people. This is higher than the Italian average of four.
- The average lifespan for closed WBOs is 11.9 years. This compares with manufacturing businesses in Italy, the average lifespan of which is between 2 and 5 years.
- WBOs that are still active are on average 13.9 years old. Of these, 22 percent have been operating for more than 25 years.

(Vieta, Depedri and Carrano 2017)

This research clearly demonstrates that WBOs are able to prolong the life of an enterprise by almost 12 years. CFI's own assessment notes that the State is able to recuperate the unemployment and severance pay paid in advance within a couple of years from the personal and company tax paid by cooperatives. CFI also emphasizes that workers' initial investment is matched by CFI, cooperative funds and other banks, thus generating up to 3–4 times the workers' initial investment (Viola 2016) These initiatives also produce positive externalities as workers improve their self-esteem and confidence from being part of a WBO. The process of getting employees, cooperative and State institutions to work together builds up social capital and trust.[14]

7.4 Developing New Cooperative Sectors and the Rise of Social Cooperatives

Cooperatives traditionally have been present in the consumer, agriculture and banking sectors. Italian cooperatives today are present in all sectors of the economy. They have adapted to emerging economic structures and people's needs. Post-war reconstruction required the country to be rebuilt, so housing, construction and manufacturing cooperatives built houses, public buildings, roads and railways. As the economy grew, a middle class emerged with time and money to spend, so cultural and tourism coopera-tives were set up to meet these new needs. When, as a result of globalization, deregulation and privatization, the public sector and large private compa-nies outsourced their services, cooperatives offered general maintenance, cleaning, gardening, security, data management, waste management and general catering services. Recent changes to the welfare state and deregula-tion have led cooperatives to open up pharmacies, general medical practices and dental clinics. The service sector produces 74 percent of Italy's GDP, and with 79 percent of its cooperatives operating in this sector, the cooperative sector has been part of this change (OECD 2017; Fondazione Censis 2012).

7.4.1 Emergence of Social Cooperatives

A key sector to emerge since the 1980s is the social services sector. It emerged at a time of economic, social, political and cultural changes. It was the end of the economic boom and full employment, which led to years of social and political activism demanding equality and social justice. The State responded and enacted legislation that strengthened the rights to work and education and promoted equal rights for disabled persons. In 1978, the Basaglia Law closed psychiatric hospitals, paving the way for people with mental illness to live in communities. The Italian State was not equipped to deal with issues such as aging, drug addiction and disability because its social welfare system was based on providing a pension, hoping that the family would take care of social welfare matters. Women, however, had entered the workforce and could no longer take care of their family members. As families could no longer take care of elderly parents or deal with emerging issues, Catholics, influenced by the Second Vatican Council, and left-wing activists, influenced by principles of equality, justice, civic responsibilities and human rights, began to form associations to look after vulnerable people in society (Marzocchi 2012).

Associations of volunteers and worker cooperatives began to provide social services. Worker cooperatives began to provide work to disadvantaged people. Many associations began to establish rehabilitation communities for drug addicts, shelters for homeless people and home-based services for the elderly. Cooperatives, associations and foundations shared the provision of these activities. Cooperatives, however, became the chosen legal form, in part because of people's preferences but also because Italian law prohibited foundations and charity organizations from carrying out any economic activities. By 1991, there were 2,000 active social cooperatives. In the same year, the Italian Parliament approved a specific law for social cooperatives (Borzaga and Galera 2016).

7.4.2 Social Cooperatives Legal Framework

The Cooperative Law 381/1991 gave formal recognition and a unique definition of social cooperatives. The key feature of social cooperatives is their mission to operate in the best interest of the community, the active role performed by volunteers and disadvantaged workers and stakeholder governance arrangements. Social cooperatives are defined as having:

> the purpose of pursuing the general interests of the community, promoting human development and the social integration of citizens through:

a) the management of social, health and educational services (via Type A cooperatives); b) the carrying out of different activities including agricultural, industrial, commercial or services with the aim of integrating disadvantaged persons into the labour market (via Type B cooperatives).[15]

Other key features include the following:

- Volunteers can become members but cannot exceed 50 percent of total members.
- At least 30 percent of the workforce in Type B cooperatives must be comprised of disadvantaged workers (such as people with mental and physical disabilities, alcoholics, drug addicts, prisoners on probation and minors with family problems).
- The stakeholder governance structure may include voluntary personnel, external investor-members and legal entities as well as worker-members.
- Social cooperatives can form consortia with private enterprises provided 70 percent of its members are social cooperatives.[16]

Social cooperatives' ownership and governance arrangements place them in a unique position within a 'business typology.' They differ from conventional capitalist firms because they are not owned by capital and are not profit-maximizing. They are not a not-for-profit firm because they do make a profit. They differ from other cooperatives because they are required to pursue the general interest of the community and not just members' interests and can opt for a stakeholder model over a member-based governance model (Borzaga 2009).

7.4.3 Social Cooperatives and the State

Social cooperatives are able to access taxation concessions because they perform a social function and because profits deposited in the reserve fund and accumulated assets cannot be distributed to members. In this way social cooperatives use profits for long-term goals and to improve services and holds assets in trust for the next generation. Tax policies that apply to social cooperatives include:

- All profits allocated to the indivisible reserves are exempt from paying corporate tax.
- Type A social cooperatives pay a value-added tax (VAT) of 5 percent instead of 22 percent.
- Type B social cooperatives pay the full VAT but are exempted from paying national insurance contributions for disadvantaged workers.
- Private donations are also tax exempt as they are for charity organizations.
(Fici 2013; European Commission 2014)

Local governments are the largest purchasers of social services.[17] It has been estimated that in 2011, 69 percent of total turnover of Type A social cooperatives and 46 percent of Type B social cooperatives comes from local government contracts (Borzaga and Galera 2016). Initially, local governments provided grants in return for services. In line with EEC directives, and in response to rising public debt, from 1992 until 2006 local governments outsourced social services via a competitive public tender process that assigned work to the lowest bidder.[18] This changed in 2006 when clauses giving social goals a higher priority were introduced in the public tender process. This was in compliance with EEC directives of 2004 (Eurocities-NLAO 2011).[19] In response, the Emilia Romagna Regional Government reviewed its practices and introduced an accreditation process to replace public tenders. Through this process, it allocates work to 905 registered, accredited social cooperatives and private enterprises. Legacoop Emilia Romagna estimates that its social cooperatives receive 50 percent of their work through this accreditation model (Alberani and Marangoni 2017).

7.4.4 Growth and Economic Performance

Social cooperatives have grown since the passing of the 1992 legislation. It has been estimated that 40 percent of all employment created in Italy since the mid-1990s has been in the health and social services area, especially in personal and family care (Brandolini 2017). Demand for these services has come from the aged, asylum seekers, single family homes (especially rentiers), immigrant families, people with mental illnesses, early childhood education and child care centers, enterprise welfare services offered to their employees and the long-term unemployed (Alberani and Marangoni 2017). The market is highly competitive. According to the Institute for Research on Social Enterprises, in 2013, social cooperatives competed with 774 private enterprises operating as social enterprises,[20] 82,231 not-for-profit organizations (charities and foundations) and thousands of private for-profit firms that operate in the same sectors as social cooperatives, such as cultural and recreational services (Venturi and Zandonai 2014b).[21] In spite of this competition, social cooperatives have increased in numbers, employment, and turnover:

- Registered social cooperatives increased from 1,293 in 1991, to 11,334 in 2008 and to 13,041 in 2013.
- Total employment increased from 27,510 in 1991, to 339,763 in 2008, and to 390,079 in 2013.
- Turnover increased from 6.8 billion in 2008 to 10.1 billion in 2013.

A review of the cooperative sector conducted by Fondazione Censis found that social cooperatives provide 23 percent of the national social and recreational sector workforce[22] and employ close to 50 percent of the national social services workforce[23] (Carini and Borzaga 2015; Fondazione Censis 2012; Zamagni and Zamagni 2008). Table 7.1 provides a breakdown of social cooperatives by sector and turnover.

Table 7.1 Social Cooperatives Turnover for Each Sector, 2013

Sector of Activity	Turnover (Million Euros)	Percentage
Agriculture	132.9	1.3
Industry	366.9	3.6
Construction and Housing	77.8	0.8
Commerce	137.0	1.4
Transport and Warehousing	178.7	1.8
Social and Health Services	6937.0	68.6
Other Services	2272.1	22.5
Other	4.2	0.0
Total	**10106.6**	**100**

Source: Carini, Chiara and Carlo Borzaga. 2015. "La Cooperazione Sociale: Dinamica Economica ed Occupazionale tra il 2008 ed il 2013." In *Terzo Rapporto Euricse sull'Economia Cooperativa*, edited by Carlo Borzaga, 171–190. Trento: Euricse.

7.4.5 Competing in the Market

Social cooperatives compete in the market at times on their own but usually via networking with other cooperatives through consortia or via other networking arrangements. The Italian experience has provided four types of business models: small cooperative; the consortia system; the Consorzio Gino Mattarelli model (a consortium of consortia); and the large cooperative model represented by Cadiai, a social cooperative from Bologna.

7.4.5.1 Small Cooperatives

The majority of social cooperatives are small cooperatives. It is estimated that 72 percent have a turnover of less than 500,000 euros per year, while 46 percent employ fewer than 19 persons (Carini, Costa, Carpita and Andreus 2014; Fondazione Censis 2012). About half of all social cooperatives join a consortium to improve their competitiveness (Venturi and Zandonai 2014a). Those that do not join a consortium compete as small cooperatives on their own, possibly focusing on providing a single service within a local community.

7.4.5.2 The Consortia Network

The traditional way for small cooperatives to compete in the market is by becoming a member of a consortium. By 2011, social cooperatives had formed 452 consortia. Their total turnover amounted to 1.2 billion euros, approximately 12 percent of the total turnover produced by social cooperatives (Linguiti 2014). A study conducted in 1995 noted that consortia became a meeting place to exchange information, develop strategies, identify projects and bid and manage contracts on behalf of its members (Borzaga and Ianes 2011). As cooperatives developed and their needs grew, consortia helped cooperatives improve their strategies and competitiveness, achieve economies of scale, access know-how, achieve synergies with other cooperatives and offer clients a one-stop-shop through which many services could be offered (Alberani and Marangoni 2009). Being part of consortia allows cooperatives to survive their early years, consolidate and be in a position to grow. Considering that consortia's turnover is 12 percent of total turnover, cooperatives eventually win market share on their own or through other forms of alliances.

7.4.5.3 Consorzio Gino Mattarelli: A National Agency Model

One unique business model is that developed by the Consortium Gino Mattarelli (CGM), which is associated to Confcooperative. This consortium was formed in 1987 to perform a complementary role to that performed by the local consortia. It soon developed into a second tier national consortia providing services to other smaller, local consortia. The idea was to promote many small cooperatives, which would become members of local consortia, which in turn would become members of CGM. Their overall strategy was named the 'strawberry field development model,' whereby cooperatives were kept small (30–40 staff at most) and new cooperatives would be created by local consortia at every opportunity. This would lead to specialization and avoid bureaucratization. CGM provided a variety of services in support of this model, including encouraging collaborative activity among consortia; providing administrative, accounting and financial services; conducting research and training; promoting economic development; coordinating stakeholder engagement relations with the government; promoting legislative reform; and promoting new cooperatives (Borzaga and Ianes 2011).

In 2005 CGM became a 'joint cooperative group.' Through this model, CGM would still lead the strategies of its affiliated consortia via having them comply with agreed contractual obligations. As stated in Chapter 2 on legislation, this aspect of cooperative law enables a cooperative to act like a quasi-holding company without having capital ownership over its members, who can leave the consortium at any time. This strategy enabled CGM to become a national agency and to promote companies such as CGM Finance (loans and financial consultancy); Welfare Italia (family medical services); Accordi (employment); Comunita' Solidali (aged care, disabled and mental health); Luoghi per Crescere (education); Mestieri (training); and Pan (child care centers and early education). This new approach has led to a closer relationship between CGM and its consortia members. Members are expected to be certified, develop an annual report on ethics and social responsibility and comply with agreed protocols, policies and tariffs (Venturi and Zandonai 2014a; Consorzio Pan 2017; Welfare Italia 2017). CGM has been very successful as it counts on the membership of 67 consortia, 766 cooperatives and not-for-profit associations that employ 42,000 people (Consorzio Gino Mattarelli 2017).

7.4.5.4 The Large Cooperative Model: Cadiai

The fourth business model is that of developing large cooperatives, which usually provide a variety of services and operate outside their municipal area. Euricse has revealed that in 2011, 1 percent of cooperatives contributed to 30 percent of the sector's turnover and 6.1 percent produced 59 percent (Carini, Costa, Carpita and Andreus 2014). Legacoop Sociale Emilia Romagna, which has promoted large cooperatives, revealed that 33 of their 186 social cooperatives based in the region produced 66 percent of their total turnover (Alberani and Marangoni 2017). The same report noted that these 33 cooperatives managed to grow for the following reasons:

- Greater efficiencies. Cooperatives developed paperless offices (invoicing, registration, payments and so on) and improved marketing services and financial management practices.
- Diversification of products. Type A cooperatives provided new services in autism, treatment of rare diseases, severe burns, dentistry and home dialysis. They have also responded to new demands, such as asylum seekers and new migrants. Type B cooperatives diversified into agriculture, maintenance services, cleaning, laundry and environmental regeneration.
- Diversification of market segments. Cooperatives serviced a number of clients, including the local government and local health authorities, private patients, cooperatives and private businesses. Percentages vary, but usually Type A cooperatives source up to 80 percent of their work from local authorities, compared to Type B cooperatives, which source only 30 percent (Alberani and Marangoni 2009). Cooperatives that sell agricultural produce or manage business archives engage only with the private sector.
- Diversification of geographic markets. There were 11 cooperatives operating outside the regional markets: two operated on a national scale, and three started to operate overseas. This expansion into other markets was made possible by providing services to other cooperatives; through the creation of networks with other cooperatives (one-stop-shops); and through acquisitions, mergers or rescue operations of other cooperatives.
- Innovative business models. These have included build-own-operate aged residential services in alliance with other cooperatives from other sectors and the provision of comprehensive services from one location (social services, social housing, maintenance, catering, gardening and care for elderly) (Alberani and Marangoni 2017).

Cadiai is a good example of a large-scale social cooperative promoted by Legacoop. Cadiai commenced in 1974, providing social services to Italians that returned after the Libyan crisis. Following the Basaglia Law, Cadiai began to care for mentally ill patients at private residences. Up to 1992, funding for its services came entirely from local government authorities, but today this reliance has been reduced to less than 50 percent, with the remaining coming from private patients, cooperatives and private companies. Cadiai employs 1,455 people, of whom 71 percent are members. Its turnover amounted to 45 million euros in 2016, which included a surplus of 468,000 euros (Cadiai 2016b).

Cadiai's business model delivers a diversified blend of quality products and services via networking with other cooperatives and the cooperatives sector's financial structures. More specifically, these include:

- Diversified products and services: social care for the aged, disabled and mentally ill (61 percent of turnover); educational area managing child care centers and services to minors (34 percent); and preventive care and occupational health and safety (5 percent).
- Diversified revenue stream including 49 percent from local authorities and health agencies, 25 percent via cooperative consortia and partnerships and 26 percent via the private sector (individuals, cooperatives and private companies).
- Diversification of partnerships via alliances with other cooperatives. Cadiai has established work arrangements with other cooperatives to provide social care and educational services on 30 sites located in Emilia Romagna and Milan. It is also a member of 13 project-based consortia. Some are multi-sector consortia formed with cooperatives that provide maintenance, catering and gardening services to complement Cadiai's provision of social services. Together they have built, owned and operated aged care and child care facilities. Cadiai also provides occupational, health and safety services to 22 cooperatives.
- Networking with cooperatives to provide services on a broader geographical scale. Ten cooperatives from five regions formed the network 'Come Te' to provide social and welfare services to individuals, families and businesses. Coopfond and CCFS financed the project.
- Along with 20 other cooperatives, and with the support of Coopfond and CCFS, it has established the Social Cooperatives Real Estate Investment Company to build, own and operate residential aged care facilities, day care facilities and child care centers.

(Cadiai 2014; Cadiai 2016a; Cadiai 2016b)

Cadiai has continuously increased its turnover and workforce: from 16 million euros and 634 employees in 2001, to 25.5 million and 1032 employees in 2007, to 36.8 million and 1296 employees in 2011, to 45 million and 1455 employees in 2016. It has made the most of the opportunities offered by a growing market through its market strategies, product diversification, close alliance with the cooperative sector, quality services and overall capabilities, which have all contributed to its success. This success has continued during the GFC, a theme which will be explored in Chapter 8.

7.5 Community Cooperatives

Community cooperatives are being established throughout Italy. These are cooperatives formed to revitalize small villages or towns by providing a variety of services and activities hoping to create jobs, attract families and look after the elderly. They are managed like a cooperative because there is not a specific law that reflects their purpose (Legacoop 2011). A key feature is that they do a variety of jobs and activities via a flexible workforce. For instance:

- The community cooperative Briganti di Cerreto has turned an old mill into a grocery and coffee shop and unused buildings and a stable into 'bed and breakfast' (B&B) accommodation; produced chestnut flour; and provided tourist excursions into the forest. They created ten jobs, revitalized the little village and created a sense of belonging (Legacoop 2016).
- The cooperative Valle dei Cavalieri was formed after the last remaining shop in the village closed. Nine members refurbished the old school building and turned it into a grocery and coffee shop. In addition, they produce their own bread, have established a B&B and a restaurant, manage a farm and produce cheese, bring students to school, provide school excursions to the national park and provide services to the elderly such as buying medicine or providing wood for winter. The cooperative has 33 members and seven employees. Employees do many jobs, such as taking kids to school in the morning, working on the farm in the afternoon and working at the restaurant in the evening during the tourist season (Grella 2016).

These cooperatives are becoming popular because there are many quasi-abandoned small villages that need support. These cooperatives are inclusive and serve the whole community. In a sense, they have an even broader mission than social cooperatives' stakeholder model. It is early to say how far this model could expand, but it provides evidence that the cooperative model can satisfy community needs that the private sector and the State could not because these are not profitable for the former and too expensive for the latter.

7.6 Concluding Remarks

The cooperative model has demonstrated that it is an adaptable and flexible model capable of meeting the needs of members and their communities. The development of new cooperatives in new sectors of the economy and by young people offers the opportunity to grow, diversify and revitalize. Its cooperative model, supported by an innovative legislative framework and the cooperative network, has also been innovative and resilient during the GFC.

The approach taken to promoting new cooperatives is via networking and stakeholder engagement. New cooperatives have generally been promoted by cooperative development funds in cooperation with other financial stakeholders. These usually have consisted of Central Associations, cooperative enterprises, cooperative development funds, financial consortia and financial companies, as well as cooperative banks and local banks. These stakeholders have shared know-how, information and risks and have ultimately co-invested in a coordinated way.

New cooperatives have been formed in diverse sectors of the economy and on a national scale. Cooperative start-up programs are introducing a new generation to cooperative values and have focused on promoting innovative cooperatives formed mainly by young people. Cooperative development funds support all types of cooperatives throughout Italy, including promoting entrepreneurship in new sectors and in Southern Italy. WBOs have mostly supported the formation of manufacturing cooperatives. This approach provides the cooperative sector with a national dimension and a presence in all sectors of the economy. It enhances the reputation and significance of the cooperative sector within the Italian economy and society and allows it to regenerate.

An effort has been made to create greater awareness of cooperative principles and to bring more people closer to the cooperative sector. This has been manifested by the variety of education and training programs that have developed throughout Italy; the provision of work experience to people on civil service duties; and the promotional work conducted by the cooperative start-up programs.

The cooperative sector has shown a strong inclination to innovate and develop new laws, new types of cooperatives and unique business models. Key innovations include the following:

- The cooperative development funds are innovative rotational funds that operate like a venture capital fund without the need to maximize profits.
- The Coopstartup program is very innovative because it promotes a holistic program that includes funding, cooperative and management education and a structured support program for 36 months that includes access to the cooperative network.
- Confcooperative's start-up programs are innovative because they promote new cooperatives via 16 incubators throughout Italy that offer consultancy, financial services and access to the cooperative network.
- The WBO program operates within a unique legislation framework that allows workers to use their termination payments and unemployment benefits to buy out enterprises in crisis. They are supported by CFI and a financial network that provides management support and long-term loans and equity capital.
- The legislation governing social cooperatives promotes cooperative models for both Type A and Type B cooperatives, the role of which is

to meet the general interest of the community and not just those of its members. The law allows for a stakeholder governance model, which differs from a members-based model.

- The CGM consortia and Cadiai have developed innovative business models. CGM is a national agency of consortia that in turn support small cooperatives and promote new cooperatives. It has developed into a national support structure promoting national brands and providing managerial and financial support across Italy. Cadiai competes in the market via forging multi-sector, inter-sectoral cooperative alliances and networks that have led to building aged care facilities and child care centers via the build-own-operate model. It has succeeded in diversifying its geographic reach, product range and client base.
- Community cooperatives are inclusive of all citizens, represent the needs of whole communities and operate as multifunctional and multi-sector providers. They are best placed to revitalize communities by building social trust and social cohesiveness.

The establishment of WBOs and the continued growth of social cooperatives demonstrate the cooperative model's resilience. The fact that WBOs have survived for at least another 12 years is a testament to the capabilities and resolve of workers, the adaptability of the cooperative model and the networking culture that permeates the cooperative sector. Social cooperatives have also continued to grow in numbers, size and employment while operating in a competitive market. A combination of sound business strategies, networking and an appropriate legislative environment have enabled them to compete and grow. As a result, they have been able to endure late payments from governments and having to bid for contracts awarded to the lowest price bidders. The capacity of cooperatives to survive and grow over time—including during the GFC—will be explored in Chapter 8.

Notes

1. Prior to the establishment of cooperative development funds, Legacoop cooperatives could access funds from large cooperatives if they had mutual interests, but it was ad hoc and limited (Bulgarelli and Viviani 2006).
2. The fee is usually jointly paid by the partners and the new cooperative.
3. Cooperatives have been established in the following areas: organic products, local tourism, urban planning, waste management, health sector, beer factory, theatre and entertainment, housing and furniture, education services and a clothing manufacturer (Coopstartup 2017).
4. In the 1980s, State debt as a percentage of GDP rose from 56 percent to 94 percent (De Micheli, Imbruglia and Misiani 2017).
5. Chapter 4 provides information on Foncooper.
6. The scheme is called Cassa Integrazione Guadagni—CIG—which pays up to 80 percent of a person's income. Workers accessing CIG are effectively employed and are to be re-instated as soon the company can afford it. The scheme is funded by employers and employees and applies to enterprises with more than 15 employees (Vesan 2015).

7. SMEs employ less than 250 people, have a turnover less than 50 million euros and have assets not exceeding 43 million euros.
8. The information for this section is based on the work conducted by Giancarlo Laurini from Coopfond and Alessandro Viola and Iolanda Esposito from CFI (G. Laurini 2016; L. Laurini 2016; Viola 2016).
9. CFI provides management training and support to its cooperative members (Cooperazione Finanza Impresa 2015).
10. These examples are based on the following WBOs: Italstick, Raviplast, Greslab, Social Pnews and Berti.
11. At Greslab, employees invested 14,000 euros each, raising 500,000 euros; CFI and Coopfond matched their investment; loans of 1.5 million were obtained from Unipol and Banca Etica via Cooperfidi (the guarantor); plus three local companies from Sassuolo became investors (De Micheli, Imbruglia and Misiani 2017).
12. Greslab, Raviplast and Italstick needed further funding to deal with unexpected events. In all cases cooperative members, CFI, cooperative development funds and local banks provided further capital.
13. CFI funded another 21 WBOs from 2015 until June 2017, saving 435 jobs (Cooperazione Finanza Impresa 2017b).
14. People involved in WBOs are very proud of managing their own enterprise or when people acknowledge their achievement.
15. Please refer to the law on social cooperatives: Law of 8 November 1991/381, Article 1.
16. Please refer to Law of 8 November 1991/381.
17. The funds come from the national government, which are transferred to local governments via regional governments.
18. The local government can assign a contract without recourse to public tender for contracts up to 300,000 euros for cleaning, laundry and gardening services assigned to Type B cooperatives (European Commission 2014).
19. The EEC passed two directives, 2004/17CE and 2004/18/CE, which supported awarding public tenders contracts to achieve social aims.
20. These are privately owned firms that operate for a social purpose. As per law 2006/155, they must generate at least 70 percent of income from business activities and cannot distribute profits. Profits should be re-invested or used to increase company assets (European Commission 2014).
21. The Institute for Research on Social Enterprises calculates that there are 61,776 capitalist firms that could provide social services.
22. The social and recreational sector includes education and training, social services and recreational and sporting activities.
23. The social services workforce includes aged care, people with disabilities and people with mental illness.

References

Alberani, Alberto, and Luciano Marangoni. 2009. *Cooperazione Sociale Legacoop in Emilia Romagna: Il Posizionamento Attuale e le Prospettive Future*. Rimini: Maggioli Editore.
———. 2017. *Cooperazione Sociale Legacoop Emilia Romagna. Oltre la Crisi*. Forli: Maggioli.
Alleanza delle Cooperative Italiane. 2016. *Le Cooperative Attive in Italia (2015)*. Annual Data Review, Rome: Alleanza delle Cooperative Italiane.
BCC-Federcasse. 2016. *Bilancio di Coerenza del credito Cooperativo: Rapporto 2016*. Annual Social Responsibility Report, Rome: BCC -Federcasse.

Bologna Today. 2016. *le coop del futuro saranno innovative, collaborative, solidali e attente all'integrazione sociale.* 26 May. Accessed June 29, 2017. www.bologna today.it/economia/le-coop-del-futuro-saranno-innovative-collaborative-solidali-e-attente-all-integrazione-sociale.html.

Borzaga, Carlo. 2009. "Impresa Sociale." In *Dizionario di Economia Civile*, edited by Luigino Bruni and Stefano Zamagni, 516–526. Rome: Citta' Nuova Editrice.

———, and Giulia Galera. 2016. "Innovating the Provision of Welfare Services Through Collective Action: The Case of Italian Social Cooperatives." *International Review of Sociology*, 31–47.

———, and Alberto Ianes. 2011. *Il Sistema di Imprese della Cooperazione Sociale. Origini e Sviluppo dei Consorzi di Cooperative Sociali.* Euricse Working Papers 48.

Brandolini, Andrea. 2017. "Lavoro e Disuguaglianza tra Rivoluzione Digitale e Invecchiamento della Popolazione." *"Cooperative Sociali Oltre la Crisi": Assemblea Annuale della Cooperative Sociali Aderenti a Legacoop Emilia-Romagna e Legacoop Sociali.* Rimini: Legacoop Emilia Romagna, 32.

Bulgarelli, Marco. 2006. "Coopfond e la Nuova Promozione Cooperativa." In *La Promozione Cooperativa: Coopfond tra Mercato e Solidarieta'*, edited by Marco Bulgarelli and Mario Viviani, 39–80. Bologna: Il Mulino.

———, and Marco Viviani. 2006. *La Promozione Cooperativa: Coopfond tra Mercato e Solidarieta'*. Bologna: Il Mulino.

Cadiai. 2014. *A Way of Caring: Social, Healthcare and Educational Services.* Press Kit, Bologna: Cadiai.

———. 2016a. *Bilancio D'Esercizio.* Annual Financial Report, Bologna: Cadiai.

———. 2016b. *Bilancio Sociale Consuntivo.* Annual Social Responsibility Report, Bologna: Cadiai.

Carini, Chiara, and Carlo Borzaga. 2015. "La Cooperazione Sociale: Dinamica Economica ed Occupazionale tra il 2008 ed il 2013." In *Terzo Rapporto Euricse sull'Economia Cooperativa*, edited by Carlo Borzaga, 171–190. Trento: Euricse.

———, Ericka Costa, Maurizio Carpita, and Michele Andreus. 2014. "Le Cooperative Sociali Italiane Negli Anni della Crisi." In *La Cooperazione negli Anni della Crisi: Secondo Rapporto Euricse*, edited by Carlo Borzaga, 105–116. Trento: Euricse.

CECOP. 2013. *Business Transfers to Employees.* Brussels: CECOP.

Compagnia Finanza Impresa. 2003. *Nuova Legge Marcora.* 10 November. Accessed November 10, 2003. www.cfi.it/Laleggemarcora/19/base.ASP.

Confcooperative. 2016. *Bilancio Sostenibilita' 2016.* Annual Sustainability Report, Rome: Confederazione Cooperative Italiane.

———. 2017. *Servizio Civile.* Accessed September 15, 2017. www.confcooperative. it/Le-Iniziative/SERVIZIO-CIVILE.

Confederazione Cooperative Italiane. 2017. *La rete dei Servizi.* Accessed September 16, 2017. www.confcooperative.it/I-Servizi/La-rete-dei-servizi.

Consorzio Gino Mattarelli. 2017. *Chi Siamo.* 4 December. Accessed December 4, 2017. http://cgm.coop/chi-siamo/.

Consorzio Pan. 2017. *Presentazione Consorzio Pan.* Milan: Consorzio Pan.

Cooperazione Finanza Impresa. 2015. *Il Lavoro Riparte dal Lavoro.* Presentation to Annual General Meeting, Rome: Cooperazione Finanza Impresa.

———. 2017a. *Chi Siamo—Investitore Instituzionale.* 12 December. Accessed December 12, 2017. www.cfi.it/public/chi-siamo/.

———. 2017b. *WBO 2011–2017.* Progress Report, Rome: CFI.

Cooperazione Trentina. 2016. *In 600 per Raccontare la Cooperazione*. Accessed May 31, 2016. www.cooperazionetrentina.it/Ufficio-Stampa/Notizie/In-600-per-raccontare-la-cooperazione-a-scuola?utm_source=Newscoop%20n.%20877& utm_medium=email&utm_campaign=Newsletter.

———. 2017a. "Promocoop: Crescono le Participazioni." *Cooperazione Trentina*, June: 2.

———. 2017b. *Crea Impresa-Coop*. 16 September. Accessed 2017. www.coopera zionetrentina.it/Crea-Impresa-Coop.

Coopfond. 2015. *Rendiconto Sociale: 2014–15*. Annual Sociale Report, Rome: Coopfond.

———. 2016 Sintesi delle *Rendicontazioni Sociali 2014/15 and 2015/2016*. Annual Accountability Report, Rome: Coopfond.

———. 2017. *Interventi su Iniziative Workers' Buyout*. Progress Report, Rome: Coopfond.

Coopstartup. 2015. *Coopstartup Unicoop Tirreno: Nuove Imprese Crescono. Saranno Cooperative*. Rome: Coopfond.

———. 2016. "10 Steps and Go." *10 Steps and Go*. Rome: Coopstartup, 28 April.

———. 2017. *Carta D'Identita' del Progetto Coopstartup*. Progress Report, Rome: Coopfond.

De Bertoli, Renato. 1993. "Foncooper: Adeguare la Normativa e le Risorse ai Bisogni Reali." *La Cooperazione*, January–February: 4–7.

De Micheli, Paola, Stefano Imbruglia, and Antonio Misiani. 2017. *Se Chiudi Ti Compro: Le Imprese Rigenerate dai Lavoratori*. Milano: Guerrini e Associati.

Eurocities-NLAO. 2011. *Social Economy in Cities: Bologna*. European Commission Programme Cities for Social Inclusion, Brussels: European Commission.

European Commission. 2014. *Country Report Italy*. A Map of Social Enterprises and their Eco-Systems in Europe, Brussels: European Commission.

Fici, Antonio. 2013. "Italy." In *International Handbook of Cooperative Law*, edited by Dante Cracogna, Antonio Fici Fici and Henry Hagen, 479–502. Heidelberg: Springer.

Fondazione Censis. 2012. *Primo Rapporto sulla Cooperazione Italiana*. Report on the Italian Cooperative Sector, Rome: Alleanza delle Cooperative Italiane.

Gherardi, Silvia. 1987. "Worker Takeovers: The Italian Experience." In *Analysis of the Experiences and Problems Encountered by Worker Takeovers of Companies in Difficulty or Bankrupt*, edited by Commission of the European Communities, 160–192. Luxemburg: Commission of the European Communities.

Grella, Diletta. 2016. "Succiso: Il Paese Cooperativa Dove Ogni Giorno si Cambia Lavoro." *Vita*. Rome: Vita, 24 December.

La Cooperazione Italiana. 1989. "I Meccanismi della Legge." *La Cooperazione Italiana*, 4 April: 23.

Laurini, Luca. 2016. *Coopfond Spa: A Company Overview*. Bologna, 18 October.

———, and Barbara Moreschi. 2016. "La Rendicontazione Sociale di Coopfond." *Le Risorse per Finanziare la Ripresa*. Rome: Coopfond.

Legacoop. 2011. *Guida alle Cooperative di Comunita'*. Guidelines, Rome: Legacoop.

———. 2016. "Lotta allo spopolamento: la comunità dei Briganti diventa l'impresa di tutti in paese." *Legacoop News*, 13 April. Rome: Legacoop.

———. 2017. *Il Servizio Civile in Legacoop*. 29 June. Accessed June 29, 2017. http:// serviziocivile.legacoop.coop/visualizza-pagina/il-servizio-civile-in-legacoop.

Legacoop Emilia Romagna. 2017. "Sviluppo e Promozione." *Legacoop Emilia Romagna.* 30 June. Accessed June 30, 2017. www.legacoopemiliaromagna.coop/sviluppo_e_promozione/seniorcoop.

Linguiti, Francesco. 2014. "I Consorzi Cooperativi." In *La Cooperazione Italiana negli Anni Della Crisi, Secondo Rapporto Euricse*, edited by Euricse, 53–72. Trento: Euricse.

Marzocchi, Franco. 2012. *A Brief History of Social Cooperation in Italy.* Forli: Aiccon.

OECD. 2017. *Economic Survey: Italy.* Country Report, Brussels: OECD.

Promocoop. 2014. *Indirizzi Srategici 2014–2016.* Policy Document, Trento: Promoop Trentina.

Reggio-Sera. 2015. *Bellacoopia, La Cooperazione Entra nell'Universita'.* 19 November. Accessed June 29, 2017. www.reggiosera.it/2015/11/bellacoopia-la-cooperazione-entra-nelluniversita/8499/.

Venturi, Paolo, and Flaviano Zandonai. 2014a. *Ibridi Organizzativi: L'innovazione Sociale Generata dal Gruppo Cooperativo CGM.* Bologna: Il Mulino.

———. 2014b. *L'Impresa Sociale in Italia: Identita' e Sviluppo in un Quadro di Riforma.* Report of the Italian Social Services Sector, Trento: IRIS.

Vesan, Patrick. 2015. "Labor Market Policy and Politics." In *The Oxford Handbook of Italian Politics*, edited by Eric Jones and Gianfranco Pasquino, 15 pages. Oxford: Oxford University Press.

Vieta, Marcelo, Sara Depedri, and Antonella Carrano. 2017. *The Italian Road to Recuperating Enterprises and the Legge Marcora Framework: Italy's Worker Buy-outs in Times of Crisis.* Research Report 015/17, Trento: Euricse.

Viola, Alessandro. 2016. *WBO.* WBO Program Review, Rome: Cooperazione Finanza Impresa.

Welfare Italia. 2017. *Accredita il tuo Studio Odontodriatico.* Milano, 25 July.

Zamagni, Stefano, and Vera Zamagni. 2008. *La Cooperazione: tra Mercato e Democrazia Economica.* Bologna: Il Mulino.

Zanotti, Antonio. 2011. "Italy: The Strength of an Inter-sectoral Network." In *Beyond the Crisis: Cooperatives, Work, Finance*, edited by Alberto Zevi, Antonio Zanotti, François Soulage and Adrian Zelaia, 21–100. Brussels: Cecop.

Zevi, Alberto. 1993. "Una Piu' Ampia Partecipazione dei Lavoratori Anche in Imprese non in Crisi." *La Cooperazione*, January–February: 18.

———, and Camillo De Bernardinis. 2016. *L'Italia che ce la fa: 1986–2016.* Rome: Cooperazione Finanza Impresa.

8 Cooperative Resilience
Managing the Global Financial Crisis

This chapter examines how cooperatives have managed to compete in the market following the GFC. The GFC commenced in 2007 with the collapse of the housing market in the United States and the subsequent loss in value of securities, which included subprime mortgages. Banks that did not have enough capital to manage financial risks either collapsed (such as Lehman Brothers Holdings Inc.) or had to be bailed out. This led to a bank liquidity crisis and a bank credit squeeze, making it difficult to obtain a loan. This loss of trust and credit squeeze had a profound effect on economies worldwide. It is estimated that 25 to 35 percent of financial wealth was wiped out in Europe and North America. The US and European governments provided billions of dollars in aid to save the banks. Twenty million people lost their jobs worldwide (Bayo and Roelantz 2011).

Italy, which was already experiencing difficulties competing in global markets, was severely affected by the GFC and the prolonged recession that followed. It experienced negative GDP growth for four years after the GFC, including −8 percent in 2009 (Battilani and Fauri 2014). It witnessed the failure of 117,000 businesses and the loss of 1.4 million jobs. Unemployment increased from 6 percent to almost 13 percent in 2014 (De Micheli, Imbruglia and Misiani 2017). Government debt increased from 110 percent of GDP in 2007 to 157 percent by 2015 (OECD 2017). This impacted a number of economic sectors with a strong cooperative presence. More specifically:

- Reduced spending on public works and infrastructure impacted the construction and service sectors.
- Less spending on social services and extended late payments to service providers[1] impacted the social, service and construction cooperatives.
- Less consumer purchasing power impacted spending in consumer and retail cooperatives.[2]
- The credit squeeze made it more difficult for all businesses to access credit.

This chapter explains how cooperatives fared during this period and the reasons for their continued growth. It is divided into six sections. The first section provides an overview of how the cooperative sector performed following the GFC. The second section compares the economic performance and behaviors of cooperatives and capitalist enterprises and identifies key features of the cooperative firm. The third section analyzes key factors that enabled cooperatives to perform well during the GFC. The fourth section discusses the anti-cyclic role performed by the cooperative banks. The fifth section examines the negative impact that the crisis had on the cooperative sector. The final section will summarize the key findings.

8.1 The Continued Growth and Resilience of the Cooperative Sector

The cooperative sector has experienced steady growth since 1971. It has demonstrated a capacity to survive and grow during periods of stagnation and negative growth, including during and after the GFC period of 2007–2009. The Italian economy grew by an average of 0.9 percent per annum from 1992 to 2012, during which time it contracted six times, with the highest contraction occurring in 2009 when the economy shrank by 8 percent (Battilani and Fauri 2014). Despite operating in a period of stagnation or state of recession, as Table 8.1 indicates, from 1991 to 2011, the number of registered cooperatives increased from 35,000 to 79,000 and employment grew from 356,000 to over 1.3 million.

A closer analysis of the data indicates the importance for the cooperative sector to promote new cooperatives and operate in emerging market segments. A sectoral analysis also indicates differences in the performance of different sectors.

- The service sector, and the social cooperatives in particular, have been growth sectors and now provide 79 percent of total cooperative employment. This is not unusual since the Italian social services sector created 40 percent of the total jobs in Italy since 1996 (Brandolini 2017).
- The anti-cyclic sectors such as agriculture and consumer/retail have shown steady employment growth but not to the extent of social cooperatives.
- The traditional, cyclic sectors of manufacturing and construction hold a lower share of cooperative numbers and employment. In 1971 they numbered 40 percent of the total number of cooperatives and 36 percent of total employment, but by 2011 their percentages were reduced to 28 and 13 percent respectively. These are the sectors most influenced by the world market, fluctuating public spending and a stagnant housing market.

During the decade that includes the GFC period, the cooperative sector was a net creator of jobs. Euricse notes that new cooperatives were responsible for most of the new jobs created by the cooperative sector over the

Table 8.1 Number of Registered Cooperatives and Cooperative Employment, 1971–2011

	Number of Registered Cooperatives					Cooperative Employment				
	1971	1981	1991	2001	2011	1971	1981	1991	2001	2011
Agriculture-Fishing*	994	1662	1766	3116	9042	32660	33795	27948	36917	101949
Manufacturing	3558	6170	6611	5319	6162	44213	90355	112762	85815	103078
Construction	768	2138	5097	10878	16454	32168	58811	61654	57796	66702
Commerce-Retail	2718	3475	7084	3553	7069	25386	44078	83611	74047	120616
Other Services**	2706	6455	13795	24853	26553	73050	135396	270837	531517	607100
Social Cooperatives			1293	5674	14425			27510	149147	309785
Total	10744	19900	35646	53393	79705	207477	362435	584322	935239	1309230

Note: *Agriculture and Fishing includes forestry employment in 2011. **Other Services include transport and storage which in 2011 employed 257,538 persons and banking and insurance which employed 99,507.

Sources: Fondazione Censis. 2012. Primo Rapporto sulla Cooperazione in Italia. Roma: Alleanza delle Cooperative Italiane; Zamagni Stefano and Vera Zamagni. 2008. La Cooperazione: tra Mercato e Democrazia Economica. Bologna: Il Mulino.

Table 8.2 Cooperatives as a Percentage of the Total Workforce, 1951–2011

	Number of Registered Cooperatives	Employees	As a Percentage of Total Workforce
1951	10,782	137,885	2.0
1961	12,229	192,008	2.2
1971	10,744	207,477	1.9
1981	19,900	362,435	2.8
1991	35,646	584,322	4.0
2001	53,393	935,239	5.8
2011	79,705	1,309,230	7.2

Source: Fondazione Censis. 2012. Primo Rapporto sulla Cooperazione Italiana. Rome 2012; and Zamagni Stefano and Vera Zamagni, *La Cooperazione: tra Mercato e Democrazia Economica*, Bologna: Il Mulino, 2008.

last decade. It found that 16,000 new cooperatives across all sectors of the economy created a total of 389,000 jobs from 2005 to 2011 (Sforzi, Zandonai and Carini 2014).[3] The mature cooperatives also continued to create jobs. The large cooperatives created 45,000 jobs from 2006 to 2011 (Alleanza delle Cooperative Italiane 2016), and the medium-sized cooperatives added another 30,000 jobs from 2008 to 2011 (Alleanza delle Cooperative Italiane 2017b).

The growth in the number of new cooperatives and new jobs increased the cooperative sector's share of total employment to 7.2 percent[4] (Fondazione Censis 2012). Table 8.2 provides data that shows the Italian cooperative sector progressively capturing a greater share of the total Italian workforce.

The relevance of the Italian cooperative sector in the economy is greater than the above statistics indicate because they do not include self-employed persons, like farmers, who entirely rely on cooperatives for their livelihoods, nor indirect employment. If one also considers these cohorts, then, according to Euricse, the cooperative sector produced close to 10 percent of GDP and contributed to 11 percent of total employment (Borzaga 2015).

8.2 Cooperatives and Private Enterprise: A Comparison

8.2.1 Key Economic Performance Indicators

A number of comprehensive studies have compared the economic performance and behaviors of cooperatives and private enterprises during the crisis. These focus on turnover, value added, employment, capitalization, investments, debt levels, salaries and profits. Key results include:

- Turnover. Alleanza delle Cooperative Italiane's (ACI) study from 2006 to 2015 found that cooperatives' turnover grew by 39.5 percent compared to 7 percent for other enterprises (Alleanza delle Cooperative Italiane 2016).[5]

- Value added.[6] Euricse's study[7] from 2007 to 2013 found that cooperative value added grew by 24 percent compared to public companies[8] (0.7 percent) and limited companies (10.6 percent; Borzaga 2015).
- Employment. Cooperatives created 29.6 percent of the total jobs created in Italy from 2001 to 2011 (Borzaga 2015). During the period 2007–2011, employment in the cooperative sector increased by 8 percent, from 1.213 million to 1.309 million, compared to a national employment decline of 2.3 percent (Fondazione Censis 2012). Data from the Italian Social Security Office confirms that from 2008 to 2013 cooperatives created an extra 80,000 jobs while private enterprises lost 500,000 jobs (Borzaga 2015).
- Capitalization. The level of capitalization, which includes shares, reserves and profits, increased by 48.4 percent for cooperatives compared to 36.6 percent for private enterprises. Cooperatives increased their reserves from 8.87 billion to 13.6 billion through the re-investment of profits and increased members' equity from 1.24 to 1.9 billion euros (Alleanza delle Cooperative Italiane 2016).
- Investments. Higher capitalization and borrowings led to higher investments, which grew by 25.4 percent for cooperatives compared to 15.2 percent for public companies and 26 percent for limited companies (Borzaga 2015).
- Debt. Cooperatives increased their level of debt from 36 billion to 47 billion euros, and their leverage was close to twice that of private enterprises (Alleanza delle Cooperative Italiane 2016).
- Salaries. During the period 2007–2013, salaries in cooperatives increased by 29 percent, compared to 13.5 percent in public companies and 23.1 percent in limited companies (Borzaga 2015).
- Profits. Cooperatives recorded lower profits compared to private enterprises: –42 percent compared to –21.6 percent for private enterprises (Alleanza delle Cooperative Italiane 2016).[9]

The above data suggests that cooperatives have increased their capitalization, which in turn has led to long-term investments. These have included the acquisition of machinery and companies, mergers and strategies that have led to the development of new products, market diversification and internationalization. This policy has led to higher levels of employment and salary increases at the expense of lower profits and higher levels of debt. The data supports the view that cooperatives have performed an anti-crisis role by increasing investments and creating more jobs. It also supports the view that cooperatives are professionally managed enterprises with a long-term horizon that allows them to manage operational and labor costs in the short term (without cutting staff) and exploit market opportunities for the long term. This is regarded as a balanced approach that provides an opportunity for future growth (Gulati, Nohria and Wohlgezogen 2010).

In comparing cooperatives with the private sector, the key finding is that in times of crisis cooperatives have focused on increasing employment, whereas the private enterprises have cut labor costs and contained debt levels in order to remain profitable. This reflects the different ownership structures and fundamental values: cooperatives are employee-owned and focus on job security while private enterprises, being enterprises owned by capital or investors, focus on maximizing profits.

The lower profits and higher debt levels—especially bank loans, which have risen from 7.7 to 12.5 billion for the large cooperatives—are a cause for concern.[10] Also, the ACI study on 250 cooperatives notes that their total turnover remained stable from 2010 to 2015. Considering that cooperatives have relied historically on profit retention as their main form of capitalization, lower profits mean lower levels of capitalization, which will negatively influence future investment. All things being equal, the continuation of borrowing will eventually increase repayments to the point that investments will be further curtailed and assets may have to be sold. This implies that cooperatives can only perform an anti-crisis function for a limited time. If the economic downturn persists, the lower profits and high debt will prevent cooperatives from continuing to fulfill this function (Fontanari and Borzaga 2015a).

8.2.2 Longevity—Survival Rates

Another key indicator of resilience is a business's capacity to be sustainable over time. Cooperatives have been long identified as resilient businesses, and when compared with similar private enterprises they have demonstrated higher survival rates (Bayo and Roelantz 2011; Smith and Rothbaum 2014). Italy is no exception, which should be no surprise considering that cooperatives are generally larger than private enterprises. Additionally, cooperatives that are members of Central Associations have access to business services, can join a consortium, access credit and equity and engage in inter-sectoral trade with other cooperatives. This chapter has already noted that WBOs have better survival rates than private enterprises (Vieta, Depetri and Carrano 2017). A Unioncamere comprehensive study comparing the survival rates of cooperatives and private enterprises from the region of Emilia-Romagna provides further confirmation that cooperatives have a better survival rate than private enterprises. Key results include:

- Long-term survival rates: 11 percent of cooperatives commenced operations more than 50 years ago compared with only 1 percent of private enterprises; 20.4 percent of cooperatives have operated for more than 35 years compared with only 4 percent for private enterprise.
- Short-term survival rates: only 17 percent of cooperatives cease to operate after five years compared with 20.4 percent of public companies, 24.6 percent of other companies and 47.3 percent of sole proprietors.

(Caselli 2014b)

8.2.3 Taxes

Italian business has argued that tax concessions favor cooperatives and are, as a result, the reason for their success. This is mainly in response to the tax incentives granted to cooperatives from 1977 to 2003, during which time all profits placed in the indivisible reserve were not taxable. The tax regime changed in 2004, and since then cooperatives must pay company tax on at least 40 percent of profits for worker cooperatives, 20 percent for agricultural cooperatives and 65 percent for consumer cooperatives.[11]

Unioncamere Emilia Romagna and Euricse have compared the level of taxes paid by cooperatives and public companies and have found that overall, cooperatives pay more taxes. Unioncamere compared all taxes paid by the Italian cooperative sector with Italian public companies. It concluded that overall, the Italian cooperative sector pays on average 36 percent of taxes on profits compared with 33 percent paid by Italian public companies (Caselli 2015).

Euricse reviewed all types of payments made to the State by businesses and cooperatives, including company tax, regional tax, personal income tax and social security and welfare contributions paid by employer and employees. It found that while public companies paid more company tax on profits, cooperatives transferred more payments to the State as a result of being more labor-intensive businesses, thus incurring higher payments for social security and welfare contributions. Euricse calculated the results by adding all taxes and payments paid as a percentage of the company's turnover and as a percentage of the company's value-added amount. It found that when considering:

• Total payments as a percentage of the company's turnover: cooperatives pay 7.7 percent of their turnover compared to 6.8 percent paid by public companies.
• Total payments as a percentage of the company's value-added amount: cooperatives paid 36.8 percent of their value-added amount, and public companies paid 34.6 percent.

(Fontanari and Borzaga 2015)

These two studies indicate that while the tax concessions on profits have been beneficial to cooperatives, their overall tax burden is higher than public companies.[12] Thus the reasons why cooperatives have successfully managed the GFC and the period following the crisis are to be found elsewhere.

8.3 Key Factors Explaining Cooperative Resilience and Anti-Crisis Tendencies

Many factors explain why the cooperative sector managed to compete and grow before and after the GFC. These include an enabling legislative environment, leadership from the Central Associations, the capacity to access capital, cooperative business culture and business strategies, flexible management practices and the role performed by the financial network structures.

8.3.1 An Enabling Legislative Environment

The Italian legislation provides a variety of avenues enabling cooperatives to manage change during a crisis. It facilitates access to capital, provides a choice of legal structure that facilitates entrepreneurship and allows the use of flexible management practices during a crisis.

The legislation facilitates access to capital through a variety of sources. In addition to the traditional ways of attracting capital such as member shares and retained profits, the law has progressively provided more avenues to attract capital. These include external investors, tax concession on a portion of the profits placed in the indivisible reserve, listings of companies on the stock exchange and the requirement for cooperatives to deposit 3 percent of their profits into a cooperative development fund.

The law also allows cooperatives to operate under various organizational structures that promote: entrepreneurship, partnerships with the private sector, consortia that help small cooperatives achieve economies of scale and company structures that facilitate internationalization. Key legal company structures include the possibility to: establish a consortium that can include private enterprises, consider a joint-group-consortia led by a cooperative thus operating as if it were a holding company,[13] operate as a group of companies that include wholly or partly owned subsidiaries and own listed companies.

As noted in Chapter 2, the Law 2001/142 contains a unique set of regulations that facilitates flexible workplace arrangements in times of crisis. This Law regulates the rights of workers as members and as workers. It states that members and non-members must receive equal pay for equal work and that internal decisions cannot contravene the collective agreement signed by the Central Associations and the trade union confederations. Law 2001/142 also formalizes the process that leads a cooperative to declare a 'state of enterprise in crisis'. This process allows a cooperative to activate 'solidarity contracts' enabling it to place members and non-members on the temporary unemployment list, reduce working hours or reduce their pay for a limited period. Solidarity contracts can be activated subject to having a restructuring plan in place and agreeing not to distribute profits to members or investors during the crisis.[14] Those employees that are placed on the temporary unemployed list will receive unemployment benefits from a temporary relief scheme (Vesan 2015).[15] This scheme allows cooperatives to retain staff on the payroll with the intention to re-employ them at a later date. While the scheme is also available to the private sector, it provides cooperatives with a formal, humane process to manage a crisis without losing experienced staff.

8.3.2 Central Associations Were Mature Organizations Experienced in Managing Crisis

When the GFC arrived in 2008, all the Central Associations were mature, experienced organizations with capabilities to provide consultancy services, financial services and work via the consortia system. All had lived through the highs and lows of Italian political and economic life and had dealt with a number of economic crisis and public policy changes, so by the time the crisis came, they were all equipped to provide assistance and support to their members.

Legacoop's experience in a number of well-publicized and reported crisis management cases illustrates their acquaintance with these situations and their approach in dealing with them. As mentioned in Chapter 3, Legacoop was directly involved in rescuing consumer cooperatives from north-west Italy, which experienced financial difficulties. It did this with the help of the national consortia, large cooperatives and Unipol insurance group. It required a new strategy, new funding, a changed business model and transfer of staff, but it was successful. From 1996 to 1998, Legacoop coordinated the activities of Unipol, its own merchant bank Finec and Coopfond to invest 265 million euros in support of 31 construction cooperatives that were experiencing financial difficulties (Zamagni and Felice 2006; Fabbri 2011).[16] Legacoop also oversaw the rationalization of its large cooperatives, which from 1988 to 2008 were reduced from 241 to 119. Of these, 52 merged, but 70 were placed under administration (Bulgarelli 2014). More recently, the consortia CNS and CCC were restructured after encountering financial difficulties.[17]

When the crisis came in 2008, the cooperative sector was as ready as it could have been. It had developed large cooperatives that through the years developed into cooperative groups. Their financial structures were more solid thanks to the cooperative development funds and financial companies that had grown. The consortia network operated across the country. The law facilitated capitalization and flexible industrial relation arrangements. The Central Associations were more likely to work together than ever before and began to co-manage national financial consortia such as Cooperfidi Italia and CFI. In addition, Legacoop had developed a de-facto crisis management approach from previous experiences with some success. This approach included gaining an understanding of the problem, assessing the economic and reputational risks for cooperatives and the cooperative movement, sharing financial support among cooperatives and its financial structures and appointing a new Board and senior management accompanied by a new strategic and implementation plan.

8.3.3 Capital Raising at Enterprise Level and Via a Mature Financial Network

At the time of the GFC, raising capital or having access to capital became crucial to: consolidate their market position; exploit market opportunities through acquisitions; invest in new products and services; and have sufficient cash flow withstand late payment from government agencies. Cooperatives have used all avenues offered by the legislation to raise capital. The ACI study on the largest 250 cooperatives found that they have been able to raise more capital throughout the period 2006–2015.[18] Key sources of capital raising have included:

- Members' shares. Members have increased their investment during the period from 1.2 billion euros to 1.9 billion euros (a 53.8 percent increase).
- Cooperative reserves. These are made up of accumulated retained profits and have increased from 8.87 billion euros to 13.6 billion euros (a 53 percent increase).
- Members' loans. Their amounts have ranged from 11.5 to 11.9 billion euros. Consumer cooperatives receive 95 percent of member loans.
- Bank loans. Cooperatives have increased their bank loans from 7.7 billion to 12.59 billion (a 63 percent increase).
- Corporate bonds. Since 2013, cooperatives have raised 921 million euros from selling corporate bonds.

Large cooperatives can access capital as a result of their size, longevity, accumulated assets, levels of profitability and established relations with banks. Small and medium-sized cooperatives and new cooperatives, however, have relied more on the support from the cooperative sector's own financial structures, whose contribution has been invaluable.

The cooperative development funds have been investing a growing pool of funds in new and existing cooperatives and companies strategic for the cooperative sectors. Promocoop had 23.5 million euros invested in over 40 cooperatives, consortia and cooperative-owned companies (Cooperazione Trentina 2017). Fondosviluppo invested approximately 165 million euros from 2007 to 2016 in support of cooperatives.[19] Coopfond invested 246.5 million euros in 354 investment projects from 2007 to 2016 (Coopfond 2016b).[20] Coopfond has directed approximately 75 percent of these investments into either new cooperatives or cooperatives with growth strategies. Other investments facilitated mergers, consolidation or restructuring. Some funds were directed into special projects; this usually required Coopfond to invest in larger cooperatives such as CNS, Unicoop Tirreno or the Consortia Integra, which were re-financing or restructuring their operations. Most investments, however, are directed at new cooperatives or existing cooperatives with growth strategies.

The cooperative development funds have also invested strategically. Promocoop has invested in consortia and financial companies associated with the Trentino cooperative sector. Fondosviluppo invests in Cooperfidi Italia, CFI, the insurance group Assimoco and the Consorzio Gino Mattarelli Finance. As of 2016, Coopfond had invested 210 million euros in Cooperare Spa, Cooperfidi Italia, CCFS, Cooperfactor and many other local credit guarantee companies and cooperative-owned financial companies (Coopfond 2016a). Coopfond has entered into agreements with Unipol Banca, Banca Popolare dell'Emilia-Romagna and Banca Etica, together with other local banks, in order to further help cooperatives access finance at lower rates.

The cooperative sector has been steadily developing its own financial support structures and cultivating partnerships with friendly local banks. This strategy proved successful, and by 2008 the cooperative sector could provide directly or facilitate via third parties sufficient capital to help new and existing cooperatives access credit, consolidate, grow and take over enterprises in crisis. Their contribution is summarized as follows:

- Cooperfidi Italia helped new and small businesses access credit. It provided 274 million euros in credit guarantees to 3,425 cooperatives from 2010 to 2016. This service allowed cooperatives to access loans valued at 605 million euros from over 40 banks.[21] Loans were made available to start-ups, to manage late payments, to overcome cash-flow issues, to buy machinery and for acquisitions.
- Cooperative banks provide loans to cooperatives directly and as partners with other financial structures. While cooperatives receive only 2 percent of their total loans from cooperative banks (Catturani and Brancati 2015), Cooperfidi Italia notes that 24 percent of its credit guarantees are arranged via cooperative banks.
- CFI funded 20 WBOs from 2008 to 2010. In addition, it invested 47 million euros into 185 projects from 2011 to 2016, which included: 56 WBOs, cooperative start-ups and existing cooperatives (Cooperazione Finanza Impresa 2017; Vieta, Depetri and Carrano 2017).
- CCFS provides loans and equity to its cooperative members, either directly or in partnership with other banks. The 2012 loan portfolio noted that it provided 692 million euros to 243 small and medium-sized cooperatives. CCFS also funded 69 cooperatives in partnership with third parties and invested 6.2 million euros in equity in 33 cooperatives (CCFS 2012).
- Cooperfactor provides factoring services to help cooperatives improve their cash-flow by managing late payments from public administration.[22] Social services and construction cooperatives benefit most from this service. In 2012, the Cooperfactor credit portfolio amounted to 118 million euros (CCFS 2012).
- Cooperare Spa has made large investments of 5 million euros or more in 16 cooperatives and subsidiaries since 2008. It currently holds equity investments worth 76.5 million euros in seven internationally focused cooperatives and cooperative-owned companies (Cooperare Spa 2016).
- At least another 40 banks, of which most are popular and savings banks, support the cooperatives. Banca Popolare Etica has become an integral part of the cooperative sector and has signed a number of agreements

with all the cooperative development funds and cooperative-owned financial companies. During the crisis, as of 2011, it had financed 216 cooperatives for a total of 125 million euros (Euricse 2012).

At the time of the GFC, accessing finance was no longer the issue it once was for cooperatives. They were now operating within an enabling legislative environment and were able to access external equity and finance via their cooperative financial support structures and a friendlier banking sector.

8.3.4 Competitive Business Strategies: Long-Term Goals, Large Cooperatives and Networking

Having a big core group of large cooperatives and an even larger cohort of cooperatives employing 50 people or more helped the cooperative sector compete and grow during the GFC. The rise of larger cooperatives is due to members having a culture that privileged long-term goals over short-term profit sharing (Zevi 2011). This culture led cooperatives to re-invest almost all their profits, normally deposited into the indivisible reserve fund.[23] This strategy to develop large cooperatives was originally promoted by Lega-coop, took off in the 1970s and eventually became accepted by all the major Central Associations. Even Confcooperative, which has always been a staunch supporter of small cooperatives, supports "fewer cooperatives and more cooperation" (Euricse 2012; Confcooperative 2016). At the time the GFC came, the cooperative sector share of all larger businesses increased dramatically. For instance, as Table 8.3 shows, the cooperative sector's share of total enterprises employing 50–249 people rose from 4.4 percent in 1971 to 17.3 percent in 2011, while their share of all enterprises employing over 250 employees rose from 3.6 percent in 1971 to 14.8 percent in 2011 (Alleanza delle Cooperative Italiane 2017b).[24]

During the crisis, the large cooperatives demonstrated that they are more competitive than smaller cooperatives. As Chapter 6 on cooperative groups has shown, these cooperatives are better able to access capital, fund growth strategies via acquisition and mergers, and internationalize their business. They are large and achieve economies of scale to lower costs and economies of scope to diversify their products and markets. Indeed, during the GFC, many of them engaged in acquisitions and expansion.[25] The Alleanza conducted a study on 58,952 cooperatives for the period 2008–2014[26] and found that: the large cooperatives with a turnover of over 50 million euros grew by 12.1 percent; medium-sized cooperatives with a turnover of 10–50 million euros grew by 5.1 percent; and small and micro cooperatives (turnover of less than 10 and 2 million euros respectively) recorded negative growth of –7 percent and –39 percent respectively. Table 8.4 provides annual data for the period 2008–2014 (Alleanza delle Cooperative Italiane 2015).

Table 8.3 Cooperatives as a Percentage of Employment Cohorts, 1971–2011

Employees per Company	Census 1971	Census 1981	Census 1991	Census* 2001	Census* 2011
Micro	**0.4**	**0.5**	**0.8**	**1.0**	**1.1**
1	0.1	0.2	0.3	0.7	0.9
2	0.3	0.4	0.5	0.5	0.8
3–5	0.9	1.0	1.5	1.8	1.6
6–9	1.4	1.6	3.0	4.2	2.9
Small	**2.6**	**4.2**	**5.1**	**6.5**	**6.3**
10–15	2.2	3.6	4.4	5.0	4.3
16–19	2.8	4.0	4.7	6.4	6.4
20–49	3.1	5.2	6.6	9.3	10.1
Medium	**4.4**	**5.9**	**8.6**	**13.6**	**17.3**
50–99	3.9	5.6	8.0	13.2	16.4
100–199	4.4	5.3	8.7	14.7	19.0
200–249	5.4	6.7	7.0	13.1	19.4
Large	**3.6**	**5.9**	**7.8**	**11.4**	**14.8**
250–499	4.5	6.8	8.0	11.8	16.3
500–999	2.9	5.6	7.8	11.5	12.1
>1000	1.6	2.9	7.0	10.0	13.5
TOTAL (Cooperatives as a Percentage of All Firms)	**0.5**	**0.7**	**1.0**	**1.3**	**1.4**

Note: *Census includes social cooperatives.

Source: Alleanza Cooperative Italiane. 2017. *Imprese Cooperative in Italia: Incidenza sul Totale delle Imprese per Classi di Addetti 1971–2011*. Comparative analysis based on 2011 Census. Rome: Alleanza Cooperative Italiane.

These 272 large cooperatives are the main anchors of the cooperative sector. They have:

- Increased their turnover from 67.1 billion euros in 2008 to 75.2 billion in 2014, which equates to 64.6 percent of the cooperative sector's total turnover for 2014;
- Increased their workforce from 237,000 in 2008 to 268,000 in 2014 (Alleanza delle Cooperative Italiane 2016);
- Been the major financial contributors to cooperative development funds;
- Focused on exports: five cooperatives from Emilia-Romagna are responsible for 79 percent of the regional cooperative sector's total exports (Caselli 2014a);
- Promoted inter-cooperative trade via winning public works or housing development projects and engaging other cooperatives operating in the housing industry; by managing supermarkets that through cooperatives purchase goods, and transport and property maintenance and security services; or managing comprehensive health care facilities in

Table 8.4 Cooperatives' Total Turnover (Million Euros) by Cooperative Size, 2008–2014

Size	Turnover	Number of Cooperatives	Turnover 2008	Turnover 2009	Turnover 2010	Turnover 2011	Turnover 2012	Turnover 2013	Turnover 2014	Difference 2008–2014
Large	>50	272	67122	67936	70585	75093	75997	76856	75214	12.1%
Medium	10–50	844	14433	13847	14258	15005	14981	15066	15168	5.1%
Small	2–10	3507	13555	12863	13386	13208	12914	12813	12611	-7.0%
Micro	<2	29426	10712	10712	10313	9473	8247	7365	6534	-39.0%
New cooperatives		24903	—	282	1495	3455	5179	7117	6817	—
Total		58952	105822	105640	110037	116234	117318	119220	116343	9.9%

Source: Alleanza delle Cooperative Italiane. 2015. *Il Movimento Cooperativo in Italia 2008–2014*. Note e Commenti, Rome: Alleanza Delle Cooperative Italiane. This data does not include cooperatives that operate in the banking and insurance sectors.

partnership with cooperatives providing catering, gardening and general maintenance services.

The medium and smaller cooperatives provide the majority of jobs and perform an important role in the sector. The medium cooperatives can become the large cooperatives of tomorrow, while the smaller ones add vitality and diversity, operate in new economic areas and attract the young. These have made use of the traditional consortia network to improve their market position, achieve economies of scale and access know-how and management expertise. A longitudinal study of consortia has revealed that in 2011, 2,005 consortia were operating in Italy, of which 546 were formed after 2006. Consortia produced 20 billion euros in turnover, which helps small cooperatives survive, consolidate and grow (Linguiti 2014).

8.3.5 Flexible Management Practices

Cooperatives are also affected by economic downturns. Those cooperatives that are not in a position to navigate the crisis by investing and exploiting market opportunities adopt cost-saving measures and flexible work practices to save jobs. These measures can be divided into cost-cutting, cost containment and flexible working conditions. More specifically:

• Cost-cutting measures are typically used by all types of enterprises and public administration in times of crisis and include measures such as reducing spending on consultants, marketing, and non-replacement of staff leaving or retiring.
• Cost containment would include reduction of over-time or use of accumulated leave.
• Flexible working conditions are implemented once solidarity contracts are activated. These include measures to reduce working hours, use of part-time work and salary and holiday pay reduction as well as placing staff on temporary unemployment benefits.

(Canonico 2011)

The measures noted above may also reflect the action taken by a socially responsible private enterprise and government agencies. What distinguishes cooperatives from other enterprises or agencies is that the key focus is on saving jobs and fostering internal cohesion. The key focus on job-saving is a fundamental principle of the cooperative mission and a direct result of democratic ownership. It is understandable that worker-members would consider job losses as a last resort. Maintaining employment levels and promoting cooperative principles such as mutuality, participation and relationship with the local community promotes internal cohesion and a bond between members and non-members. Cooperatives have fostered internal cohesion by promoting equal pay for equal work, re-investing almost all of their profits, adhering to the principle of limited return on capital, signing collective workplace agreements that apply to the whole workforce and providing workers with time for union activities. These practices galvanize the workforce and facilitate change and decision-making. Indeed, research conducted on 47 worker cooperatives from various sectors indicates that in some cases all workers voluntarily agreed to cut their holiday pay or to place themselves on a temporary relief scheme for a set period. This non-discriminatory approach between members and non-members facilitated dialogue and change (Accornero and Danieli 2011). This culture is present because, in a cooperative, it is the members that ultimately make the decisions that ensure that when economic performance improves, so too will their salaries and work conditions.

The policy to keep the existing workforce provides benefits in addition to internal cohesion and an effective decision-making process. It allows the retention of experienced staff, making it easier to exploit future market opportunities. It also provides a pool of loyal employees who could become future members of the cooperative, thus contributing to cooperative renewal and internal capitalization.

8.4   Cooperative Banks and Their Anti-Cyclic Function

Cooperative banks have performed an anti-cyclic role since 2007. These banks met the challenges of the economic crisis while undergoing structural changes. Since 1993, cooperative banks have extended their membership to all individuals and local businesses residing in the local area covered by a bank. In addition, to combat greater competition from large Italian and global banks, they started to merge, and their numbers were reduced from 726 in 1988 to 337 in 2016. They were now more capitalized but still too small compared to larger banks (Cusa 2009; Carretta and Boscia 2009; Federcasse 2016).

During the GFC, cooperative banks lived up to their reputation as good local community banks that put people before profits. Research from the Bank of Italy has revealed that throughout the crisis cooperative banks paid higher interest rates on deposits and charged a lower interest rate on loans made by at least one percentage point compared to other banks. They also increased lending to members and customers. This, again, was contrary to practices from other banks (Stefani and Vacca 2016). Additionally, they offered support to clients in financial difficulty by suspending or extending their repayments rather than initiating debt recovery procedures. Data from 2014 to 2016 reveals that cooperative banks have continued this practice, suspending payments of 4,865 loans and extending repayment schedules to 477 clients (BCC-Credito Cooperativo 2016).

These policies led the cooperative banks to initially increase their market share for business and family loans from 8.1 percent in 2007 to 9.4 percent by 2014 (Stefani and Vacca 2016). Their market share subsequently fell slightly to 9 percent for business loans and 8.5 percent for family loans by 2016 (Federcasse 2016). During this period, cooperative banks extended their coverage but also increased their non-performing loans. The latter was a result of lending to a more diverse clientele, larger businesses and businesses that could not get loans at other institutions. This is also a direct result of accepting a greater share of risks from clients, operating in risky local economies (for instance with a high level of construction activity) and, possibly, highlighting the negative side of relationship banking. The latter refers to when a local bank is captured by its clients (Arnone 2015; Catturani and Brancati 2015).

The period 2008–2016 has demonstrated that cooperative banks have performed a counter-cyclic function. However, as noted earlier in this chapter, cooperatives cannot perform this function indefinitely. In fact, during the GFC over 50 local banks, of which 30 were cooperative banks, were placed under administration. Of these, 15 were liquidated, nine merged and the others were under review (Stefani and Vacca 2016). Cooperative branches rose to 4,450 by 2015 but fell to 4,382 in 2016. In 2016, overall employment fell by 1,000 to 36,000. In addition, from 2010 to 2015, the Cooperative Banks Guarantee Fund invested 286 million euros to support 35 cooperative banks that were having financial difficulties (Federcasse 2015; Federcasse 2016).

During the 2008–2016 period, cooperative banks merged in order to remain competitive, and their numbers fell from 438 in 2008 to 337 by 2016. Despite this, the Government still deemed them too small, and in 2016 conducted a review that led to a major recommendation requiring cooperative banks with less than 200 million in assets to join a Cooperative Banking Group (CBG) and those with more than 200 million to transform into a public company. The CBG is to be 50 percent owned by cooperative members and has oversight over its members' governance arrangements (Cooperazione Trentina 2016).[27] The Government has given the cooperative banks until July 2018 to decide whether to be independent or join a CBG. Initial discussions have led to the formation of two groups: one led by the Trento-based Banca Cassa Centrale with over 100 cooperative banks; and the other led by the larger Gruppo Bancario ICCREA, based in Rome, which represents the remaining cooperative banks.

8.5 Cooperatives Are Not Immune to a Prolonged Economic Crisis

While cooperatives performed an anti-cyclic function, they are not immune to a prolonged economic crisis. Many cooperatives also failed during the crisis. It has been estimated that from 2009 to 2014, some 11,995 cooperatives ceased to operate (Alleanza delle Cooperative Italiane 2015).[28] It is also important to note that all types of cooperatives were impacted. More specifically:

- As noted earlier, the turnover of micro and small cooperatives was reduced during the GFC by 39 percent and 7 percent respectively. Small and new cooperatives, just like private enterprises, have a high failure rate within the first five years, so most of the cooperative failures represent this cohort (Alleanza delle Cooperative Italiane 2015).

- Medium sized cooperatives—that is, those with a turnover of 10–50 million per year—lost 115 cooperatives with a combined turnover of 1.5 billion euros and a workforce of 16,000 (Alleanza delle Cooperative Italiane 2017a).
- The large cooperatives managed the crisis better than the other cohorts but also had failures. Alleanza's review of the top 250 cooperatives noted that 90 cooperatives merged, and while some would merge because of aligned objectives, some merged because of economic need.[29] Others were no longer viable and were placed under administration (Alleanza delle Cooperative Italiane 2016).
- Sixty-five cooperative banks either folded or were rescued by the Cooperative Banks Guarantee Fund.

8.5.1 The Construction Sector

One sector that has suffered most as a result of a prolonged crisis and stagnation has been the construction sector. It has been estimated that from 2008 to 2013, the turnover generated by construction cooperatives was 11 percent lower than previous years for cooperatives and 3.5 percent lower for consortia (Carini, Borzaga and Fontanari 2015). Some high profile large cooperatives failed, leaving large amounts of debts behind and hundreds of people without jobs. The construction cooperatives hold a unique place in cooperative history because they are a demonstration of working people being able to develop businesses over time. This has ranged from building local roads to major highways; from local railways to underground and subways; from soccer stadiums to water purification plants. Construction cooperatives have also prided themselves on being able to provide long-term employment and have a culture of preserving jobs. A survey conducted in Emilia-Romagna has identified a number of reasons why these construction cooperatives failed:

- They had focused on the national public works and housing market, ignoring the international market. Public investments were down for many years, and the demand for the housing market was down at a time when cooperatives had become property developers, making it difficult to sell the apartments. This eventually led to losses and closure.
- Leadership's inability to read the market and to speak openly with members, suppliers and stakeholders and deal with the issues through a change in strategy and market repositioning.
- Some did not use the flexible management options available via the solidarity contracts or social security payments via temporary unemployment benefit schemes.
- Governance was found to be inadequate. The leadership team had been in place for decades. They no longer had the pre-requisites to lead the cooperative, yet members continued to vote for them, and there was no succession plan.

(Ricciardi 2014)

The failure of these construction cooperatives reinforces the view that cooperatives can perform an anti-cyclic function for a limited period. In a prolonged recession they would be required to change strategies, otherwise they would not be able to continue as debts rise and competitors improve their market positioning. Their experience has raised questions about their cooperative governance and their succession planning arrangements. It also highlighted the importance of finding a balance between the principles of mutuality (job security at all costs) and economic performance. Most importantly, these events can generate distrust toward the cooperative sector and also weaken inter-cooperative ties as a result of the high losses incurred (Ricciardi 2014; Baroni 2015).

What the experience of construction cooperatives also revealed was the limited capacity of Legacoop to foresee and intervene in support of these large construction cooperatives before they reached a critical point. The situation was difficult to resolve because cooperatives asked Legacoop for help at a late stage, making it difficult to find solutions. The fact that the whole sector was experiencing difficulties also made it difficult to find solutions.

8.6 Concluding Remarks

The Italian cooperative sector confronted the impact of the GFC as a mature sector operating within an enabling legislative environment and well-versed in dealing with and managing the crisis. To this end, it could count on an entrepreneurial culture focused on long-term goals and being well-supported by a network of large and medium-sized cooperatives, two thousand consortia and a number of key financial structures that were able to assist cooperatives throughout their lifecycle. As a result, the cooperative sector was able to:

• Access equity capital and loans from members, investors and banks. The financial support structures performed a vital role by helping cooperatives access credit from third parties, providing loans and, importantly, making available equity capital to new and existing cooperatives to implement growth plans and to deal with difficulties.
• Access factoring services to overcome cash flow problems resulting from late payments from government agencies.
• Create new cooperatives, including WBOs, whose numbers far exceeded cooperatives that failed.
• Exploit the market opportunities offered by the growing social services sector, which created the most jobs during this period.
• Manage economic and financial difficulties via flexible management practices, restructuring, repositioning, rescue operations and mergers with support from the sector's financial structures.
• Grow their business via product diversification, market diversification and internationalization or, in the case of smaller cooperatives, via the consortia network and inter-cooperative trade linkages.
• Choose a legal structure that best suited their business strategy and business model.

The data supplied via Table 8.4 demonstrated how vital it is to grow larger cooperatives. It showed that the large and medium-sized cooperatives grew their turnover by 12.1 and 5.1 percent respectively, while the smaller cooperatives experienced negative growth. Overall these 1,116 large and medium-sized cooperatives comprise only 1.9 percent of total cooperatives but produce almost 78 percent of the total turnover. This highlights that the strategy to create larger cooperative enterprises has been successful.

The cooperative sector did perform better than the private sector during this period and did perform an anti-crisis function. In part, this was because most cooperatives operated in sectors that were not severely affected by the crisis. The major reason, however, is to be found in the cooperative principles of mutuality, values and business culture. This is demonstrated by their ability to raise capital and continue to invest, by creating new cooperatives and new employment and, in the case of banks, by providing business and family funding at lower rates and offering support when facing financial difficulties. This was achieved at the expense of lowering profits and increasing debt, which is not sustainable should the crisis continue for prolonged periods. Therefore, cooperatives need to perform a balancing act that protects the sustainability of the business in the long term as well as meeting the needs of employees and local communities, which expect cooperatives to continue to perform an anti-cyclic role in difficult periods. When this balance is not achieved, cooperatives will also face economic difficulties.

The Euricse and ACI studies have confirmed the differences between democratically owned cooperatives and capitalist-owned public companies and businesses. Cooperatives have put people before profits, focusing on maintaining employment at the expense of profits. Private enterprises have put profits before people by cutting staff and preserving profits. This also confirms that people who work in a well-managed cooperative fully integrated with the cooperative network have a greater level of job protection through the use of solidarity contracts, collective use of flexible arrangements, collective use of temporary unemployment benefits and access to financial support from the cooperative sector.

The longer longevity rate of cooperatives compared to other firms further confirms cooperatives' higher level of resilience compared to capitalist enterprises. This is due to cooperative's competitive business model, strategies and networking arrangements.

Cooperatives are not immune to a crisis. While they live longer than private enterprises, they do fail. Competing in the market requires cooperatives to produce goods and services that the market wants and constantly monitor the market and manage change by introducing new products, services and markets. The financial and non-financial networks from the cooperative sector can help, but there are limits to what they can do. The greater autonomy within which the cooperative construction enterprises had been operating from Legacoop is problematic because their eventual failure will have an economic and reputational impact on Legacoop's network, the whole cooperative sector and future generations. Thus, a better balance needs to be found, one that preserves the autonomy of cooperatives but enables the Central Associations to monitor them and intervene prior to a crisis developing in order to find common solutions that benefit the cooperative, the cooperative sector and their communities. Solutions may be market repositioning, financial management, better governance arrangements or change of leadership. The next two chapters will discuss these issues in more detail.

Notes

1. Late payments of up to 12 months caused cash flow problems for public sector providers.
2. The purchasing power of Italian families in 2016 was 105 billion euros lower than 2007 (Coop Italia 2016).
3. Unioncamere found that active new cooperatives doubled their employment within five years from five to ten employees (Caselli 2014).
4. The percentage rises to 9.9 percent in the service sector and 8.6 percent in the agricultural sector.
5. The ACI study compared the performance of the largest 250 cooperatives with Mediobanca's sample of 2,060 enterprises for the period 2006 to 2015 (Alleanza delle Cooperative Italiane 2016).
6. Value added refers to total revenue minus intermediate costs (primary, services and consumption costs). The value-added amount is then used to pay labor costs, taxes and amortizations after which a profit or loss is made.
7. Euricse's study comprised all businesses (public companies, limited companies and cooperatives) that submitted financial statements for the duration of the period reviewed (Borzaga 2015).
8. In Italy public companies are called Societa' per Azioni (SPA) or joint stock companies. I will use the term public companies to refer to SPA.
9. Profits ranged from a high of 824 million euros in 2006 to a low of 134 million euros in 2008.
10. ACI studies on 793 medium-sized cooperatives and 7,184 social cooperatives found a similar pattern of higher turnover and higher employment levels as well as lower profits and higher debt (Alleanza delle Cooperative Italiane 2017a; Alleanza delle Cooperative Italiane 2014).
11. Please refer to Chapter 2.
12. Italian cooperatives pay more taxes than any other cooperative sector. Chinese cooperatives pay the next highest tax rate at 29 percent, while Portugal had a tax rate of less than 4 percent (Caselli 2014).
13. Please refer to Chapter 5 for more information.
14. Please refer to Law 2001, n. 142. 2001.
15. Please refer to Chapter 7, Section 7.3 and Endnote 7 for more information.
16. These cooperatives had a turnover of 1.5 billion euros and workforce of 11,000.
17. Please refer to Chapter 5 for more information.
18. These 250 cooperatives represent 97 percent of all large cooperatives and 98 percent of their turnover.
19. This is the author's estimate based on Fondosviluppo investing 16.5 million euros per year (total investment of 396 million euros divided by 24 years of operation).
20. Coopfond invested 184 million euros in 256 projects 2007–2011.
21. The data is taken from Cooperfidi Italia Annual Financial Reports from 2010 to 2016. Prior to the formation of Cooperfidi Italia there were nine credit guarantee companies offering the same service.

22. Public bodies pay on average 177 days late and owed the construction industry 8 billion euros in 2015 (Atradius 2016).
23. A Legacoop study of its largest 361 cooperatives revealed that 88.5 percent of profits were deposited in the indivisible reserve account (Petrucci 2009).
24. I would like to thank Francesco Linguiti of the ACI Centro Studi for kindly updating this data.
25. A Bank of Italy study indicated that 16.7 percent of cooperatives acquired another firm and 6 percent acquired an existing supplier, compared with private enterprises: 2.3 percent and 1 percent respectively (Bentivogli and Viviano 2012).
26. The 58,952 cooperatives do not include: banks and insurance companies; those cooperatives that were established in 2009 but ceased operations before 2014; and those that were established in 2014 but had not yet submitted their financial statement (Alleanza delle Cooperative Italiane 2015).
27. Cooperative banking groups are to be majority owned by cooperative banks and have the authority to provide leadership, coordination, invest in each cooperative and intervene in governance arrangements including the removal of directors.
28. From 2009 to 2015, 24,000 new cooperatives were formed (Alleanza delle Cooperative Italiane 2015).
29. Coop Adriatica incorporated La Triestina because it was in financial difficulties.

References

Accornero, Aris, and Marini Danieli. 2011. "Una Normale … Eccezzionalita'. Quando le Politiche del personale e le Strategie D'Impresa fanno la differenza: Il Caso della Cooperazione in Italia." In *Le Cooperative alla prova Della Crisi*, edited by Aris Accornero and Marini Danieli, 1–13. Venezia: Fondazione Nord Est.

Alleanza delle Cooperative Italiane. 2014. *La Cooperazione Sociale Negli Anni Della Crisi*. Note e Commenti, Rome: Alleanza delle Cooperative Italiane.

———. 2015. *Il Movimento Cooperativo in Italia 2008–2014*. Note e Commenti, Rome: Alleanza Delle Cooperative Italiane.

———. 2016. *Le Grandi Cooperative Italiane*. Osservatorio Grandi Imprese, Rome: Alleanza delle Cooperative Italiane.

———. 2017a. *Le Medie Cooperative nel Periodo 2008–2015*. Note e Commenti, Rome: Alleanza delle Cooperative Italiane.

———. 2017b. *Imprese Cooperative in Italia: Incidenza sul Totale delle Imprese per Classi di Addetti 1971–2011*. Cooperative Census, Rome: Alleanza delle Cooperative Italiane.

Arnone, Massimo. 2015. "Il Credito Cooperativo Negli Anni della Crisi. Un'Analisi Territoriale." In *Economia Cooperativa. Rilevanza, Evoluzione e Nuove Frontiere della Cooperazione Italiana*, edited by Carlo Borzaga, 191–200. Trento: Euricse.

Atradius. 2016. *Market Monitor: Italy Construction Industry*. 18 February. Accessed September 2, 2017. https://group.atradius.com/publications/market-monitor-construction-italy-2016.html.

Baroni, Paolo. 2015. *Cosi Il Crollo dell'Edilizia ha Messo in Crisi il Modello Coop*. 17 March. Accessed August 2016. www.lastampa.it/2015/03/17/economia/cosi-il-crollo-delledilizia-ha-messo-in-crisi-il-modello-coop-lhyjmg38hnbphut1xfnril/pagina.html.

Battilani, Patrizia, and Francesca Fauri. 2014. *L'Economia Italiana dal 1945 a Oggi*. Bologna: Il Mulino.

Bayo, Claudia Sanchez, and Bruno Roelantz. 2011. *Capital and the Debt Trap*. Hampshire: Palgrave Macmillan.

BCC-Credito Cooperativo. 2016. *L'impronta del Credito Cooperativo: Rapporto 2016*. Annual Report, Rome: BCC-Credito Cooperativo.

Bentivogli, Chiara, and Eliana Viviano. 2012. "Le Trasformazioni del Sistema Produttivo Italiano: Le Cooperative." *Banca D'Italia Occasional Papers*, 35.

Borzaga, Carlo. 2015. "Introduzione e Sintesi." In *Economia Cooperativa: Rilevanza, Evoluzione e Nuove Frontiere della Cooperazione Italiana*, edited by Carlo Borzaga, 5–35. Trento: Euricse.

Brandolini, Andrea. 2017. "Lavoro e Disuguaglianza tra Rivoluzione Digitale e Invecchiamento della Popolazione." *Cooperative Sociali Oltre la Crisi*. Rimini: Legacoop Sociali, Emilia Romagna, 32.

Bulgarelli, Marco. 2014. *Relazione sulla Gestione*. Bilancio D'Esercizio, Bologna: Cooperare Spa.

Canonico, Marina. 2011. "Le Cooperative e la Crisi." In *Le Cooperative alla Prova della Crisi*, edited by Aris Accornero and Daniele Marini, 108–142. Venezia: Fondazione Nord-Est.

Carini, Chiara, Carlo Borzaga, and Eddi Fontanari. 2015. "Le cooperative Italiane tra il 2008 e il 2013: Dinamica Economica, Patrimoniale ed Occupazionale." In *Economia Cooperativa: Rilevanza, Evoluzione e Nuove Frontiere della Cooperazione Italiana*, edited by Carlo Borzaga, 113–149. Trento: Euricse.

Carretta, Alessandro, and Vittorio Boscia. 2009. *Il Ruolo Economico delle Banche di Credito Cooperativo nel Sistema Finanziario*. Rome: Ecra.

Caselli, Guido. 2014a. *Lo Scenario Economico e le Prospettive della Cooperazione*. Report on the Regional Cooperative Sector, Bologna: Unioncamere Emilia-Romagna.

———. 2014b. *Osservatorio della Cooperazione in Emilia-Romagna: Partire dai Numeri*. Cooperative Sector Review, Bologna: Unioncamere.

———. 2015. *Cooperazione 4.0: I numeri di Oggi, Le Traiettorie di Domani*. Annual Report, Bologna: Unioncamere.

Catturani, Ivana, and Raffaele Brancati. 2015. "Cooperative di Credito e Imprese Italiane nella Seconda Fase della Crisi." In *Economia Cooperativa. Rilevanza, Evoluzione e Nuove Frontiere della Cooperazione Italiana*, edited by Carlo Borzaga, 201–218. Trento: Euricse.

CCFS. 2012. *Bilancio Sociale*. Annual Report, Reggio Emilia: Consorzio Cooperativo Finanziario per lo Sviluppo.

Confcooperative. 2016. *Bilancio di Sostenibilita'*. Annual Sustainability Report, Rome: Confederazione Cooperative Italiane.

Cooperare Spa. 2016. *Biliancio D'Esercizio*. Annual Financial Report, Bologna: Cooperare Spa.

Cooperazione Finanza Impresa. 2017. "CFI-Marcora Law." *Home Page*. Accessed August 29, 2017. www.cfi.it/public/.

Cooperazione Trentina. 2016. "Riforma BCC." *Cooperazione Trentina*, March: 4–11.

———. 2017. "Promocoop: Crescono le Partecipazioni." *Cooperazione Trentina*, June: 33–34.

Coopfond. 2016a. *Rendicontazione Sociale 2015–2016*. Annual Accountability Report, Rome: Coopfond.

———. 2016b. *Rendicondazione Sociale 2014–2016*. Annual Report, Rome: Coopfond.

Coop Italia. 2016. *Rapporto Coop Consumatori, 2016*. Annual Report, Bologna: Coop Italia.

Cusa, Emanuele. 2009. *Lo Scopo Mutualistico delle Banche di Credito Cooperativo*. Rome: ECRA.

De Micheli, Paola, Stefano Imbruglia, and Antonio Misiani. 2017. *Se Chiudi ti Compro*. Milano: Angelo Guerini Associati.

Euricse. 2012. *Cooperative e crisi: gli effetti della crisi economica sul mondo cooperativo, visti dalla stampa italiana ed europea*. Media Coverage Review, Trento: Euricse.

Fabbri, Fabio. 2011. *L'Italia Cooperativa*. Rome: Ediesse.

Federcasse. 2015. *Bilancio di Coerenza delle BCC*. Rome: Federcasse.

———. 2016. *Bilancio di Coerenza delle BCC*. Annual Report, Rome: Federcasse.

Fondazione Censis. 2012. *Primo Rapporto sulla Cooperazione in Italia*. Roma: Alleanza delle Cooperative Italiane.

Fontanari, Eddi, and Carlo Borzaga. "Chi Contribuisce di Piu' alla Finanza Pubblica: Coop e Spa a Confronto." In *Economia Cooperativa: Rilevanza, Evoluzione e Nuove Frontiere della Cooperazione Italiana*, edited by Carlo Borzaga, 159–170. Trento: Euricse.

Gulati, Ranjay, Nitin Nohria, and Franz Wohlgezogen. 2010. "Roaring Out of Recession." *Harvard Business Review*, 63–69.

Linguiti, Francesco. 2014. "I Consorzi tra Societa' Cooperative." In *La Cooperazione Italiana Negli Anni Della Crisi*, edited by Carlo Borzaga, 53–72. Trento: Euricse.

OECD. 2017. *OECD Data—Italy*. Accessed August 23, 2017. https://data.oecd.org/italy.htm.

Petrucci, Paola. 2009. "La Distribuzione degli Avanzi di Gestione e la Practica del Ristorno nelle Imprese Cooperative." Edited by Iris Network. In *Colloquio Scientifico Annuale Sull'Impresa Sociale*, 11. Trento: IRIS Network.

Ricciardi, Mario. 2014. *I Risultati della Ricerca su Partecipazione dei Soci e dei Lavoratori e Relazioni Industriali: Primi Risultati*. Report to the XI Regional Congress, Bologna: Legacoop Emilia-Romagna.

Sforzi, Jacobo, Flaviano Zandonai, and Chiara Carini. 2014. "Le Nuove Cooperative: Un Modello di Innovazione Sociale?" In *La Cooperazione Italiana negli Anni della Crisi: Secondo Rapporto Euricse*, edited by Carlo Borzaga, 133–148. Trento: Euricse.

Smith, Stephen C., and Jonathon Rothbaum. 2014. "Cooperatives in a Global Economy: Key Issues, Recent Trends and Potential Development." In *Co-operatives in Post-Growth Era: Creating Co-operative Economics*, edited by Sonja Novkovic and Tom Webb, 221–242. London: Zed Books.

Stefani, Maria Lucia, and Valerio Vacca. 2016. *Le Banche Locali e Il Finanziamento dei territori: Evidenze per L'Italia (2007–2014)*. Occasional Papers 324, Rome: Banca D'Italia.

Vesan, Patrick. 2015. "Labor Market Policy and Politics." In *The Oxford Handbook of Italian Politics*, edited by Eric Jones and Gianfranco Pasquino, 15 pages. Oxford: Oxford University Press.

Vieta, Marcelo, Sara Depetri, and Antonella Carrano. 2017. *The Italian Road to Recuperating Enterprises in Crisis and the Legge Marcora Framework: Italy's Worker Buyouts in Times of Crisis*. Trento: Euricse.

Zamagni, Vera, and Emanuele Felice. 2006. *Oltre il Secolo*. Bologna: Il Mulino.

Zevi, Alberto. 2011. "La Cooperazione Italiana nel Mercato Globale: Tendenze, Dimensioni, Sfide." *Italiani Europei*, 28 March.

9 Principles and Social Responsibility
People and Communities
Before Profits

The previous chapters have examined how the Italian cooperative sector has managed to grow and to navigate the GFC. This chapter assesses the extent to which cooperatives have achieved economic performance while operating in alignment with cooperative principles. Competing in the market in alignment with cooperative principles distinguishes cooperatives from other enterprises. It is what makes them unique.

This chapter is divided into four themes: mutuality, democracy, cooperation and community. Each theme will describe the cooperative principle or principles that apply and discuss how the cooperative law,[1] Central Associations[2] and cooperative practices[3] address them. The discussion will also identify issues and problems and suggest ways to further promote economic development in alignment with the International Cooperative Alliance (ICA) cooperative principles.

Table 9.1 notes the four themes and ICA cooperative principles.

9.1 Mutuality

The concept of mutuality is a core principle of cooperation. It affirms that people cooperate to solve problems or to get a benefit that they were not able to obtain on their own. This may be a job with better job security and working conditions, access to credit or being able to market their produce at better and consistent prices. The two ICA principles that underpin this concept are:

- Principle 1: open and voluntary membership. This requires cooperatives not to discriminate against anyone and to be open to all who are prepared to accept the responsibilities of membership.
- Principle 3: member economic participation. This requires members to contribute financially, democratically control capital and distribute profits to set up reserves (some indivisible), pay limited dividends on shares, pay members a rebate based on the transactions held with the cooperative and fund other activities approved by the membership.

9.1.1 Italian Cooperative Law and Mutuality

Italian law promotes open membership and economic participation. Open membership is promoted via regulations that set the minimum joining

Table 9.1 International Cooperative Alliance—Cooperative Principles

Cooperative Theme	International Cooperative Alliance—Cooperative Principles
Mutuality	Principle 1: Voluntary and Open Membership
	Principle 3: Member Economic Participation
Democracy	Principle 2: Democratic Member Control
	Principle 4: Autonomy and Independence
	Principle 5: Education, Training and Information
Cooperation	Principle 6: Cooperation Among Cooperatives
Community	Principle 7: Concern for Community

membership fees low (from 25–500 euros) to facilitate new membership, while also requiring cooperative statutes to establish non-discriminatory procedures. They also promote 'trainee members,' who are entitled to membership after five years subject to meeting the membership criteria, and offer tax concessions only to cooperatives that demonstrate that at least 50 percent of their transactions are with members.

Economic participation is encouraged by enabling members to invest or engage with the cooperative and to receive a rebate in recognition of their work or transactions. Members are required to purchase shares and, in return, receive a limited return on their investment that cannot exceed the postal bond rate by 2 percent. Members can also supply loans that are remunerated annually. Investor members can purchase ordinary or preferential shares, which can be remunerated at 2 percent more than member shares. Cooperatives can pay rebates, which cannot exceed 30 percent of a member's salary in worker cooperatives, or provide other forms of rebates, such as enterprise welfare services or discounts on food prices. At least 30 percent of profits are to be deposited in the indivisible reserve fund.

9.1.2 Central Associations and Mutuality

All Central Associations promote an open membership. They see membership as being tied to cooperative success because new members invest capital and facilitate succession planning. They emphasize the importance of managing the cooperative well because its assets will ultimately be transferred to the next generation and are to be managed in the interests of the community. All Central Associations review their members' financial statements and administration every two years (they review the larger ones every year) to ensure that engagement with members, profit distribution and share remuneration are applied according to the law.

9.1.3 Cooperatives and Mutuality

Cooperative enterprises have been operating in alignment with these principles. Most transactions are conducted with members. For instance, more than 80 percent of the workforce of Legacoop's worker cooperatives from construction, manufacturing, services and social services are members (Legacoop Centro Studi 2014). Confcooperative notes that 79 percent of cooperative transactions are conducted with members (Confcooperative 2016) and over 77 percent of consumer cooperatives' revenue derives from sales to members (ANCC-Coop 2015).

All cooperatives report in their annual reports how they distribute profits in compliance with the regulations. The key finding is that most cooperatives deposit more than the required 30 percent of profits into the indivisible reserve fund. Legacoop's Centro Studi conducted a study on 361 large and medium-sized cooperatives and found that 88.5 percent of profits were deposited into the reserve fund; 7.9 percent were used in capital remuneration; less than 1 percent was spent on rebates, and 3 percent went to Coopfond (Petrucci 2009). This trend has continued. Cooperatives surveyed from 2015–2016 deposited between 60 to 97 percent of profits in the indivisible reserve (3 percent went to the cooperative development fund).

Rebates are provided in many forms. Members are offered a variety of services in lieu of cash rebates. These rebates may include payment toward private health cover to pay health benefits gaps; supplementary pension fund; social activities such as cheaper holidays; scholarships for their children; intra-cooperative loans; free medical tests/examinations; summer holidays for children; free lunch; financial support for maternity leave; and tax returns support. It is important to note that because there are few prescriptive regulatory provisions, and cooperative memberships have different needs, these rebates are not consistently applied across all cooperatives. In short, the larger cooperatives provide more generous rebates (Sacmi 2015; Cooperservice 2014; EmilBanca 2015; Coop Adriatica 2015; Cooplat 2016; Camst 2015).

While in most cooperatives members comprise the majority of the workforce, the membership level of a few large cooperatives—especially those that have expanded overseas or have formed groups via holding companies—represents less than the 50 percent of the workforce. This deserves attention because it may slow generational change, limit access to member capital and limit the democratic nature of the cooperative. A closer look at three cooperatives reveals real barriers to increase their membership. More specifically:

- Some cooperatives are employing more staff via their subsidiaries. Manutencoop, a multi-service property management cooperative, employs 517 persons, of whom 499 are members. However, via its majority-owned holding company, MFM, it controls five major companies that directly, or via other subsidiaries, employ more than 16,000 people. The members of the cooperative work in these subsidiaries. In fact, the cooperative has transformed itself into a labor-hire company for the companies owned via MFM. All employees can become members subject to having worked for the cooperative or a subsidiary for three years, completed the cooperative induction program and committed to purchasing 7,700 euros worth of shares payable within five years. A difficulty faced by Manutencoop is that whenever it wins a new public contract, the law requires that it employs the existing firm's employees, who may not believe in or understand the cooperative ideals and thus may not want to become members.[4] It is also difficult to offer long-term employment and membership as a result of the short-term tenure of contracts. While membership is low, it is important to note that Manutencoop offers health coverage and other benefits to all employees, not just members (Manutencoop 2015).

- Cooperatives working overseas also find themselves with a workforce that is comprised mostly of employees. CMC of Ravenna employs 1,441 persons in Italy and a further 5,876 employees via overseas subsidiaries. CMC finds real barriers in attracting members because overseas staff are hired on a project-based basis, so full-time employment cannot be guaranteed. They are also hired via joint ventures with private sector partners registered overseas, so it cannot enforce cooperative principles on private partners. Even in Italy, CMC can provide full-time ongoing employment only to 456 employees, of whom 389 are members.[5]

- Some cooperatives prefer smaller memberships because this promotes a greater level of participation and democratic management. Sacmi employs 385 members out of a possible 1,084 persons in Italy and 4,180 worldwide. It adheres to strict membership rules, which include: need to be between 24–40 years of age; five years' employment with the cooperative; demonstrated technical competencies, discipline and cooperative spirit; and willingness to pay the membership fee. There have been as many as 300 persons on the membership waiting list of this highly successful cooperative (Benati and Mazzoli 2009). Some of the reasons for low membership are similar to those outlined above with CMC. Cooperatives from Imola, however, are of the view that the combination of having a small membership base comprised of committed members who are willing to make a high investment leads to high participation levels that enhance the democratic life of the cooperative. They believe that a large membership leads to apathy, low participation levels and lack of promotion of democratic management (Hancock 2007). It is also true, however, that fewer members can also share the portion of the profits distributed as capital remuneration. In 2015, the sum of 5.74 million euros was distributed as dividends to 389 members. All things being equal, this amounts to a return of 14,755 euros each.[6] As is the case with Manutencoop, Sacmi offers health coverage and other benefits to all employees, not just members (Platoni 2009).

9.1.4 Comments on Mutuality

Cooperatives in Italy have demonstrated that they operate in alignment with the open door principle and economic participation of members. The development of large cooperatives with an international base or a dual legal structure where cooperatives own holding companies has led a few larger cooperatives to have fewer than 50 percent of members. This does not appear to have led to members exploiting non-members because the return on capital is limited and their salaries are based on collective agreements that treat everyone as equals. According to the statistics and data available, it has also not led to members keeping their jobs at the expense of non-members, as the flexible management policies designed to keep jobs during and following the GFC applied to all staff. It does, however, reserve democratic participation to less staff, and this is a concern for a cooperative movement that has always prided itself on promoting democratic management.

Cooperatives have distributed profits in accordance with the ICA principles. Profits are mostly deposited into the indivisible reserve fund preferring long-term investments while a smaller portion is made available for capital remuneration and member rebates (profit sharing or bonus payments). The provision of making available a rebate to members is a typical cooperative feature that is not present in any conventional enterprise. It is unique because it rewards the work performed for or the transaction held with the cooperative. It rewards labor or the level of engagement with the cooperative. Unlike capitalist enterprises, it does not reward capital. Antonio Zanotti[7] supports the payment of rebates because this improves member engagement and makes it more attractive for non-members to join a cooperative. This, in turn, could attract more capital and facilitate succession planning. The Sacmi experience is an example where participation at annual assemblies and demand for membership is quite high. According to Zanotti, the cooperative movement needs to find an acceptable balance that, while prioritizing long-term investment, also makes a portion of profits available for rebates if economic results allow it (Zanotti 2016).

9.2 Democracy

If the concept of mutuality defines the reason why people form cooperatives, the principle of democracy defines how they are governed. Democratic governance is the decision-making framework through which members elect the board, keep it and management accountable and participate in key decisions to ensure the cooperative achieves economic performance in compliance with the law, mutual goals and community expectations. The relevant ICA principles are:

- Principle 2: democratic member control. Members should control the organization by participating in setting policies, making decisions and serving as elected members. The principle of one-person-equals-one-vote should apply to primary cooperatives.
- Principle 4: autonomy and independence. Cooperatives are to be controlled by members and should be autonomous from other organizations, governments or financial institutions.

- Principle 5: education, training and information. Cooperatives are required to train their members so that they can contribute to the development of their cooperative. This means training in technical skills and all the skills necessary to govern the cooperative. They should also educate the public on the history of cooperatives, their ideals and practice.

9.2.1 The Law and Democracy

The cooperative legislation promotes the practice of democracy by regulating voting rights, forms of participation and governance structures that allocate decision-making powers and responsibilities. More specifically:

- Voting rights are based on the principle of one-person-equals-one-vote. Institutional members can have five votes. Members are guaranteed two-thirds of the votes at the annual general assembly (AGA), with the remaining third left to external shareholders. This allows members to have always control of their cooperative. In consortia, a weighted voting system applies, giving the larger cooperatives up to 10 percent of the votes while restricting their combined vote to one-third of total votes.
- Participation is encouraged. The law allows proxy voting, enabling members to delegate up to ten votes to a delegate. Voting can take place via post or electronically. Large cooperatives are required to hold separate general meetings before the AGA, allowing members to participate at a location close to their residences.
- Education is not covered specifically, but it is covered indirectly via the cooperative development funds, which are allowed to spend a portion of their funds to promote cooperative education and training.
- Three governance models are available to cooperatives: the tripartite, dualistic and monistic models.[8] The first is the traditional model that allows members to elect their board, management and the oversight committee at their AGA. Members approve the annual budget and annual accounts, admit new members and approve the dividend and rebate remuneration policies at their AGA. This is the most widely used governance structure and the only one used prior to 2003. Today, this model is viewed as better suited to small cooperatives but not for larger cooperatives, especially cooperative groups. These require the clear division of powers between the board and management and clearer forms of accountability that are better served by the dualistic governance model.[9]
- Oversight. The Ministry of Economic Development is responsible for conducting annual oversight reviews of the larger cooperatives[10] and every two years for other cooperatives. This function is delegated to the Central Associations, who have the authority to review their members. The reviews ascertain whether cooperatives have complied with the principles of mutuality; whether the functioning of the board and

AGA comply with the legal requirements; and whether the cooperative is financially sound. If found to be in financial difficulty, the Ministry can place it under administration.

(Bonfante 2011)

9.2.2 Central Associations and the Promotion of Democratic Practices

The law provides general guidelines on democracy, leaving it to the Central Associations and cooperatives to develop fit-for-purpose democratic practices. All Central Associations promote cooperative democracy. It is common knowledge that democracy is more difficult to apply in a large cooperative than in a small one where everyone knows each other, the products or services are few, knowledge is widespread, information flows are more informal and the focus is on a local market.[11] However, the formation of large cooperatives has made cooperative governance more difficult. The recruitment of managers outside of the cooperative movement who focus on economic growth more than the goals of mutuality has raised further concerns.[12]

Vera Zamagni and Emanuel Felice provide a very good analysis of the steps taken by Legacoop in understanding and dealing with the issue of cooperative governance. This is not surprising considering it promoted large cooperatives and cooperative groups. They note that since 1980, Legacoop leadership has realized that cooperative governance has become more complicated. Key issues that were noted include cooperative territorial expansion, which raised the issue of participation from members located in different locations, and executives now making the more technical decisions. Other key issues include financial management becoming increasingly complex and challenging for members to understand; fewer members having an adequate knowledge of the economy and the market; and the increased specialization and segmentation of the workplaces (Zamagni and Felice 2006).

In 1997, working groups led by the current Unipol president, Pierluigi Stefanini, considered the role of members, cooperative democracy and efficient enterprises. It identified 20 areas to focus on for improving democracy. These included the open door principle, the electoral process, increasing voting participation and developing and monitoring codes of conduct. It also included committees to monitor and review policies and procedures; clearer roles and responsibilities for executives and committees; enterprise oversight committees to be more independent from management; developing guidelines on when to use conventional companies; and promoting the production of an annual social report to complement the annual financial statement (Zamagni and Felice 2006).

Corporate governance had by now also become a topical issue worldwide. Key discussions, investigations, reports and laws were initiated in response to company collapses, fraud and concern about the lack of competitiveness if companies failed in their corporate governance practices. Key reports of international note included the United Kingdom's Cadbury report in 1991; the King report in South Africa in 1994; and the Sarbanes-Oxley Act of 2002 in response to the collapses of Enron and WorldCom. The OECD, the EEC and countries such as Australia have also produced corporate governance guidelines. These reports and guidelines vary but generally cover the role of the board, the separation of roles for the board and management, the duties of directors and independent directors, risk management and compliance, remuneration committees and strong and independent audit functions (Du Plessis, Hargovan, Bagaric and Harris 2015). In Italy, political corruption scandals also hit a high in 1992, with company fraud such as that taking place in Parmalat being hotly debated and, as stated, some large cooperatives also failed.

The cooperative sector responded to these scandals with Legacoop producing a code of ethics in 1993 (Legacoop 1993), governance guidelines in 2008 (Legacoop 2008) and a good practice guide to encourage member participation in 2012 (Legacoop 2012). Confcooperative and Federazione Trentina also developed membership charters for their members (Federazione Trentina 2011; Confcooperative 2017; Credito Cooperativo 2017). In 2017, Legacoop Emilia-Romagna set up a governance working group to report on how the gap between governance theory, knowledge and implementation was being reduced, on applying the 2008 governance guidelines and on supporting education and training (Benini 2017).

These guidelines, while not yet fully implemented, are contributing to finding a right balance between economic performance, compliance with the law, alignment with cooperative principles and community expectations. These guidelines also communicate that cooperatives take governance seriously. Key statements and suggestions emanating from these documents included:

- Autonomy. Central Associations declared their full autonomy from political parties and made it incompatible to simultaneously hold office at a Central Association and a political or social organization.
- Education and training. Provide induction training for all potential cooperative members, including the history and principles of cooperation, and provide formal training for board members. Provide funding for university-based courses on cooperative studies and professional training via Fon.Coop. Develop websites to inform on cooperative principles, legislation, finance and governance.
- Information and participation. Members need to be informed in order to participate in decision-making, and the flow of information via the intranet and newsletters is encouraged. Ad hoc committees and work groups should discuss key topics before the AGA to facilitate informed decision-making. The AGA needs to discuss key investment decisions as well as decisions on dividend payments, rebates and admission of new

members. Cooperatives to arrange AGA at family-friendly times, transport for members designed to encourage participation and produce bilingual information to assist migrant workers.

- Governance arrangements. This is possibly the most important topic, and Central Associations have suggested many improvements. These include improving accountability in large cooperatives by separating the role of the board (direction and control) with the role of management (operational responsibilities); electing independent directors to the board; promoting a stakeholder model that includes different categories of board members; limiting mandates for board members to three consecutive terms, especially the chair; succession planning allowing potential members to sit on the board; and limiting board appointments to other boards.
- Cooperative groups. Cooperatives that head a group of companies should make sure that members are aware of decisions being made, that the decision supported the principles of mutuality and that controlled companies operate in alignment with cooperative principles and practice to the maximum extent allowable by the law. To this end, cooperatives need to have strategic control of subsidiaries; align subsidiary's goals with goals of mutuality and principles of cooperation; establish a formal relationship with the subsidiaries via ad hoc committees; and ensure the head cooperative leads and controls its subsidiaries.
- Oversight. The Central Associations, either directly or via external reviewers, conduct reviews of their members and through them suggest how to improve democratic management and member participation.

9.2.3 Enterprise Level Democracy

As cooperatives vary in size and complexity and operate in different sectors of the economy, different cooperative governance models and democratic practices have developed. All cooperative members of the Central Associations comply with the formal aspects of cooperative governance. This includes having the AGA elect the board every three years and approving the budget and financial statements, complying with the principle of one-person-equals-one-vote, and having members hold the majority of board positions. Information on AGA agenda is regularly supplied. There are different governance models adopted that influence the relations between board and management and varying participation levels. The results of a few studies will now be illustrated, followed by a comparison of two types of cooperative governance models.

A survey on governance conducted by Antonio Zanotti on participation and one conducted by Mario Ricciardi on industrial relations attempt to assess the level of substantial democracy present in cooperatives. Zanotti's research involved 84 cooperatives from the services sector (logistics, multiservice and transport) employing more than 250 persons. He found that all provided information to members; 59 percent provided immediate approval for new members; 36 percent provided training to board members; 44 percent had more than one AGA per year; key items discussed at general assemblies included the budget, strategy, rebates, remuneration and subsidiaries; 34 percent had working groups, including one that focused on subsidiaries; and most adopted the tripartite governance structure where the president was chair of the board and also CEO (Zanotti 2012).

Ricciardi reviewed 35 cooperatives in 2011 and followed up with 25 interviews in 2014. He found that cooperatives paid above award wages and conditions; encouraged the participation of members and non-members at the AGA; supplied a reasonable level of information to members; provided formal induction programs; and some introduced maximum terms for board members. Ricciardi also found that participation in the AGA was passive; participation was also low except when they had to vote to elect board members; there was no formal succession planning; the chair and board members also held executive positions; and power was concentrated in few hands (Ricciardi 2014). These two studies indicate that cooperative practices are not homogenous. The formal side of democracy is consistently applied, and while participation is encouraged, the level of participation differs among cooperatives.

This author's review of the sustainability reports of 12 large cooperatives from the social, banking, manufacturing, consumer, construction and services sectors for 2014–2016, confirmed that there are differences between cooperatives but also noted many good practice examples. The review found that all cooperatives provided a good level of information via various means; the tripartite governance model was most commonly used; all organized more than one AGA to inform their members; all had put in place sub-committees; most had established member branches in different cities to encourage member participation; and most had in place a formal cooperative induction program. Key good practice examples include:

- Cadiai, Manutencoop and the consumer sector provide formal cooperative induction courses.
- Banca Popolare Etica has trained 392 members to review business loan applications to determine whether they meet the bank's ethical requirements.
- CMC, Camst, Cadiai, Manutencoop and Coop Adriatica publish their own magazines to inform members about the life of the cooperative.
- Emilbanca has established 19 members' branches to encourage participation in developing products and services and to create stronger links with the local community.
- Coop Adriatica held 198 meetings across regions to discuss the annual budget that attracted 44,000 members.
- Cadiai has established environment, participation, communication and social responsibility committees to encourage member participation.

9.2.4 Two Different Approaches to Governance: Sacmi and the Construction Cooperatives

Sacmi uses the dualistic governance model. It separates the powers of the Board (direction, control and representing members) and those the chief executive officer, who is appointed by the board, endorsed by the AGA, and responsible for operational matters along with senior managers. Membership is kept low to encourage participation. Each member is required to invest more than the minimum requirement (the average member has invested more than 60,000 euros). Members are highly qualified and expect a share of the profits in the form of dividend payments and profit sharing arrangements within the legal limit. Members are expected to comply with management directions but keep a check on management powers via participating in the budget process and approving the strategic and business plan at the AGA; hold discussions with management at work and in specialized committees; and attend 8–10 AGA meetings each year where key issues are raised and key decisions are made (80 percent of members attend). A culture permeates the organization where the Board will either delay for further discussion or refer to the AGA any issue that lacks a broad consensus. The AGA also decides on any issue affecting membership, key strategic directions and any decision that overrides the strategic plan or matters relating to the cooperative movement (Sacmi 2015; Hancock 2007; Benati and Mazzoli 2009).

Sacmi has been a very successful cooperative because it has been able to blend economic success and cooperative principles and goals. Its model is based on a trade-off that accepts low membership (below 50 percent) in return for an active membership that is willing to invest and actively participate in the decision-making process. While no longer a prevalent mutual cooperative, it is still behaving like one, placing most of its profits into the indivisible reserve fund, engaging with the cooperative sector and supporting the community.

The governance arrangements adopted by construction cooperatives illustrate the other side of governance. Construction cooperatives adopted the tripartite model of governance. In this model, the AGA appoints the board, the chair (who also acts as CEO) and senior managers with executive responsibilities, as well the oversight committee. There is no separation of duties between the board and management. While there are many large, successful cooperatives that adopt this model,[13] at times it results in weak accountabilities as it is difficult for board members to hold themselves to account. These older construction cooperatives also displayed a poor governance culture. For example, during the GFC, when they were accumulating losses from investments in the housing sector and lack of public infrastructure works available, they did not manage costs well, implement solidarity contracts or inform members of the difficult financial situation. Members did not question the leadership until it was too late. They approached Legacoop to remedy the situation when they realized that their investments were at risk. These cooperatives did not have a succession plan and had been led by an executive group that had held the key positions for close to 20 years. These are usually led by long-standing charismatic leaders who had previously successfully managed the cooperative. In return, they received cooperative members' loyalty even when they were no longer able to steer the cooperative toward a positive economic outcome (Ricciardi 2014).

What is important to note is that the leaders' behavior, supported by a passive workforce, led a number of cooperatives to fail and lose all accumulated reserves that should have been preserved for the next generation. It is widely accepted that these leaders behaved more like owners of the cooperative than custodians. This was to the detriment of their cooperative and the cooperative movement.[14] It is also a failure of Legacoop's oversight function. As part of their annual review (as these were large companies), the auditors should have known their precarious financial situation and called the cooperative to account before it was too late to save the cooperative assets.

Antonio Zanotti has noted that this state of affairs underlines a weakness of the working cooperative environment compared to listed companies, because in the latter's case the market provides adequate oversight as a result of investors, brokers and superannuation funds seeking action whenever results do not meet market expectations (Zanotti 2013). Listed companies are required to produce quarterly reports and operate under disclosure requirements leaving them open to shareholder and public scrutiny. In more serious cases, a well informed and knowledgeable media intervenes in the debate, seeking answers on behalf of the public interest and leading to further action by boards to protect their reputation and shareholder interests.[15] In the case of construction cooperatives, there appears to have been a poor level of external oversight by Central Associations (and the government), and by the media, which only reports economic performance, industrial relations matters or cases of failure but does not adequately scrutinize overall cooperative performance, investment decisions or alignment with cooperative principles.

It is important to note that before the late 1980s, in Legacoop's case, oversight was exercised by political parties who, via their members—who were also members of cooperatives, and political appointees in the Central Association—were able to coordinate member intervention and make changes. Intervention would occur either at the cooperative level, via Legacoop or, in certain circumstances, at party headquarters. The fact that members, cooperative leaders and the Legacoop leadership were members of the same parties, predominantly the Communist party, facilitated information flow, discussions and decision-making. On many occasions, this led to a change of leadership, subject to members' formal approval. Legacoop, unlike today's situation, had more resources then, was better informed, was more aligned with its member cooperatives and was able to identify and proactively intervene when problems arose. It could be argued that the political parties, thanks to their large membership and strong links with civil society, performed the external oversight role that the market, regulators, investors, brokers, institutional investors and the media perform for listed companies. In doing so, they served as the guarantors of cooperative values and inter-generational assets and created a link between cooperatives, Legacoop, local governments and the community (Viviani 2013; Turci 2015; Ammirato 1996).

9.2.5 A New Cooperative Governance Approach?

The question of oversight raises a key question: how can cooperative governance be improved considering that cooperative members have the right to govern the cooperative though they do not own it? The law makes it clear that cooperative members are entitled to govern the cooperative, but they do not own the cooperative. Cooperatives have received some tax concessions because indivisible reserves cannot be distributed to members. These are regarded as inter-generational assets and, indeed, if cooperatives fold, the remaining assets must be deposited into the cooperative development funds. These assets need to be grown and preserved on behalf of the next generation. This raises more questions: who should formally intervene when a cooperative is being mismanaged and risks losing the inter-generational assets? Who should protect the rights of future generations and the communities in which they live? Who can most likely perform the external oversight function that the market, financial institutions, brokers, regulators and the media perform on behalf of shareholders of listed companies?

In the author's view, the Central Associations should be in a position to perform this oversight function, with assistance from the Ministry of Economic Development, cooperative investors, cooperative brokers and the media. The first step, however, is to develop a definition of cooperative governance that uniquely represents cooperatives. Cooperative governance cannot be confused with corporate governance, which sees the role of companies as profit maximization on behalf of shareholders. It should also not be confused with the more progressive definition of corporate governance that embraces stakeholders and the Triple Bottom Line reporting on economic, social and environmental matters, yet still sees the company as primarily pursuing profit maximization on behalf of shareholders.[16]

9.2.5.1 Defining Cooperative Governance

Cooperative's role is not profit maximization but one that supports the needs of current members, future members and the communities in which they live. Thus, a more appropriate definition for cooperative governance could be:

> the system of governance comprising rules, policies, processes, participatory culture and oversight through which a cooperative is democratically

governed so that it can achieve long term sustainable growth and the preservation of wealth created on behalf of its current members, future generations and the local community.

This is achieved:

- Via competing in the market through the production of goods and services that meet the needs of their members and their community and by making a profit sufficient to promote sustainable development.
- Via democratic decision-making processes that include forms of direct, indirect and participatory democracy by well-informed members and by the agreed separate division of powers among the general assembly, the board and management.
- In compliance with the law and in alignment with cooperative values and principles and the broader principles of equality, integrity, solidarity, reciprocity and openness.
- In full support of the needs, aspirations and expectations of their communities.
- Through the internal oversight provided by the board, its oversight committee and members and the external oversight provided by Central Associations and independent directors on behalf of current and future generations and with the intent to safeguard cooperative values, cooperative assets and the reputation of the cooperative sector.

9.2.5.2 *A New Cooperative Governance Framework*

In support of the above-offered definition, a number of changes can be made to the overall cooperative governance framework. These include internal and external oversight arrangements supported by public disclosure requirements and an effort to create a knowledgeable cooperative society, one that can report critically and truthfully on the cooperative sector and at the same time keep it publicly accountable. The following should be considered:

- The Central Associations should not conduct a review of their members that ultimately determines whether they should or should not be eligible for tax concessions, as it constitutes a conflict of interest. These reviews should be conducted by the Ministry of Economic Development. They should be fundamentally accounting reviews to determine whether cooperatives have complied with the mutuality requirements.
- The Central Associations should be given statutory powers to enforce their governance guidelines on their cooperative members. They could conduct annual or biennial qualitative reviews that could examine whether cooperatives are managed democratically and assess their financial risks. An assessment of their financial and democratic governance risks should enable the Central Associations to make timely

interventions. The Central Associations should have the powers to compel the cooperative to discuss and implement options for improvement. These reviews should be conducted by experienced personnel, with cooperative experience or with a good understanding of the principles of cooperation, and who are familiar with cooperative governance and have sufficient standing to influence the discussion.[17]

- Boards should include independent directors that promote cooperative values and represent future generations and the community. The Central Associations should have a seat on the board of all cooperatives with turnover exceeding 10 million euros and recommend independent directors to sit on the board of every cooperative with turnover above 2 million euros.

- The duties of directors should be clearly spelled out, taking into consideration the key principle of cooperative governance and the cooperative law. They should focus on the promotion of cooperative principles and values, economic performance, compliance with the law, promotion of inter-cooperative trade and support and the preservation of cooperative assets for future generations and local communities.

- The level of information and type of information to be made available to members during the year and before the AGA should be prescribed. To ensure members are fully informed, agendas could include: strategic directions, budget decisions, key acquisitions and subsidiaries, key financial investments, levels of debts, understanding key risks and so on.

- Cooperatives with a turnover of more than 2 million euros per annum should be subject to public disclosure requirements. This may include any information of materiality that may affect the financial stability of the cooperative, the reputation of the cooperative sector or social cohesion and stability of the local community. Disclosures should be made to the Central Associations, the Ministry of Economic Development, the public and cooperative investors.

- The cooperative sector should consider establishing a Cooperative Institute, possibly associated with one or more universities, the role of which would be to conduct research and teaching. This could lead to a unique cooperative approach to economics, democracy and governance; provide specific courses and qualifications for cooperative managers and directors; provide specialist courses for media commentators and financial brokers; and provide short courses for the general public and cooperative members. This should help the cooperative sector develop robust governance arrangements and better engagement with the public. The cooperative institute could be funded by the cooperative development funds, which could increase their share of profits from 3 to 8 percent.

This new cooperative governance approach will promote a more knowledgeable public about cooperatives, which will better understand why cooperatives are successful, how they differ from capitalist enterprises and why at times they fail. It will hold cooperatives and Central Associations to account and strengthen their reputation. This new governance approach could also attract more retail external investors (currently missing) because they will be better informed and will trust an independent and robust oversight framework. External investors could invest directly or via brokers of specialist cooperative investment funds.

9.3 Cooperation

The sixth ICA principle supports 'cooperation among cooperatives.' It encourages cooperatives to form consortia, achieve economies of scale, efficiency and market competitiveness and work together to compete in a global market. It also encourages them to join a cooperative movement at all levels so that they can provide services, educate the public and media and represent cooperatives vis-à-vis governments.

9.3.1 The Law and 'Cooperation Among Cooperatives'

The Italian State has supported via legislation and funding cooperation among cooperatives. In 1909 it passed a law allowing cooperatives to form consortia and bid for public works. The 1947 Basevi Law promoted the formation of consortia among cooperatives, and the Civil Code enabled cooperatives to form a 'joint group' consortia. The 1992 law promoted cooperative development funds, through which the Central Associations can set up new cooperatives, help existing cooperatives and develop the cooperative sector. The State has developed a co-regulatory environment that allows Central Associations the authority to have oversight over their members and to conduct regular reviews to ensure compliance with the cooperative law. Finally, the State through Invitalia is an investor with CFI and the Trento local government is an investor in Promocoop.

9.3.2 Central Associations and 'Cooperation Among Cooperatives'

The Central Associations and the Trentino Federation all promote cooperation among cooperatives. Their statute, guidelines and codes all support this principle. Legacoop's statute states that one of its objectives is to promote inter-cooperative relations to improve their economic competitiveness and the capacity of the cooperative system (Legacoop 2014). Confcooperative stresses that the best way to promote social justice and solidarity is via a common union and not the promotion of particular sectional interests (Concooperative 2017). More specifically, they promote cooperation via the following activities:

- Central Associations together lobby the Italian State to promote the interest of the cooperative movement. This level of cooperation has been strengthening over the years and has resulted in forming the unitary Alleanza.

- They provide legal, industrial relations and administrative assistance to all cooperatives. All Central Associations have signed collective agreements with the three major trade union confederations, which are binding on their members.
- Central Associations govern the financial consortia Cooperfidi and CFI and their services are open to all cooperatives. Other financial consortia and companies provide services to their associates from different sectors of the economy.
- All Central Associations have promoted sectoral associations, consortia and inter-sectoral cooperation. The inter-sectoral cooperation and trade between the consumer-agricultural-manufacturing-transport-services cooperatives is a key feature of the Italian cooperative sector. Cooperatives that are members of different Central Associations trade with each other and are joint members of consortia.[18]
- The cooperative development funds receive money and operate on behalf of all their cooperative members.
- The Central Associations and the three trade union confederations have formed Fon.Coop to provide training and education to cooperative members.

9.3.3 Cooperatives and 'Cooperation Among Cooperatives'

The available data indicates that cooperatives do embrace cooperation among cooperatives in a variety of forms. Cooperatives are reviewed at least every two years, and all reviewed comply with contributing to cooperative development funds at least 3 percent of their profits. They also regularly pay fees to the Central Associations to help them fulfill their political and service-related function. In addition, the following forms of cooperation have taken place:

- Economic cooperation via consortia. There are 2,005 consortia in operation, which usually require a minimum of nine members.
- Financial cooperation via consortia and local companies. Cooperatives are members of financial consortia, with 3,500 becoming members of Cooperfidi Italia, 1,061 of CCFS and 306 of CFI. Cooperatives are also members of cooperative-owned local financial companies, insurance companies like Unipol and Assimoco, Banca Etica and cooperative banks. Emil-Banca notes that 88 percent of its total investments are within the cooperative sector.
- Inter-cooperative cooperation and trade. Many cooperatives engage and trade with other cooperatives, with this taking place in a variety of forms. Cooplat, a transport company from Florence, receives 40 percent of its work from other cooperatives. Emil-Banca notes that 38.4 percent

of its preferred suppliers are cooperatives or cooperative banking sector related companies. Camst notes that it engages 29 cleaning and catering cooperatives and 89 cooperatives that supply goods and services. Cadiai provides occupational, health and safety education to 24 cooperatives. The consortia CCC facilitates 100 million euros of trade between construction cooperatives and cooperative suppliers of raw materials and fixtures.

- Non-economic activities that support cooperative development. Cooperatives support various educational, research and cultural institutions. These include the Fondazione Barberini, which conducts research on cooperative enterprises; Impronta Etica, an organization that promotes corporate social responsibility reporting; the Centro di Documentazione sulla Cooperazione e L'Economia Sociale, which houses a library and promotes research and cooperative publications; Aziende Modenesi per la Responsabilita' Sociale D'impresa; and many others.

9.4 Community

The seventh cooperative principle is 'concern for the community.' It says that: "Co-operatives work for the sustainable development of their communities through policies approved by their members. It promotes the principle of sustainability,[19] the promotion of social justice and the need to combat inequalities and poverty" (International Cooperative Alliance 2015).

9.4.1 The Italian Cooperative Law and the Community

The cooperative law does not specifically say that cooperatives should have concern for their community. However, it promotes sustainable development and concern for the community via two provisions. First, it requires that at least 30 percent of profits (70 percent for cooperative banks) be deposited in the indivisible reserve fund, which, along with cooperative assets, cannot be distributed to members and is transferred to future members and the next generation. Second, it requires cooperatives to deposit 3 percent into their cooperative development funds, which is then used to promote cooperatives and jobs throughout Italy, including WBOs and community cooperatives serving villages in remote areas.

9.4.2 Central Associations and the Community

Central Associations have always promoted cooperatives as enterprises committed to their local communities. This is the result of people being proud of the local communities and having a sense of civic duty. It is also a result of the universal views of Italy's Catholic and Socialist/Communist subcultures that all human beings are born equal, and they should be treated with dignity. To this end, Legacoop sees cooperatives performing their economic role in support of their members, future generations and the social community (Legacoop 1993). It expects its members to contribute by resolving national social and economic issues such as good functioning of the market, social cohesion, equal opportunity, integration of migrants, environment protection,and development and reskilling of the workforce (Legacoop 2014). Confcooperative stresses that the cooperative movement is to safeguard the local businesses, place people and their needs at the center of their activity and promote responsible and equal development for all communities (Confcooperative 2016). The cooperative banking charter stresses that cooperative banks promote social cohesion and sustainable and responsible economic development and re-invest their profits in local communities (Credito Cooperativo 2017).

9.4.3 Cooperatives and the Community

Cooperatives have been formed over the years to solve problems faced by people, families and communities. In addition to the obvious benefit derived from cooperatives not de-locating their activities abroad, as has been practiced by capitalist firms, they have been supporting the local, national and international community in a variety of ways. Key examples include:

- Local community. Social cooperatives provide social services to the aged, disabled and early childhood learning. Coop Italia purchases 90 percent of its products from local suppliers. Cassa Rurale Trento spends 63 percent of its purchasing budget on local suppliers. Sacmi paid 499 million euros to suppliers from the region of Emilia-Romagna. Cooperative banks lend 96 percent of their loans portfolio to families and small businesses that operate in their local catchment area.
- National community. Conserve Italia donates food to many not-for-profits, foundations and parishes throughout Italy. Camst provides thousands of free meals to people in need as well as employing 11 women who experienced family violence in 2015. Most large cooperatives support Libera Terra, an organization that forms cooperatives to manage land confiscated from organized crime (some cooperatives provide funding; Granarolo helped it start a cheese factory, while consumer cooperatives sell its products). It is estimated that Coop Italia sells 70 percent of Libera Terra's total produce at its supermarkets. Cooperative banks donate 7 percent of their profits, with which they funded 780 community activities in 2015.
- International community. Granarolo is promoting a dairy farm in Tanzania. Conserve Italia supports a number of projects in Central and South America. CMC funds three community projects overseas. Federcasse, Confcooperative and cooperative banks have funded over one hundred agricultural cooperatives, small businesses and women entrepreneurs in Togo and Ecuador. Consumer cooperatives sell under their label Solidal over 40 percent of all Fairtrade products in Italy.

9.5 Sustainability Reporting and Cooperative Principles

The discussion so far has noted that the combined effort of the cooperative law and Central Associations' guidelines and charters promote all ICA principles. The surveys and reviews conducted also note that there are inconsistent approaches to the way cooperatives implement ICA principles and good governance practices and the way they report on them. The large cooperatives produce large and informative sustainability reports that are mostly based on global reporting methodologies, such as the Global Reporting Initiative, or global standards on accountability or human rights. These standards, however, are not suitable for cooperatives since they are not aligned with cooperative principles (Rixon and Beaubien 2015; Herbert 2015). The large Italian cooperatives have attempted to blend the ICA principles with international reporting requirements, but not consistently, making it difficult for both the reader and the public to assess the extent to which the cooperative and the cooperative sector are operating in alignment with the ICA principles. A key omission, for instance, is the qualitative reporting of how democratic participation and decision-making are encouraged and practiced.[20] Some reports do not inform the reader of the policies, practices and extent to which cooperatives trade and engage with other cooperatives. Knowing the extent of the cooperative sector's alignment with ICA principles is made even more difficult because cooperatives are not obliged to produce a sustainability report nor to demonstrate compliance with all ICA principles.

The Italian cooperative sector as a whole, in the author's view, would benefit if cooperatives with a turnover above 2 million euros were required to produce a fit-for-purpose sustainability report. The larger cooperatives would be expected to produce a more comprehensive report. This would allow cooperatives and the sector to demonstrate to their members, stakeholders and the community that they are fulfilling their mission in alignment with the law, cooperative principles and community expectations. In addition, the inter-sectoral data could be collected nationally and regionally and used to produce collated reports that would indicate the broader impact of the cooperative sector.[21] These reports could educate not only cooperative members but also a skeptical media about the virtues of cooperatives. The data could also provide valuable information to identify areas where the movement is performing well and where it needs to improve to meet member and community expectations.

The cooperative sector has been at the forefront of promoting sustainability reporting. It would be desirable for the Alleanza, in association with key enterprises, academics and consultants, to develop a Bilancio Sociale Reporting Framework that, while keeping the necessary elements of the international reporting standards, includes comprehensive reporting on the ICA principles, key community expectations and key data that convey the broader social impact of the cooperative sector.

9.6 Cooperatives Not Members of any Central Association

Finally, the cooperative sector also includes a number of spurious cooperatives that may not comply with ICA principles or cooperative law.[22] It is generally acknowledged that these may not comply with cooperative principles, may not pay taxes and may practice dubious industrial relations (Menzani 2015). Some are family-owned and are not truly open nor democratic. These cooperatives are not members of any Central Association, and when they do try to join, hoping to access their services, their membership is withdrawn once they are reviewed, and their failings noted. Indeed, Confcooperative reports hundreds of cooperatives to the Ministry of Economic Development every year, recommending they be de-registered from the cooperative register on the grounds of operational irregularities (Confcooperative 2016).[23] The cooperative law states that those cooperatives that are not members of a Central Association should be reviewed by the Ministry of Economic Development. Unfortunately, evidence suggests that the Ministry does not conduct regular reviews of these cooperatives. The Alleanza has been petitioning the government to act on this, but so far no action has been taken (Alleanza delle Cooperative Italiane 2017).

9.7 Concluding Remarks

The Italian cooperative sector, through a mixture of regulation, guidelines and practice, has demonstrated a sincere commitment to upholding all of the cooperative principles. Those cooperatives with a deep commitment have demonstrated, via their sustainability reports, to uphold all cooperative principles. At the same time, as the qualitative application of the principles is left to individual cooperatives, it is difficult to get a consistent application of principles across the whole cooperative sector.

The size of cooperatives, their level of internationalization and their governance arrangements have also revealed that low membership among some large cooperatives, ineffective governance practices with a few cooperatives and lack of external oversight need to be addressed. To this end, the Central Associations could seriously consider seeking statutory powers to allow them to enforce governance changes that would lead to more robust cooperative governance arrangements and democratic practices. Statutory powers should also require cooperatives with turnover exceeding 2 million euros to produce a sustainability report so that they demonstrate their alignment with the cooperative law, principles and mission.

The cooperative sector should construct a new external oversight environment that can hold cooperatives accountable. To this end, giving mandated powers to the Central Associations to enforce their cooperative governance guidelines and to monitor cooperative disclosure requirements will help. The appointment of independent directors in cooperatives with a turnover exceeding 2 million euros will improve governance and compliance with cooperative principles. Public disclosure requirements should keep all stakeholders informed. The formation of a Cooperative Institute will also support better internal governance and external oversight. It will do this by developing cooperative-specific approaches to democratic governance and economic development while educating directors, managers, journalists, cooperative brokers and the public about the unique characteristics of cooperatives. The Ministry for Economic Development should conduct the financial-regulatory audits and share the information with the Central Associations. The latter cannot review its members as this constitutes a conflict of interest.

Notes

1. The legislative framework was covered in detail in Chapter 2.
2. The Central Associations considered include Legacoop, Confederazione and Federazione Trentina, plus Federcasse, which represents cooperative banks. Documents perused include: statutes, annual reports, good practice guides, code of ethics, key speeches and press releases.
3. The author reviewed the following: Emilbanca, Banca Etica, Cassa Rurale di Trento, Cooplat, Cooperservice, CFT, Coop Adriatica, Camst, Cooperativa Muratori e Cementisti, Cadiai, Cooperativa Dolce, Manutencoop, Sacmi, Granarolo, Caviro, Conserve Italia, Cavit, Federcasse, CCC, CNS, Cooperfidi Italia, CCFS and the WBOs Greslab, Raviplast and Italstick.
4. The Mondragon-based Eroski supermarket chain had similar problems in convincing staff from the acquired conventional companies to become members (Barandiaran and Lezaun 2017).
5. Mondragon-owned foreign subsidiaries employ 11,000 people who are not members and are facing the same difficulties encountered by Italian cooperatives (Barandiaran and Lezaun 2017).
6. This is the author's calculation and is based on information supplied in Sacmi's 2015 Annual Sustainability Report (Sacmi 2015).
7. Antonio Zanotti has worked with Legacoop and is the accomplished author of books and reports on cooperative governance and economic performance.
8. Please refer to Chapter 2 for a definition of the three models.
9. Please refer to Chapter 2 for more information on the three governance models.
10. Please refer to Chapter 2 for more information on the oversight functions.
11. Concern over democratic practices has long been a concern of the international cooperative movement (McPherson 2012).
12. Managers recruited outside of the cooperative sector possess management and technical skills but are not familiar with cooperative history, culture and governance.
13. Camst, Cadiai and Coop Adriatica use the tripartite model and are very successful.
14. Mauro Gori explains how this attitude damaged the reputation of CPL Concordia (Gori 2017).
15. A recent scandal affecting the Commonwealth Bank of Australia, whose lax controls were aiding the recycling of money from organized crime, led to the eventual resignation of the CEO (Janda 2017). The Prime Minister of Australia announced a Royal Commission of Inquiry into the banking sector on December 1, 2017.
16. A good discussion on the debate on corporate governance can be found in the book *Principles of Contemporary Corporate Governance* (Du Plessis, Hargovan, Bagaric and Harris 2015).
17. Accounting firms are not suitable to conduct cooperative governance reviews or to assess the quality of democratic practices.

18. For instance, cooperatives from the Trentino region use Coop Italia as their wholesaler.
19. This refers to the principle of sustainability defined by the Brundtland Report as "development that meets the needs of the present without compromising the ability of future generations to meet their own needs."
20. The author is referring to forms of participation at the enterprise level: number of work-committees; number of AGA held; topics for discussion and participation level; attendance at induction programs; education and information sessions explaining strategies, policies and financial data.
21. Federcasse produces a national annual report, Bilancio di Coerenza, that demonstrates the impact of the cooperative banking sector on the Italian economy and society.
22. It is estimated that 12,000 cooperatives are not members of any Central Association. These have approximately 50,000 members and employ 75,000 persons (Zamagni and Felice 2006).
23. Confcooperative withdrew membership of 382 cooperatives in 2016 and from 2013 to 2016 it reported on average 500 cooperatives per year to the Ministry for Economic Development, recommending de-registration for operational irregularities (Confcooperative 2017).

References

Alleanza delle Cooperative Italiane. 2015. *Il Movimento Cooperativo in Italia.* Cooperative Sector Data, Rome: Alleanza delle Cooperative Italiane.

———. 2017. "Alleanza delle Cooperative alla CGIL: Insieme per Intensificare Controlli e Vigilanza." *Alleanza delle Cooperative Italiane.* Accessed October 30, 2017. www.alleanzacooperative.it/?s=cooperative+spurie.

Ammirato, Piero. 1996. *La Lega: The Making of a Successful Cooperative Network.* Aldershot: Dartmouth.

ANCC-Coop. 2015. *Rapporto Sociale Nazionale della Cooperazione di Consumatori.* Annual Report, Rome: ANCC-Coop.

Barandiaran, Xabier, and Javier Lezaun. 2017. "The Mondragon Experience." In *The Oxford Handbook of Mutual, Co-operative, and Co-Owned Business,* edited by Jonathon Michie, Joseph Blasi and Carlo Borzaga, 279–294. Oxford: Oxford University Press.

Benati, Marco, and Marco Mazzoli. 2009. *Partecipazione Ricerca e Innovazione: Un'Analisi Economica del Gruppo Sacmi.* Imola: Editrice La Mandragora.

Benini, Andrea. 2017. *Le Nuove Linee Guida per la Diffusione della Buona Governance Cooperativa.* Report to the Assembly of Delegates, Bologna: Legacoop Emilia-Romagna.

Bonfante, Guido. 2011. *Manuale di Diritto Cooperativo.* Bologna: Zanichelli.

Camst. 2015. *Bilancio Sociale.* Annual Social Report, Bologna: Camst.

Concooperative. 2017. "Statuto della Confederazione Cooperative Italiane." *L'Associazione.* Accessed October 3, 2017. www.confcooperative.it/Portals/0/File Associazione/STATUTO-CONFCOOPERATIVE.pdf.

Confcooperative. 2016. *Bilancio di Sostenibilita'.* Annual Sustainability Report, Rome: Confcooperative.

———. 2017. "L'Associazione." *Confederazione.* Accessed September 22, 2017. www.confcooperative.it/LAssociazione.

Coop Adriatica. 2015. *Bilancio di Sostenibilita'.* Annual Sustainability Report, Bologna: Coop Adriatica.

Cooperservice. 2014. *Bilancio D'Esercizio e Bilancio Sociale*. Annual Report, Reggio Emilia: Cooperservice.

Cooplat. 2016. *Bilancio Sociale*. Annual Social Report, Florence: Cooplat.

Credito Cooperativo. 2017. "La Carta della Coesione del Credito Cooperativo." *BCC Credito Cooperativo*. Accessed September 21, 2017. www.creditocoopera tivo.it/template/default.asp?i_menuID=10611.

Du Plessis, Jean Jacques, Anil Hargovan, Mirko Bagaric, and Jason Harris. 2015. *Principles of Contemporary Corporate Governance*. Cambridge: Cambridge University Press.

EmilBanca. 2015. *Bilancio Sociale 2015*. Annual Social Report, Bologna: Emilbanca.

Federazione Trentina. 2011. *Linee Guida per un Nuovo Patto Associativo della Federazione Trentina*. Cooperative Association Agreement. Trento: Federazione Trentina.

Gori, Mauro. 2017. "Dalla Crisi Reputazionale a un Rinnovamento per un Nuovo Sviluppo." *Legacoop- Emilia-Romagna: Assemblea di Meta' Mandato*. February 23, 2017. Bologna: Legacoop Emilia-Romagna.

Hancock, Matt. 2007. *Compete to Cooperate: The Cooperative District of Imola*. Imola: Bacchilega Editore.

Herbert, Yuill. 2015. "Leadership in Hegemony: Sustainability Reporting and Cooperatives." In *Cooperatives for Sustainable Communities*, edited by Leslie Brown, Chiara Carini, Jessica Gordon Nembhard, Lou Hammond Ketilson, Elizabeth Hicks, John McNamara, Sonja Novkovic, Daphne Rixon and Richard Simmons. Saskatchewan: Centre for the Studies of Cooperatives.

International Cooperative Alliance. 2015. *Guidance Notes to the Cooperative Principles*. Brussels: International Cooperative Alliance.

Janda, Michael. 2017. *Commonwealth Bank CEO Ian Narev to Retire Before July 2018 as Bank Deals With Money-Laundering Scandal*. 14 August. Accessed September 29, 2017. www.abc.net.au/news/2017-08-14/commonwealth-bank-ceo-ian-narev-to-retire-by-july/8803302.

Legacoop. 1993. *I Valori Guida*. Code of Ethics, Rome: Legacoop.

———. 2008. *Linee Guida per la Governance delle Cooperative Aderenti a Legacoop*. Governance Guidelines, Rome: Legacoop.

———. 2012. *Partecipazione in Cooperativa: Instruzioni per l'Uso*. Good Practice Guide, Bologna: Legacoop.

———. 2014. *Statuto Legacoop Nazionale*. Association Statute, Bologna: Legacoop.

Legacoop Centro Studi. 2014. *Legacoop in Cifre*. Annual Data Statistics, Rome: Legacoop.

Manutencoop. 2015. *Bilancio Sociale*. Annual Report, Bologna: Manutencoop.

McPherson, Ian. 2012. "'…What Is the Purpose of It All': The Centrality of Values for Cooperative Success in the Marketplace." In *The Cooperative Business Movement, 1950 to the Present*, edited by Patrizia Battilani and Harm G. Schroder. New York: Cambridge University Press.

Menzani, Tito. 2015. Cooperative: Persone Oltre che Imprese. Soveria Mannelli: Rubbettino.

Petrucci, Paola. 2009. "La Distribuzione Degli Avanzi di Gestione e la Pratica del Ristorno nelle Imprese Cooperative." Edited by Iris Network. In *Iris Network, Colloquoio Scientifico Annuale sull'Impresa Sociale*, 1–11. Trento: Iris Network.

Platoni, Silvia. 2009. "Lo scambio mutualistico fra il socio e la cooperativa: incentivi, azzardo morale e selezione avversa." In *Partecipazione, Ricerca, Innovazione*, edited by Benito Benati and Marco Mazzoli, 322–328. Imola: Editrice La Mandragora.

Ricciardi, Mario. 2014. "I Risultati della Ricerca su Partecipazione Dei Soci e dei Lavoratori e Relazioni Industriali: I Primi Risultati." In *Rapporto Sulla Cooperazione in Emilia-Romagna: Una Prima Sintesi*, edited by Legacoop Emilia-Romagna, 63–78. Bologna: Legacoop Emilia-Romagna.

Rixon, Daphne, and Louis Beaubien. 2015. "Integrated Reporting for Cooperatives: A Case Study of Vancity Credit Union." In *Cooperatives for Sustainable Communities*, edited by Leslie Brown, Chiara Carini, Jessica Gordon Nembhard, Lou Hammond Ketilson, Elizabeth Hicks, John McNamara, Sonja Novkovic, Daphne Rixon and Richard Simmons, 337–352. Saskatchewan: Centre for the Study of Co-operatives.

Sacmi. 2015. *Bilancio di Sostenibilita'*. Annual Sustainability Report, Imola: Sacmi.

Turci, Lanfranco. 2015. "La Cooperazione e Il Lavoro: Intervista a Lanfranco Turci." *Inchiesta*, 20 July.

Viviani, Marco. 2013. *Piccola Guida alla Cooperazione: Un Avvicinamento, non un Manuale*. Soveria Mannelli: Rubbettino Editore.

Zamagni, Vera, and Emanuele Felice. 2006. *Oltre il Secolo: Le Transformazioni del Sistema Cooperativo Legacoop alla Fine del Secondo Millennio*. Bologna: Il Mulino.

Zanotti, Antonio. 2012. *La Governance Nelle Imprese Cooperative. Il Caso delle Cooperative Aderenti a Legacoopservizi*. Working Paper, Trento: Euricse.

———. 2013. *La Governance Societaria: Societa' per Azioni e Cooperative a Confronto*. Soveria Mannelli: Rubbettino Editore.

———. 2016. *Cooperative e Imprese di Capitali. Quanto Sono Diverse e Quanto Sono Uguali: Una Analisi Comparata Dell'Analisi Cooperative*. Soveria Mannelli: Rubbettino Editore.

10 Cooperative Identity
In Search of a New Vision

Cooperative identity is multi-faceted and comprises a cooperative's mission, ownership structures, principles, unique business model and public perceptions. To understand it, we must consider why cooperatives were established, what they did, how they did it and what they hoped to achieve. This includes their overall vision of a better society, their role in key moments in history and how they have responded to key economic and political crises. Cooperative identity also reflects the views and expectations of the community, political parties, civil society and the public. These groups expect cooperatives to operate within certain values, comply with the law, uphold the highest of moral standards and contribute to developing a new society where people control capital and invest for the common good.

The previous chapters have already revealed a number of features that would constitute part of the cooperative identity. These include:

- A business model that includes community (inter-generational) ownership, democratic management and limited return on capital and limited member rebates.
- A networked, inter-sectoral, cooperative sector comprising Central Associations and economic and financial consortia supported by cooperative owned financial companies.
- Economic behavior that is anti-cyclic, operates with a long-term horizon and puts people before profits, even during the GFC.
- Broad alignment with the seven ICA principles, including the open door principle, and support for local communities.

These constitute an important part of cooperative identity, but they are not the only factors that define it. To provide a better understanding of cooperative identity, this chapter will review seven other key factors that have defined cooperation in Italy.

The first section of this chapter focuses on the sector as a broad-based, inter-classist, inter-sectoral movement and considers whether this has changed. The second section will describe the relationship between politics and cooperative legitimacy. The third section discusses how the development of large cooperatives and holding companies have impacted on democratic management. The fourth, fifth and sixth sections will focus on three key areas that have defined cooperatives in Italy: equality, good citizenship and jobs for all. The final section explores how a united cooperative sector is dealing with the identity question today, namely the development of a new vision for society and cooperative's role within it.

It is important to note that the Italian cooperative sector is diverse and has been aligned to diverse political ideologies and political parties. Some of the matters that will be discussed in this chapter—such as the broad-based pluralist model, relationships with politics, the development of large cooperatives and good citizenships—apply to all parts of the political movement. The sections on equality and jobs for all, while also relating to the whole cooperative sector, relate in particular to Legacoop cooperatives.

10.1 A Broad-Based, Pluralist Cooperative Movement

The Italian cooperative sector, like its counterparts across Europe and throughout the world, came into being to satisfy the needs of workers, peasants, farmers and small businesses who had been alienated and excluded by the processes unleashed through the industrial revolution and the rise of capitalism.

The cooperative sector has always had a political and economic pluralist dimension. The first period of cooperative development spans from the 1850s to 1926. During this period, conservatives promoted mutual aid societies to provide welfares services, consumer cooperative in Turin in 1854 to provide food at lower prices and popular banks to provide small businesses with access to credit. Artisans formed cooperatives in 1856. Socialists promoted construction cooperatives to provide jobs to landless laborers and collective farms. The Catholics, following the Encyclical Rerum Novarum of 1891, established rural banks (now cooperative banks) to provide loans to farmers and set up agricultural cooperatives to help farmers cut costs and bring produce to market. Everyone set up consumer cooperatives to provide food at low prices (Zangheri, Galasso and Castronovo 1987).

The second period of cooperative development spans from 1944 to the 1980s. After the Second World War, the cooperative sector reorganized itself once more, following two decades of Fascism. Under Fascism, cooperatives had been destroyed, controlled and incorporated into fascist organizations. By the fall of Fascism in 1943, 12,000 cooperatives remained in operation, much fewer than the 19,500 in operation in 1921.[1] Following the defeat of Fascism, the cooperative sector continued to evolve as a pluralist, inter-classist and inter-sectoral movement. Legacoop established construction, manufacturing and consumer cooperatives, thus providing jobs and food at lower prices for working people. Confcooperative promoted rural banks and agricultural cooperatives in support of farmers, thus promoting social cohesion in the countryside. All supported housing, though Legacoop promoted collective ownership while Confcooperative promoted private ownership. This division also existed in agricultural cooperatives. Over time these two organizations broadened their activities, with Legacoop expanding into supporting retail cooperatives and agricultural and fishing cooperatives while Confcooperative also promoted worker cooperatives as well as WBOs of private companies in crisis.

The third period of cooperative development commenced in the 1990s. The rise of the service sector, the fiscal crisis of the State and the policies of privatization, outsourcing and deregulation that followed provided further opportunities for cooperatives. Cooperatives expanded to bid for outsourced public services, to provide social services to the aged and disadvantaged, and to enter professional services markets such as pharmacies, medical services, optometrists and dentists. Recently, migrants and women have been forming many cooperatives, and community cooperatives have also been established.[2]

It could be strongly argued that the Italian cooperative movement has always been about providing jobs, improving working and living conditions and practicing policies of inclusion for all classes. It is organized through Central Associations that have welcomed cooperatives from all economic sectors. This is still a key feature of cooperative identity today.

10.2 Political Legitimacy

Political legitimacy has been a big part of cooperative identity. Political parties have always viewed cooperatives as part of broad political projects that could change society. They encouraged their followers to establish, work with and support cooperatives because cooperatives supported higher goals and long-term visions of a political and social order that would ultimately lead to the creation of a democratic, civilized society of equals. This came to be known as cooperatives having 'external legitimacy.'

Political parties always have enlisted cooperatives in their political projects. In the 1850s, Liberals and Conservatives supported cooperatives hoping they would support the Liberal State and the capitalist system. Mazzini's Republican movement wanted mutual aid societies and cooperatives to support the unification of Italy, support universal suffrage and promote democracy (Mazzini 1978). The Socialists acknowledged that cooperatives supported the ideas of freedom and liberty, educated workers and were anti-capitalists. Andrea Costa of Imola wanted cooperatives to work with the Socialist party and the unions and win local elections so that local government resources could be used to improve working and living conditions (Pelliconi 1990). In 1906–1907, Legacoop formed the triple alliance with mutual aid societies and the trade union movement to promote democracy and improve social conditions. It had a political program that aimed to reduce working hours and introduce social security measures and old age pensions as well as supporting cooperatives to obtain public works and tax concessions (Briganti 1976). The Catholic Italian Popular Party was formed in 1919 and promoted inter-classist policies inspired by the Catholic Social Doctrine, which aligned with the role that Catholic cooperatives were performing in the countryside (Zangheri, Galasso and Castronovo 1987).

These activities were short-lived because in 1926 the Fascist government dissolved Legacoop together with the Catholic Confederation and placed all cooperatives under State control. After 1945, the relationship between political parties and cooperatives re-emerged. More specifically:

- The National Committees of Liberation formed cooperatives all over northern Italy because they had supported anti-Fascist struggles and were seen as promoting a democratic society.
- Communists and Socialists held leadership positions in Legacoop and wanted cooperatives to be part of the class struggle that would ultimately lead to a socialist society. The Communists' 'Italian Road to Socialism' strategy proposed that working people, cooperatives and small businesses work together against the power of monopolies and promote structural economic reforms (L'Unita' 1986). In 1978, the Communists promoted the cooperative sector as the third sector of the economy that would work alongside the State and the private sector (Prandini 1982). Cooperatives were to play a more significant role in the mixed economy by promoting economic pluralism and economic democracy.
- The Catholics formed Confcooperative in 1947. It was one of many organizations supported by Christian Democratic Party and the Catholic Church.[3] It promoted cooperatives within a mixed-market economy by promoting inter-classist alliances, private property among farmers and artisans and housing ownership in urban areas and supporting local communities hoping to improve people's civil and spiritual needs (Williams 2015). Its long-term project was to humanize the market in accordance with the Catholic Social Doctrine.
- The Republicans and Social Democrats formed another Central Association in 1952, which was inspired by Mazzini's view that cooperatives could contribute to the gradual transformation of society through consensus within a democratic state (Mazzini 1978).

The relationship between cooperatives and political parties and their participation in broad political projects provided the cooperative sector with more than just political representation toward the State; it provided a common worldview and influenced the strategy, structure and culture of the cooperative sector. It has been noted that the cost of this relationship with political parties led to duplication costs, political competition among factions (Negri-Zamagni 2015) or slower growth up until the 1970s as a result of an anti-capitalist culture. The Christian Democratic Party, in alignment with the Catholic Social Doctrine, promoted small cooperatives in support of private property. They saw the cooperative sector as an inter-classist movement operating within the current capitalist economy. This led Confcooperative to develop a cooperative model based on small cooperatives, supported by consortia and cooperative banks, in support of farmers, small businesses and families wanting to own their own home. Confcooperative, though many members of parliament defined as 'friends of cooperation,' influenced the Christian Democratic Party, which through a number of government bodies provided funding and support, especially to agricultural cooperatives (Castronovo 1986; Menzani 2007; Cafaro 2008; Williams 2015; Baldini 2016).

The positive contribution that the Communist and Socialist political parties made to Legacoop's overall growth, innovation and identity is unquestioned. They led people with strong ideals and values who favored collective interests above individual interests to join cooperatives. The anti-monopoly strategy led cooperatives to expand in other economic sectors, create alliances with the middle class and small businesses and create large cooperatives that became the mainstay of the cooperative sector. They supported the development of a national consortia network and inter-sectoral trade. Cooperatives facilitated leadership development by providing leaders with work opportunities in various structures, including cooperatives, consortia, territorial structures, financial companies and even the trade union movement. They facilitated change management strategies, especially when a cooperative or group of cooperatives encountered difficulties through the support offered by other cooperatives and consortia. Cooperatives inspired the development of a national movement that enabled cooperatives to grow and have more influence in public affairs. They promoted a strict ethical code that ensured that cooperatives were not a place for careerists or get-rich-quick schemes or individualists. They gave cooperatives a worldview that allowed them to focus on meeting the needs of all people and not just their members. Finally, Left political parties, their members and Central Associations acted as an external oversight body that made sure that cooperatives were law-abiding and worked in the interest of their members and the community. This operating environment ensured that cooperatives were good citizens, and until 1992, when still in effect, Legacoop cooperatives were never involved in any wrongdoing (Ammirato 1996; Silvia and Campesato 2002; Bertagnoni and Menzani 2010; Viviani 2013; Menzani 2015).

The link between the cooperative sector and political parties waned in the 1980s. The traditional parties of Christian Democrats, Communists, Socialists and Republicans started to lose their appeal. The Central Associations and new political parties did not re-establish the close relationship they once had. The new generation recruited had lived in a democratic society all their life and harbored more individualistic tendencies. Since the 1980s, large cooperatives wanted more of a say and replaced political appointees at the head of Legacoop, slowly transforming it to resemble a more traditional employer association. These changes led to inevitable consequences for Legacoop that can be summarized as follows: a weakening of the cooperative cohesion; a refocusing on the cooperative enterprise rather than the movement; a weakening external economic and moral oversight function; and an increasing difficulty in proactively managing cooperatives in crisis. In this period there also emerged a visible disconnect between the cooperative movement, political parties and the State.

10.3 Large Cooperatives and Industrial Relations

Cooperatives started as small, undercapitalized and under-resourced enterprises that used the consortia system to achieve economies of scale in order to compete against the larger companies. Since the 1970s, cooperatives have grown, and today the large cooperative groups are also some of the largest companies in Italy. Some are market leaders and have extended their presence overseas. Large cooperatives have provided the cooperative sector with heightened credibility among the business community and increased confidence in their ability to manage and grow large businesses. This development has also led to changes in organizational structure, democratic management and industrial relations. More specifically:

- Worker participation in large cooperatives became more difficult. Large cooperative enterprises diversified their operations into different product lines and different markets, and also changed their organizational structures to suit their strategies. It led to multi-divisional structures aiding cooperatives that now worked on a national level and overseas and that had also developed complex financial portfolios. Cooperatives had become enterprises of some repute, but this created a distance between members, the Board and management. While members still had powers to elect and dismiss board members and approve the budget, rebates, dividend payments and membership, their participation in the decision-making process was diminishing. Committees and work commissions have been established, but in these large cooperatives, it is not unusual for members and employees to call on the unions to voice their grievances. Indeed, the 2001 Law formalized this, confirming that in industrial relations matters the union represents all employees. To the external observer, this makes cooperatives resemble conventional companies. The resemblance is even more apparent when workers go on strike.
- Large cooperatives have formed holding companies that own many subsidiaries. These companies may be wholly or partially owned but operate as conventional companies. In these companies, the union represents employees versus management as they would in capitalist enterprises. To external observers, this type of company structure and industrial relations is similar to that of conventional holding companies where employees neither own nor participate in profit sharing or the decision-making process.

While these developments are making it difficult for cooperatives to be differentiated from capitalist enterprises, it is important to note that the pay and conditions offered by cooperatives are above the minimum standards of the union collective agreements. All employees are given time off to conduct union affairs. Relationships with unions are formal but cordial, as was the case during the aftermath of the GFC—leading to agreeable change in management initiatives that put people before profits. Cooperatives encourage participation, and members do ultimately choose the board and make key decisions.[4] It is also understandable why outsiders would start to see more similarities between cooperatives and capitalist enterprises, especially if the latter adopt socially responsible policies and triple bottom line reporting. The cooperative movement needs to encourage participation through education, information, participatory mechanisms and power-sharing arrangements in both cooperatives and their subsidiaries. In the latter, unless the subsidiaries are re-absorbed into the cooperative structure, policies should be developed that enable employees of subsidiaries to participate in the decision-making processes and to access financial and material benefits that may be reserved for cooperative members.

10.4 Equality

Equality is a key principle of cooperative movements. Chapter 2 and Chapter 9 have noted that the Italian legislation and the ICA principles promote an open membership and that the workforce of cooperatives is mainly comprised of members (with few exceptions), thus giving everyone the opportunity to become a member. Cooperative policies of inclusion have given workers, artisans, farmers, migrants, women, the aged and the long-term unemployed the opportunity to meet their needs via forming or joining a cooperative. In this section, other aspects of equality that are at the heart of cooperative identity are discussed. These are low salary differentials, a more equitable distribution of wealth between capital and labor and a better distribution of wealth among communities.

Equal pay for equal work and low salary differentials between management and workers have been key aspects of Legacoop's cooperative identity. Up until the 1970s, cooperatives paid management and workers almost identical salaries. The principle was "from one according to his/her means and to each according to their needs" (Bertagnoni 2010, 184), with the basic premise being that because "food was sold to everyone at the same price," salaries needed to be the same. It was not uncommon for members, managers and board members to spend extra time to do their work. These early co-operators regarded it as a privilege to serve as the chair or CEO and lead the cooperative. The CEO would earn little more than a worker. This approach is similar to that adopted by the Communist Party, whose leaders, members of parliament and trade union leaders were paid the same as a worker (Bertagnoni and Menzani 2010).

In the 1990s, in response to cooperative managers being paid much less than their counterparts in the private sector, Legacoop introduced Hay Group pay scales. These were to be based on competencies and duties and resulted in a pay increase for managers designed to reduce the gap between cooperatives and the private sector. This policy did attract external managers, but it introduced higher wage differentials within cooperatives, which until then were low (Battilani 2001). Generally in the early 1970s, wage differentials would have been less than 2:1. In the late 1980s, they rose to 3–4:1 (Ammirato 1996). In 2007, Imola cooperatives practiced salary differentials of up to 10:1 (Hancock 2007). Today, while on average salary differentials are lower than 6:1,[5] some large cooperative groups practice salary differentials that are greater than 10:1.[6] Today, the strict egalitarian culture of "from each according to his/her ability to each according to their needs" no longer applies (Bertagnoni 2010). At the same time, while salary differentials have increased, they are still lower than those observed in the private sector.

In addition to salary differentials, Picketty's work demonstrated that it was the ownership of capital assets (past wealth) that, as a result of growing more than output and wages, mostly contributed to wealth disparities (Piketty 2014). He found that capital's share of value-added amounts[7] in the OECD consistently averaged between 30–35 percent, while labor's share was less than 65–70 percent (Piketty 2015). Of course, capital in private companies is privately owned, and its owners are entitled to leave it to their children, thus transferring wealth and the inequalities that it generates from one generation to the next. The combination of salary differentials and income from wealth capital has led to the top 1 percent of the world's population owning more wealth than the rest of the world. Oxfam has revealed that over the past 25 years, the top 1 percent have gained more income than the bottom 50 percent put together. These inequalities pose a risk to world stability (Oxfam 2017).

Cooperatives can avoid the inequalities arising as a result of capital-labor distribution of national income because their business model focuses on achieving mutual goals, not profit maximization and high capital remuneration. In the cooperative business model, capital is a means to an end, so capital remuneration is not the goal of cooperatives. This is reflected in the cooperative law, which limits the remuneration of capital. In addition, profits are mostly deposited into the indivisible reserves in line with cooperative's long-term goals, and the allocation to capital in the form of amortization (machinery replacements and so on) are part of the cooperative assets that are indivisible and passed on to the next generation. A survey of how two hundred cooperatives from Reggio-Emilia distributed the value-added amount created in 2009 (Legacoop Reggio Emilia 2011) demonstrates this:

- Labor received 68.3 percent (of which 14.5 percent are social welfare payments, and 0.3 percent are profits distributed to members).

- Capital received 31.4 percent, of which:

    - 6.9 percent was paid to financiers (mainly banks);
    - 20.5 percent consisted of amortization (16 percent) and retained profits (4.5 percent);
    - 4 percent was spent on taxes.

- The Cooperative movement received 0.3 percent, which is the amount forwarded to the cooperative development fund.

In alignment with the cooperative business model and the cooperative law, the amount that goes to capital is only 6.9 percent, which is significantly less than the amount that conventional companies distribute to capital. The remaining amount goes to the State (4 percent) or cooperative assets (20.5 percent), which cannot be distributed to current members. In fact, this is wealth that can be used by current members to manage the cooperative, and that is simultaneously held in trust for the next generation. Cooperative assets then are at the same time community-owned assets. The 0.3 percent distributed to the cooperative fund is also a community asset because it is an inter-generational fund that can be invested to create or support existing cooperatives. A more realistic representation of how cooperatives distribute value-added amounts is as follows:

- Labor: 68.3 percent;[8]
- Private capital: 6.9 percent;[9]
- Enterprise/community capital for current and future generations: 20.8 percent;
- Government taxes: 4 percent.

It is also interesting to compare the distribution of profits between cooperatives and conventional companies. Based on the above data, cooperative profits amounted to 4.8 percent of value-added amounts, of which 4.5 percent were retained in the cooperative, and 0.3 percent were distributed to members. The amount distributed to members represents 6.25 percent of total profits.[10] This is much less than the average percentage of profits that listed companies distribute to shareholders. Oxfam has found that in the United Kingdom 70 percent of profits are returned to shareholders, whereas in Australia and New Zealand the percentage rises to 86 and 84 percent respectively (Oxfam 2017).[11] This confirms that listed companies distribute the majority of profits to shareholders, thus contributing to the wealth inequalities.

Cooperatives also contribute to sharing and distributing or maintaining wealth within local communities. This is achieved by not de-localizing to other countries to exploit cheaper labor or cheaper production or regulatory costs at the expense of local employment. It is also achieved by policies to engage with the local business communities as was the case with Sacmi,

CMC or the local cooperative bank Emil-Banca. It has also been reported that many cooperatives have bought local companies in financial difficulties because they were a local company with local employment (Bitossi 2008). Finally, the cooperative development funds extend the concept of mutuality to the rest of society by using funds to promote new cooperatives all over Italy (including areas of high unemployment) and to help employees buy out enterprises in crisis.

The combination of low salary differentials and the greater share of value-added that cooperatives transfer to labour and the community compared to private firms, and their embeddedness within local communities indicates the inherent potential of cooperatives to reduce inequalities and distribute income and wealth more equitably. As a result, it would be beneficial to the debate on inequalities if public policy makers and researchers consider the extent to which cooperatives can reduce inequalities. The presence of cooperatives in the economy can structurally reduce inequalities at the firm level that are the cause of the problem. Picketty does suggest that new forms of property and democratic control of capital are needed (Piketty 2014). Policy makers would do well to consider promoting cooperatives alongside the other proposals made by Piketty and Atkinson on how to reduce inequalities. These include a more progressive taxation system, inheritance and gift tax, a guaranteed minimum wage, more powers to unions, social insurance scheme, policies to increase employment and a sovereign wealth fund to invest in companies.[12]

10.5 Cooperatives as Good Citizens

The public perception of cooperatives is that they are enterprises that can be trusted and that they to do the right thing at all times. The previous chapter demonstrated how cooperatives uphold socially responsible practices. The behavior of cooperatives during the GFC also demonstrated how cooperatives put people before profits. Frequently cooperatives have come to the rescue of other cooperatives through mergers or accepting surplus labor, and many have bought private companies in economic difficulties to maintain employment in local communities. They have often supported good causes in Italy and abroad and have donated to developing countries. Many qualified co-operators gave up more highly paid jobs to work in a cooperative that for many years paid less and provided a lower social status than that offered by the private or public sector.

In the last decade, however, some cases were widely reported in the media that tainted the reputation of cooperatives. Two social cooperatives belonging to two Central Associations bribed officials in Rome to access public works (Balducci 2015). In 2016, the consortium CNS and one of its members were fined 110 million euros for collusive behavior by the anti-trust authority (CNS 2016). Management from one cooperative bought shares of a subsidiary prior to it being listed and then sold the shares once the company was listed, making a substantial personal capital gain.[13] Many registered cooperatives register as cooperatives but do not comply with cooperative law and related regulations.[14]

Those major cases reported by the media, despite numbering less than 20 (Gardini 2017a), have blemished their reputation. Once aware of wrongdoing, the Central Associations should be commended for acting with alacrity. Cooperative boards were replaced and new CEOs installed to manage them in accordance with the law and cooperative principles. In 2016 alone, Confcooperative withdrew the membership of 382 cooperatives because of noncompliance (Confcooperative 2017).

In the long term, however, Central Associations need to implement policies and procedures to prevent these events from re-occurring. Governance arrangements should be improved so they can prevent unethical behavior. Internal mechanisms should be able to detect and prevent management from misbehaving. The cooperative board and the internal legal and risk management controls should detect and prevent any form of collusion and anti-competitive behavior. Management recruitment should focus on cooperative values as much as technical and managerial competencies. The screening processes for admitting cooperatives as members should also be strengthened to prevent spurious cooperatives and members without cooperative values from joining. In addition, new registered cooperatives should be reviewed after twelve months rather than after two years.

Central Associations are aware of these issues and in response have promoted good governance guidelines, the dualistic governance model, independent directors, induction programs for members and educational programs for managers, and have condemned directors who were not aware of cooperative history and identity. The Central Associations, however, do not have the powers to force large cooperatives to apply their guidelines. To this end, as stated in Chapter 9, they should be given statutory powers to enforce good governance guidelines and be in a position to appoint independent directors to Boards of cooperatives with a turnover of 2 million euros or more. In light of the events that have taken place, an independent Cooperative Ombudsman could be established with powers to independently review complaints from cooperative members on governance and maladministration. This may give voice to passive members, identify risks and systemic issues early and promote better governance and administrative practices.

10.6 Jobs for Life and Jobs for All

A key part of the cooperative mission or reason to exist is to create jobs. Tito Menzani informs us that in the 1950s Legacoop cooperatives applied the open door principle, employing as many people as possible. It is said that even people that had personal problems, were unproductive and would not have found a job elsewhere were employed (Menzani 2007). Imola cooperatives proudly boasted of having a "no layoff policy" (Hancock 2007).

Working in a Legacoop cooperative had become synonymous with having a job for life.

Chapter 8 noted how the cooperative sector created more jobs during the GFC. As is the case with private enterprises, however, cooperatives also face the risk of closure if unable to compete in the market. Before the GFC, previous economic crises lasted only a few years, and cooperatives could count on a system of support from other cooperatives and the consortia network in times of difficulty. This practice was especially evident in the construction industry where cooperatives helped each other, the consortia distributed work and mergers would take place in which the strong would help the weak. It was also common for a cooperative to distribute excess labor to another cooperative. Through this system, they would either manage to survive or be absorbed by another cooperative. The GFC and its aftermath were devastating because it lasted many years and hit the whole construction sector; because of this, it made it difficult to activate the supporting mechanisms that had worked in the past. Hence, many construction cooperatives failed, and thousands of people lost their jobs. This led commentators to question the validity of the cooperative system (Baroni 2015).

A similar response took place in the region of Trento, where the Consorzio delle Cooperative di Consumo Trentine (consortium for the Trentino consumer sector) underwent a restructure leading to loss of jobs. Critics argued that the cooperative model was in crisis and not adequate for the times. Carlo Borzaga, however, noted how cooperatives in Trento had created more jobs, paid more taxes than public companies and dismissed employees only as a policy of last resort (Borzaga 2017). The constant questioning of cooperative's legitimacy as an alternative to the capitalist firm is not confined to Italy. In the United Kingdom, the failure of the Cooperative Bank was also greeted with cries that the cooperative system was in crisis. This is despite the fact that many shareholder-owned banks had to be bailed out after the GFC. As William Davies correctly points out: "despite shareholder banks creating costs to the public for hundreds of billions of pounds," no one has questioned the existing system. He goes on to say that "the endurance of neo-liberalism is partly down to the fact that it accommodates failure, is able to explain it, and can recommend solutions, all of which involve more competition and more explicitness of evaluation" (Davies 2017).

This is the problem: how can the cooperative sector stop people questioning its legitimacy every time something does not live up to expectations? Once again, Davies suggests that what is needed is "a careful building up of theory and practice, of a new vision for normality, that can cope with the occasional failures, through trial and error, without being condemned as idealistic" (Davies 2017). Capitalists and other critics have always questioned the cooperative system, and the cooperative sector has not been able to respond effectively. The Italian cooperative sector should maintain its ideals of creating jobs for all and providing jobs for life, but it should also communicate to co-operators, journalists and all stakeholders how cooperatives work and provide realistic expectations of what can be expected of both them and the cooperative movement. Cooperatives have already demonstrated, during the GFC, the various policies, practices and support mechanisms available to create and maintain employment. If cooperatives, as a movement, communicate openly with the public about their employment goals and their approach in dealing with a crisis and explain what has gone wrong, what they have learned and what improvements they have made, then people may no longer question the cooperative model. This may lead future discussions, perhaps, to focus on whether cooperatives have consistently applied their policies and the measures they have put in place to prevent failure and job losses, rather than questioning their legitimacy.

10.7   Cooperative Unity: In Search of a Cooperative Vision and in Need of a Political Project

The cooperative movement derived a lot of its legitimacy from being affiliated to political parties and their vision for society. This legitimacy, which came from affiliation to political parties that led the resistance movement, has dissipated since 1992. Indeed, in that year, Legacoop said it was no longer affiliated with any party. In 2002, it said it no longer had any preconceived positions toward any political party (Legacoop 2002). Confcooperative also distanced itself from political parties once the Christian Democratic Party ceased to exist in 1994 (Negri-Zamagni 2015). As a result, the cooperative sector today is not formally part of a political project with a long-term vision of society. Moreover, while it may be economically stronger than before, it does not have the political and social support it once had.

10.7.1   Toward a Unified Movement

The major Central Associations have responded by promoting cooperative values and embarking on a journey that will lead to economic and administrative unification. Their first response was to highlight the values, ethics and integrity of the cooperative movement at a time when Italian society was facing a political and moral crisis in 1992.[15] This was basically an attempt to uphold the values and principles of cooperatives and to seek legitimacy in their own right. Central Associations asked the Italian political and social community to accept cooperatives because they promote solidarity and principles of democracy; provide services to their members, the community, and new generations; accept a pluralist economic system; and promote a transparent and competitive market economy (Legacoop 1993).

The second response by Central Associations was to initiate forms of economic integration. In the 1990s, the three Central Associations jointly signed collective industrial relations agreements with the three trade union confederations. The Central Associations and the trade unions jointly manage CFI, the consortium that promotes WBOs, and Fon.Coop, a training agency for cooperative workers. They formed one national credit consortia, Cooper-fidi Italia, out of nine small ones. They jointly established health mutual and health and safety companies. The cooperative development funds have jointly funded cooperatives. The consumer cooperative sector is operating as one under Coop Italia's leadership (Alleanze Cooperative Italiane 2017).

The third response has been to initiate political and administrative uni-fication. In 2011 the Central Associations formed the Alleanza delle Coop-erative Italiane with the aim of forming a unitary organization by 2018. Alleanza has since represented the interests of the Central Associations to the State. They have merged their research units, which now produce data for the whole cooperative sector. Alleanza is also encouraging the respective Central Associations to hold joint discussions at the local level. At the time of writing, however, cooperatives are still members of individual Central Asso-ciations, and the cooperative development funds are managed separately.

10.7.2 In Search of a Common Vision and a Long-Term Political Project

The key goal is finding a common vision that can represent all Central Asso-ciations and give the cooperative sector the external legitimacy and political support that it no longer has. Mauro Gardini, the current president of the Alliance and Confcooperative, raised this issue at the 130th anniversary of Legacoop, stating that it would not be too difficult to merge, but the key issue was defining a 'common project.' He did not elaborate on this, which obviously highlights the difficulty of the task ahead (Gardini 2017b).

Confcooperative in its Statute notes that the Catholic Social Doctrine inspires it and that it promotes family property and social cohesion, equal opportunity, social equity and participation, and that it supports cooperatives so they can compete against private and state monopolies (Confcooperative 2017). In Confcooperative's 2015 annual report, Gardini stated that coop-eratives are a valid instrument of solidarity and democratic participation. He also stated that cooperatives should promote a circular economy, economic democracy, fight poverty via policies of inclusion, promote social welfare via a cooperative/public partnership and support local communities (Gardini 2015). These are all activities that would humanize the market. These goals, however, are limited to what cooperatives themselves could achieve within the current political-economic system but do not contain a holistic view of society that explains the relationship between the State, economy and society.

Legacoop has also struggled to develop a holistic vision. Ivano Barberini[16] stated in 2009 that the cooperative project consisted of:

- The liberty to form cooperatives in open and free communities in soli-darity with others;
- The provision of security of employment and good working conditions for everyone, especially the disadvantaged;

- A form of entrepreneurship that puts people first, that creates and distributes wealth and develops cooperative networks;
- Participation in cooperatives, meaning the promotion of economic democracy, policies of inclusion and collective leadership.

(Barberini 2009)

Legacoop's discussion document presented at the 39th Congress held in 2014 confirmed that its legitimacy comes from members and went on to say that it supported a collaborative, sustainable, innovative and regulated market economy and social inclusion and equity, as well as supporting the formation of new cooperatives and improved governance arrangements (Legacoop 2014a; Legacoop 2014b). While the above goals are commendable, they do not form a holistic vision of the role of the State, the economy and society. Giovanni Monti, the President of Legacoop Emilia-Romagna, made the following observation in his presentation to the regional council in 2017:

> The cooperative sector has always contained a set of values and expectations that went beyond the economic goals. It may have been called: cooperative project; cooperative humanism; self-management; Catholic social doctrine; call them as you wish but each time co-operators felt part of a long term social project. Lastly, notwithstanding ideological divisions, over the past 50 years we have all been part of the great project of civilising capitalism which has been known as construction of the social state or social democratic compromise, if you wish.
>
> (Monti 2017)

The dilemma facing the cooperative sector is that while it is economically stronger than before, it lacks a unitary vision for the cooperative movement, and it is not part of a long-term political project. More specifically, the cooperative unitary vision needs to combine the concepts dear to the Left and the Catholic tradition. The Left upholds equality, community (collective) ownership and universal human rights to a job, a home, education, welfare and essential services (water, electricity, gas, water) that only the State can universally guarantee (directly or indirectly). The Catholics support primarily private property holders, families and small businesses and privilege the role of the civil economy over the State. Both views could co-exist provided they be seen as equally legitimate. In addition, there would need to a be a strategy that defines where cooperative growth should be prioritized; whether it should grow via creating and supporting many small cooperatives, or via large cooperative groups, or via the consortia model, or via mergers; the strategic use of investments and the relationship between the State and cooperatives. It should also note the type of businesses that cooperatives would engage with in promoting economic development and its values.

A long-term political project would be one that understands the virtues and limits of the capitalist market economy and delineates a clear role for the State, the economy and society in pursuit of common goals that would benefit all citizens. The social democratic welfare state is an example of a cohesive, long-term political project. It supported a regulated capitalist market economy; regulated industrial relations; introduced a progressive taxation system; introduced progressive education, housing and social security programs; and managed a universal social welfare system.[17] In any long-term project, the promotion of economic democracy should be a core foundation. The concept of economic democracy, however, is broader than cooperative ownership and could include public banks; public-cooperative partnerships; superannuation funds; community and sovereign wealth funds; participatory budgeting; public and tax policies directed at supporting cooperatives; and other businesses that promote local economic development and redistribute wealth fairly between capital, labor and the community (Malleson 2013).

The cooperative movement is facing a difficult decision: isolation from the political system or being part of a long-term political project that considers the well-being and aspirations of all citizens. If it becomes involved in a political project, it can become part of a political, social and economic alliance that brings positive change to society and regain external legitimacy. If the cooperative movement remains distant from politics, then it risks losing influence. This is clearly demonstrable by the fact that the 2003 changes to the civil code (concept of mutuality and governance arrangements), the 2003 tax laws (reducing tax concessions) and the 2016 cooperative banks reforms (creation of bank groups) were initiated by center-right and center-left governments, respectively, with little consultation with the cooperative movement. In the past, the legislative changes were initiated by the cooperative sector in close alliance with political parties. This is what happened in 1971, 1983 and 1992. What this also means is the inability of late of the cooperative sector to think long-term and propose legislation that would further develop the cooperative sector.

10.8 Concluding Remarks

A neutral observer may find it difficult to comprehend that a cooperative sector that has grown so much and that continues to uphold the ICA principles would even contemplate that it is experiencing an identity crisis. It is fairer to say that the core aspects of its identity have been maintained, but some are being tested. The key aspects of cooperative identity that have been maintained include:

- A business model that includes community (inter-generational) ownership, democratic management and limited return on capital and limited member rebates.
- A networked, inter-sectoral, pluralist cooperative sector comprising Central Associations and economic and financial consortia supported by cooperative-owned financial companies.
- Economic behavior that is anti-cyclic, operates with a long-term horizon and puts people before profits, even during the GFC.

- Broad alignment with the seven ICA principles, including the open door principle, and support for local communities.
- Promoting policies of inclusion by supporting women and immigrant-led cooperatives, WBOs and new cooperatives in areas with high unemployment levels.
- An egalitarian culture that promotes limited salary differentials (although some cooperatives practice high differentials) and an equitable distribution of the value-added produced between capital, labor and communities.

The identity crisis, however, can be felt at the enterprise, associational and the political levels. At the enterprise level, cooperative identity is being questioned because some of the large cooperatives have a dual structure, while some have displayed inappropriate behavior. To an outsider, the large cooperatives' industrial relations resemble those of a private company, with salary differentials wider than in previous decades and the promise of jobs for life not always met. These issues can be overcome. A stronger external, independent oversight environment should prevent unacceptable behavior. Better governance should enable cooperative groups to introduce forms of democratic participation, transform subsidiaries into cooperatives or, if they cannot do so, govern subsidiaries with similar cooperative-like principles and benefits. Policy on salary differentials should be binding on all cooperatives, as is the case in Mondragon.[18] The promise of jobs for life may not always be fulfilled, but a clear policy of what cooperatives intend to do to fulfill this promise would benefit public understanding of what cooperatives can and cannot do.

The Central Associations may have lost some of their influence, but they still perform a vital role in the movement. Legacoop, in particular, lost the external legitimacy that it once had and the authority it enjoyed over a cohesive network of cooperatives. Its lack of influence perhaps is most evident in their inability to get the large companies to comply with their governance guidelines or to limit salary differentials. Confcooperative had also benefited from having a close relationship with the party of government from 1948–1992, but it too has lost influence, as shown by its inability to influence many of its members to wholly comply with the cooperative law and regulations. The cooperative sector's loss of influence since it distanced itself from political parties is clearly demonstrable by the fact that the State initiated legislative changes with little or no consultation before their announcement.

The Central Associations, however, are still relevant in that they can provide a variety of services, promote consortia and manage substantial assets via the cooperative development funds and the national financial consortia, through which they can promote entrepreneurship and give direction to the cooperative sector. The economic crisis has also demonstrated that cooperatives do turn to the Central Associations for help and support when facing economic difficulties. The Central Associations could regain a greater level of influence and be able to direct the movement if they are given more statutory powers to enforce good practice governance arrangements and cooperative values. This could be supplemented by raising the percentage of profits deposited into the cooperative development funds from 3 percent to 8 percent. This would allow them to promote new cooperatives; support restructuring and growth of existing cooperatives; and become an equity partner of the large cooperatives. This would allow the Central Associations to nominate Board members, create closer economic linkages and promote a cohesive, cooperative culture. They could promote an Institute for Cooperative Studies providing cooperative education courses to managers, senior managers and cooperative directors and conducting state of the art research that would promote economic democracy and cooperative development.

The key issue, however, is political. The Alleanza is having difficulty developing a shared vision for the cooperative movement and to be part of a long-term political project that represents the Left, the Catholic and lay traditions. Considering that Legacoop and Confcooperative seem to support similar economic concepts and social values, a joint cooperative vision may be possible. The development of a long-term political project may be more difficult because it has distanced itself from political parties and because the center-eft, which includes among others ex-Communists, Social Democrats and Catholics, has not yet found the necessary stability to develop such a project (Mauro 2017).[19] If the cooperative movement is not able to be part of a long-term project that promotes a new vision of society that includes economic democracy, equality and social justice for all within a project that defines the roles of the State, the market and all the economic actors, it runs the risk of becoming a politically neutral business association. This would be a departure from the identity of the Italian cooperative movement and may alienate those political parties that had been allies.[20]

Notes

1. The Fascists initially used violence and destroyed cooperatives; forced co-operators to join fascist organizations; threatened to withhold public works unless members joined the fascist union; governed cooperatives in a hierarchical way, making the general assembly redundant; and replaced workers with members loyal to the regime. During later years, cooperatives were established to lower food prices or build affordable homes as a way to build consent for the regime. Overall, the 19,500 cooperatives operating in 1921 were reduced to 6,124 by 1927. The number of cooperatives increased to 12,000 by the time the regime collapsed (Zangheri, Galasso and Castronovo 1987; Nejrotti 1986; Garotti 1990; Fornasari and Zamagni 1997).
2. Female cooperatives (those where the majority are women and are women-led) number 18,500, or over 23 percent of the total cooperatives; cooperatives led by under-35 number 7,700 (9.7 percent); and those led by migrants 4,800 or 6.1 percent (Alleanza delle Cooperative Italiane 2016).
3. Other organizations included Federconsorzi, a state organization supporting farmers, ACLI (Christian Workers Association) and CISL (the Catholic Trade Union).
4. In a study conducted on the Imola cooperatives, Mark Holmstrom described members' participation as "self-management by exception." When things went well, members would be less inclined to participate; but when things went bad, they would get involved and make decisions (Holmstrom 1989).

5. Some cooperatives have salary differentials lower than 5:1. CCFS salary differentials are less than 5:1; Greslab, a worker buyout, and Cadiai, a social cooperative, adopt a maximum ratio of 3:1. A recent Government law limits salary differentials in ethical banks to 5:1 (Ardu 2016). It is safe to assume that salary differentials in small and medium-sized cooperatives are less than 5:1.
6. In some cooperative groups of enterprises, the salary differentials have risen to more than 10:1. Mondragon cooperatives apply salary scales up to 9:1.
7. Value added refers to the difference between the firm's revenue minus the cost of intermediate consumption (the goods and services that the firm buys from other firms and consumes to produce its own goods and services). What is left are capital costs (dividends, interest on loans, taxes on profits, replacement of worn machineries and equipment (depreciation of capital or amortization) and labor costs (wages, employer social contribution and employee paid social contribution) (Piketty 2015).
8. Some cooperatives pay a higher portion of value-added amounts to labor: Camst's pays more than 90 percent of value added to labor; Cadiai, more than 95 percent; and CMC, 77 percent.
9. Some of this capital may have been paid to cooperative-owned financial companies or cooperative banks whose profits also end up as indivisible reserves.
10. This was calculated as 0.3 percent / 4.8 percent × 100 = 6.25 percent.
11. Some of these returns may go to superannuation funds with broad memberships.
12. Antony Atkinson has made 15 key proposals in his most recent book (Atkinson 2015).
13. The money was subsequently returned to the cooperative.
14. These are cooperatives that are not members of Central Associations.
15. This was the period when judicial inquiries uncovered widespread corruption, initiating a new political era dubbed 'the second republic' because all previous political parties were replaced.
16. Ivano Barberini was head of Legacoop consumer sector; then from 1996–2002 was the President of Legacoop; and from 2001–2009 was President of the International Cooperative Alliance. He passed away in 2009.
17. The author is not proposing the social democratic project, but is suggesting that a holistic, long-term project should be developed that includes economic democracy.
18. This author's view is that salary differentials should not exceed 6:1. If managers are seeking more money, then their cooperative credentials should be questioned.
19. As of November 2017, there were three parties of the Left. The Democratic Party (PD) is a center-left party formed by Catholics, members of the Democratic Party of the Left and social Liberals. Democratic and Progressive Movement is to the left of the PD and disagrees with Matteo Renzi's leadership style. Sinistra Italiana is further to the left and includes ex-Communists and other left-leaning members of parliament.
20. The Democratic Party only mentions cooperatives for the provision of social services in partnership with the State (Partito Democratico 2008).

References

Alleanze Cooperative Italiane. 2017. *L'Associazione*. Accessed October 24, 2017. www.alleanzacooperative.it/l-associazione.

Alleanza delle Cooperative Italiane. 2016. *Le Cooperative Attive in Italia (2015)*. Note e Commenti Number 41, Rome: Alleanza delle Cooperative Italiane.

Ammirato, Piero. 1996. *La Lega: The Making of a Successful Cooperative Network*. Aldershot: Dartmouth Publishing Company.

Ardu, Barbara. 2016. "Via libera alla prima legge sulla finanza etica." *La Repubblica*, 7 December: 1.

Atkinson, Anthony. 2015. *Inequality: What Can Be Done?* Boston: Harvard University Press.

Baldini, Gianfranco. 2016. "Christian Democracy: The Italian Party." In *The Oxford Handbook of Italian Politics*, edited by Eric Jones and Gianfranco Pasquino, 14 pages. Oxford: Oxford University Press.

Balducci, Silvia. 2015. "il terremoto giudiziario che ha sconvolto Roma." *Rai News: Il Punto.* 2 November. Accessed October 21, 2017. www.rainews.it/dl/rainews/articoli/Mafia-Capitale-punto-indagini-ff82d4de-60a9-415f-97c2-21cc8a49ab59.html.

Barberini, Ivano. 2009. *Come Vola il Calabrone: Cooperazione, Etica e Sviluppo.* Milan: Baldini Castoldi Dalai editore.

Baroni, Paolo. 2015. *Così il Crollo dell'Edilizia ha Messo in Crisi il Modello Coop.* 17 March. Accessed August 10, 2016. www.lastampa.it/2015/03/17/economia/cos-il-crollo-delledilizia-ha-messo-in-crisi-il-modello-coop-lhYJmG38HNBphut1xfNRiL/pagina.html.

Battilani, Patrizia. 2001. *Co.Ind: un Successo Costruito Sulla Diversità.* Bologna: Il Mulino.

Bertagnoni, Giuliana. 2010. "Work and Values: The Cooperatives in the New Millennium." In *Cooperation Network Service*, edited by Patrizia Battilani and Giuliana Bertagnoni, 177–224. Lancaster: Crucible Books.

———, and Tito Menzani. 2010. *Servizi, Lavoro e Impresa Cooperativa.* Bologna: Il Mulino.

Bitossi, Serena. 2008. *I Gruppi Cooperativi.* Bologna: Il Mulino.

Borzaga, Carlo. 2017. "Conoscere per Capire." *Cooperazione Trentina*, January: 3–6.

Briganti, Walter. 1976. *Il Movimento Cooperativo in Italia, Vol. 1° 1854–1925.* Rome: Editrice Cooperativa.

Cafaro, Pietro. 2008. *Una Cosa Sola.* Bologna: Il Mulino.

Castronovo, Valerio. 1986. "Dal Dopoguerra ad Oggi." In *Storia del Movimento Cooperativo in Italia*, edited by Renato Zangheri, Giuseppe Galasso and Valerio Castronovo, 497–839. Torino: Einaudi Editore.

CNS. 2016. *Relazione Sulla Gestione al Bilancio Chiuso al 31 Dicembre 2015.* Annual Report, Bologna: Consorzio Nazionale Servizi.

Confcooperative. 2017. "L'Associazione." *Confederazione.* Accessed September 22, 2017. www.confcooperative.it/LAssociazione.

Davies, William. 2017. "Corporate Governance Beyond Neo-Liberalism." In *The Oxford Handbook of Mutual, Co-Operative, and Co-owned Business*, edited by Jonathon Michie, Joseph R. Blasi and Carlo Borzaga, 445–455. Oxford: Oxford University Press.

Fornasari, Massimo, and Vera Zamagni. 1997. *Il Movimento Cooperativo in Italia: Un Profilo Storico Economico (1854–1992).* Florence: Vallecchi Editore.

Gardini, Maurizio. 2015. "Dentro il Paese, Accanto alla Gente." In *Bilancio di Sostenibilita*, edited by Confcooperative, 2. Rome: Confcooperative.

———. 2017a. "Le Cooperative non sono Belzeblu." *La Repubblica*, 3 August: 1.

———. 2017b. "Presentazione al Congresso Legacoop dei Delegati e Delegate." *Legacoop—Home.* 2 March. Accessed October 24, 2017. www.legacoop.coop/riviviassemblea2017/.

Garotti, Giuliana Ricci. 1990. "La Cooperazione in Emilia Romagna nel Periodo Fascista." In *Emilia Romagna Terra di Cooperazione*, edited by Angelo Varni, 37–45. Bologna: Eta-Analisi.

Hancock, Matt. 2007. *Compete to Cooperate: The Cooperative District of Imola.* Imola: Bacchilega Editore.

Holmstrom, Mark. 1989. *Industrial Democracy in Italy.* Avebury: Aldershot.

Legacoop. 1993. *I Valori Guida.* Rome: Legacoop, 14 July.

———. 2002. "Dal 35o and 36o Congresso." *Legacoop 360 Congresso.* Rome: Legacoop, 9.

———. 2014a. "Documento di Mandato." *39o Congresso Nazionale.* Rome: Legacoop, 8.

———. 2014b. "Documento Congressuale." *39o Congresso Legacoop.* Rome: Legacoop, 17.

Legacoop Reggio Emilia. 2011. *Rapporto sulla Cooperazione Reggiana 2006–2010.* Congressional Report, Reggio Emilia: Legacoop Reggio Emilia.

L'Unita'. 1986. *Il PCI e la Svolta del 1956.* Rinascita Supplement, Roma: Editrice L'Unita'.

Malleson, Tom. 2013. "Economic Democracy: The Left's Big Idea for the Twenty-First Century." *New Political Science*, 84–108.

Mauro, Ezio. 2017. "La Sinistra che non c'e'." *Politica.* 7 November. Accessed November 8, 2017. www.repubblica.it/politica/2017/11/07/news/la_sinistra_che_non_c_e_-180446860/?ref=RHPPLF-BH-I0-C8-P1-S3.3-T1.

Mazzini, Giuseppe. 1978. "Lavoro e Capitali nelle Stesse Mani." In *Il Movimento Cooperativo in Italia: 1854–1925*, edited by Walter Briganti, 26–29. Roma: Editrice Cooperativa.

Menzani, Tito. 2007. *La Cooperazione in Emilia-Romagna: Dalla Resistenza alla Svolta degli Anni Settanta.* Bologna: Il Mulino.

———. 2015. *Cooperative: persone oltre che imprese.* Soveria Mannelli: Rubbettino Editore.

Monti, Giovanni. 2017. "Relazione Programmatica." *Legacoop Emilia Romagna: Verso il Dodicesimo Congresso.* July 28, 2017. Bologna: Legacoop Emilia-Romagna

Negri-Zamagni, Vera. 2015. "The Cooperative Movement." In *The Oxford Handbook of Italian Politics*, edited by Erik Jones and Gianfranco Pasquino, 15. Oxford: Oxford University Press.

Nejrotti, Mariella. 1986. "La Lunga Notte Dell'Era Fascista." *La Cooperazione Italiana*, 181–188.

Oxfam. 2017. *An Economy for the 99%.* Oxford: Oxfam.

Partito Democratico. 2008. *Manifesto dei valori del Partito Democratico.* Political Party Programme, Rome: Partito Democratico.

Pelliconi, Marco. 1990. "Uomini e Strutture della Cooperazione Imolese." In *Emilia-Romagna: Terra di Cooperazione*, edited by Angelo Varni, 121–122. Bologna: Eta/Analisi.

Piketty, Thomas. 2014. *Capital in the Twenty-First Century.* Cambridge: Harvard University Press.

———. 2015. *Economics of Inequality.* Cambridge: Harvard University Press.

Prandini, Onelio. 1982. *La Cooperazione.* Rome: Editori Riuniti.

Silvia, Biondi, and Gildo Campesato. 2002. "1992–2002: Dieci Anni Che Sconvolsero … il Mondo Cooperativo." In *360 Congresso di Legacoop*, 1–29. Edited by Legacoop. Rome: Legacoop.

Viviani, Mario. 2013. *Piccola Guida alla Cooperazione.* Soveria Mannelli: Rubbettino Editore.

Williams, Walter. 2015. "Per un Progetto Riformatore all' Insigna della Cooperazione." In *Giovanni Bersani: Una Vita per gli Altri*, edited by Fondazione Giovanni Bersani, 85–120. Bologna: Bononia University Press.

Zangheri, Renato, Giuseppe Galasso, and Valerio Castronovo. 1987. *Storia del Movimento Cooperativo in Italia 1886–1986.* Torino: Giulio Einaudi Editore.

11 Conclusion
Toward a More Pluralist and Democratic Market Economy

The Italian cooperative sector's continued growth demonstrates that a democratic economic alternative is not only desirable, but already exists. The sector has grown despite political and economic crises in Italy, increasing globalization and the GFC. In 2011, 61,398 active cooperatives with a turnover of approximately 130 billion euros employed 1.3 million people. They employed 7.2 percent of the total workforce and produced 8.5 percent of the GDP. If one considers the number of self-employed people that rely on cooperatives for their livelihoods (for example, farmers) and the indirect employment they create, the figures rise to 10 percent of the GDP and 11 percent of the workforce. The cooperative sector is a pillar of the Italian economy and quite remarkably created 29.6 percent of all new jobs in Italy from 2001 and 2011 (Fondazione Censis 2012; Borzaga 2015).

11.1 Key Factors Contributing to Cooperative Growth

A number of key factors enable the Italian cooperative sector to grow, innovate and be resilient. These factors are inter-linked to the cooperative sector's capacity to promote and manage change through its inter-sectoral networks, its ability to influence public policy and its entrepreneurial and resilient business model. The most critical factors are:

- Cooperative legislation. The legislation has facilitated economic development, access to capital and the upholding of cooperative principles. It facilitates economic development providing cooperatives with a choice of legal structures such as consortia, joint consortia and holding companies. The legislation enables cooperative's access to capital via member shares and loans, external capital from individuals, cooperative financial structures, joint ventures, listed companies and limited tax concessions on profits that are deposited into the indivisible reserve fund. Additionally, the law facilitates economic development while upholding cooperative principles and democratic governance.
- Central Associations. The Central Associations represent cooperatives from all economic sectors. They provide comprehensive business services

and offer linkages to consortia as well as financial structures to improve their market competitiveness. They have influenced the State to pass a suite of cooperative and taxation laws and to fund cooperative development programs. The Legacoop case studies demonstrated Legacoop's leadership and coordination of member activities in developing new cooperative sectors. They also describe how it has conducted rescue operations, supported large cooperatives, endorsed financial structures and national consortia, encouraged inter-sectoral trade and promoted new cooperatives. Central Associations have created a networked cooperative economy whereby the individual cooperative does not compete alone but, instead, as part of a network.

- The financial network. The financial network supports cooperatives throughout their life-cycle. It comprises financial consortia, insurance companies, banks, cooperative-owned financial companies and cooperative development funds. Financial services offered include credit guarantees, loans, equity, long-term patient capital and strategic investments that promote international trade and global expansion. The cooperative development funds will become crucial as they perform a strategic role for the cooperative sector.

- The consortia network. The consortia network allows cooperatives to compete, grow, innovate and be resilient. They provide access to cheaper raw materials, a market for products and an avenue to win public works or to develop brand products. They have changed from local to national consortia, from sectoral to multi-sector and from performing a coordinating function to one promoting managerial excellence and quality improvement. The consortia network has enabled cooperatives to grow, exchange know-how and merge into large specialized enterprises. They have promoted inter-sectoral trading among cooperatives from different sectors.

- Cooperative groups. While networks help cooperatives to grow, once they reach a certain size consortia networks can no longer fully satisfy their needs. This is one reason why cooperative groups have emerged. They have developed since the 1990s and permitted cooperatives to access know-how, enter global markets, be part of joint-ventures, manage risks better, take more risks and grow into very large cooperatives employing more than 15,000 people. They are the main contributors to cooperative development funds and demonstrate that cooperatives can compete against large multinational firms and in all sectors of the economy.

- Entrepreneurship. Cooperatives have continuously promoted new cooperatives in emerging sectors and formed new types of cooperatives. They are promoting cooperative start-ups, WBOs and social and community cooperatives. These cooperatives have contributed to cooperative growth and diversity by building critical mass and promoting cooperatives in all economic sectors and low cooperative density areas. They facilitate generational change. They also demonstrate cooperatives' relevance and adaptability in meeting people's current needs.

- A resilient business model. There are a number of reasons that explain the resilient business model of cooperatives. First, co-operators have always prioritized long-term goals and have re-invested most of their profits into the indivisible reserve fund. Second, they improved their competitiveness via being part of the consortia network that reduced costs and improved access to public works and markets. Third, the financial network has provided loans and equity, overcoming cash-flow problems, conducting rescuing operations and facilitated restructuring. Fourth, they have adopted flexible industrial relations to manage costs and maintain employment. Fifth, they are embedded in local economies, and this local knowledge enables them to identify community needs, start up new cooperatives, engage with local businesses and support community activities. Cooperative resilience was manifested in the way cooperatives were able to survive and grow during the GFC, through the formation of WBOs and through their business longevity.

- Innovation. Cooperatives have always changed and innovated to meet people's needs and to compete in the market. These changes were accompanied by new laws, organizational structures, mindsets, cooperative models, and governance models that facilitated change. The approach to financing cooperatives changed from internal financing to a mix of internal and external financing. The cooperative financial structures have continuously evolved to meet the needs of all cooperatives. Cooperatives have formed cooperative groups of companies and own subsidiaries and listed companies. The Union represents all employees in industrial relation matters, including members. Social and community cooperatives have expanded the concept of mutuality by promoting the general interests of the community, not just those of their members. Democratic governance was modified by allowing different governance models, external shareholders with voting rights and independent directors. Some cooperatives operate a stakeholder governance model.

11.2 A More Successful and Humane Way to Deal With the GFC

The Italian cooperative sector dealt with the GFC more successfully and humanely than the private sector. Overall, the cooperative sector with 1.4 percent of all businesses created 29.6 percent of all jobs in Italy from 2001 to 2011, which includes the period of the GFC.

A number of reasons explain this achievement. First, the cooperative financial network promoted new cooperatives, funded existing cooperatives with growth plans, re-financed cooperatives with restructuring plans and rescued cooperatives in financial difficulties. Second, the growth of social cooperatives and the service sector more than made up for the contraction of the manufacturing and construction sectors. Third, new cooperatives exceeded the number of cooperatives that folded. Fourth, the strategy of creating large and medium-sized cooperatives paid off because they increased employment during the GFC, whereas the smaller cooperatives did not. Indeed, some large and medium-sized cooperatives that invested during the GFC made acquisitions, expanded internationally and continued to grow. Fifth, the cooperative's flexible industrial relation arrangements placed them in a good position to face the crisis. These arrangements allowed cooperatives to adopt solidarity contracts and flexible working conditions in order to keep people employed.

The cooperative business culture of putting people before profits and maintaining employment even in difficult times was evident during the GFC. Evidence has suggested that to maintain employment levels, the cooperative sector lowered their profits and increased their debt levels. Some cooperatives also failed, indicating that they are not immune to the challenges of a prolonged recession. There are three key points to make here:

- First, cooperatives created employment during the crisis while the private sector lost jobs.[1]
- Second, cooperatives have put people before profits and treated employees with dignity, increased their salaries and maintained employment until the business was no longer able to. In contrast, the private sector put profits before people, made lower salary increases than cooperatives and reduced their workforce in order to maximize shareholder returns.
- Third, the cooperative sector performed an anti-cyclic function. Cooperatives, however, cannot perform this function for prolonged periods of time. Otherwise, their survivability will be at risk.

11.3 Economic Success, Cooperative Principles and Social Responsibility Are Compatible

Cooperatives have achieved economic success in compliance with the law while upholding the cooperative principles and behaving with social responsibility. A combination of the cooperative business model, cooperative legislation and the promotional and coordinating role performed by the Central Associations enabled cooperatives to operate with social responsibility. Cooperatives operate as democratically managed enterprises with policies promoting open memberships, limited return on capital, inter-sectoral cooperation and community support at home and abroad. As discussed, a few large cooperative groups have a membership of less than 50 percent of their total workforce and have subsidiaries that practice traditional employer-employee relation. These are socially responsible cooperatives that face difficult real-world challenges to which practical solutions would need to be found.

Social responsibility has been demonstrated by investing profits to create employment; putting people before profits during the GFC; establishing trade relations with local suppliers; selling quality food at low prices; establishing social cooperatives to provide employment to the disadvantaged and services to the aged and disabled; establishing community cooperatives to cater for remote communities; investing cooperative development funds to create employment in high unemployment areas; and supporting new cooperatives from the young, women and migrants.

There could be no greater social responsibility than that of creating a more equitable society. Cooperatives contribute to an equitable and egalitarian society by distributing the value-added created more equitably between labor, capital and the community. The study has shown that cooperatives distribute a small share of the value-added amounts to external capital. The majority of value-added amounts, which in a private enterprise are distributed to capital, are deposited in the indivisible reserves in a cooperative. These are inter-generational assets and cannot be distributed to members. The evidence also shows that cooperatives distribute a small proportion of profits as dividends and practice lower salary differentials when compared with private enterprises.

11.4 A Cooperative Movement for the Twenty-First Century: Key Challenges to Overcome

The cooperative movement has grown to become a key player in the Italian economy. It has continually evolved in a changing society. The political ideals and linkages to political parties are no longer in place and the oversight regulatory environment, put in place since the Basevi Law, was best suited to guide a locally based cooperative sector. The movement needs to overcome a few key challenges so that it can continue to promote economic democracy and a more inclusive and just society. The key challenges that have been identified are: having a common shared vision for the cooperative movement and becoming part of a long-term political project; developing an appropriate external cooperative oversight environment; enhancing the cooperative development fund; and developing policy frameworks to deal with salary differentials and improve the functioning of cooperative groups.

The Alleanza, representing the three Central Associations, has the difficult task of developing a common shared vision for the cooperative movement and becoming part of a political project that can promote an alternative society. It is slowly developing a vision that ultimately may lead to the formation of one Central Association. This could lead to synergies in all sectors of the economy, even more competitive cooperatives, more efficient use of financial and non-financial resources and a consistent level of services throughout Italy. The success of a united cooperative movement will also depend on it being part of a political project that can communicate its vision of a better society and the role assigned to the State, the economy, civil society and the role of cooperatives in building such a society. Being part of a political project has been difficult, partly because the Italian political system is in turmoil but also because of the difficulty in reconciling the different views held by Central Associations historically. Without being part of a political project, cooperatives may focus more on economic matters, and the Central Associations may perform the more limited role of a business association, which would limit their reach, influence and capability to coordinate and provide cooperatives with long-term directions.

A fit-for-purpose external oversight environment needs to be developed to reflect the size of cooperatives, protect investors and the resilience of local communities and attract further external investments. First, the cooperative reviews that determine whether a cooperative is a prevalent mutual cooperative and is therefore eligible for tax concessions should be conducted by the Ministry of Economic Development, not the Central Associations, as this constitutes a conflict of interest. Second, the Central Associations should be given statutory powers so that they can promote and enforce cooperative governance principles and practices. This should allow the Central Associations to appoint directors in all cooperatives with turnover exceeding 2 million euros, and promote democratic governance and cooperative values more effectively. Third, a definition of cooperative governance should be developed, and the unique roles of cooperative directors should be defined. Fourth, the cooperative law should prescribe disclosure requirements for all cooperatives with turnover above 2 million euros. Fifth, an independent Cooperative Ombudsman with statutory powers should be in place to investigate any complaint of cooperative maladministration or wrongdoing. Sixth, regulatory oversight should be complemented by informing and educating the media and finance sectors so that they can provide a balanced and holistic view of cooperatives. Finally, a Cooperative Sustainability Reporting Framework should be developed with all cooperatives with turnover exceeding 2 million euros, making the Report publicly available and providing key indicators on economic, legal, social and environmental and cooperative principles-related goals. The Central Associations could collate this information and communicate their findings.

A cooperative development fund is a tool that the Central Associations can use for promoting new cooperatives, strategically coordinating all investments, encouraging internationalization and promoting cooperative education and training. It would be desirable to raise the current deposit of 3 percent of profits to 8 percent so that the funds can perform an even more significant role in promoting cooperatives and establishing a Cooperative Institute. The Institute, in cooperation with existing cooperative centers, would conduct research and educate and train managers and directors as well as the public on cooperative values, the cooperative business model and democratic governance.

The Alleanza needs to develop two key policies. The first needs to state clearly the level of salary differentials allowed in cooperatives. Perhaps indicative salary differentials of 4:1 rising to 6:1 for CEOs of large international cooperatives could be a starting point. Allowing salary differentials to rise to more than 10:1 will damage the reputation of cooperatives, leading some to question their egalitarian and social justice credentials. High salary differentials may also attract managers whose ideals may not be aligned with cooperative values.

The second policy should be directed at cooperative groups. They provide a clear demonstration of cooperative's ability to grow and manage a large company. The cooperative group model allows cooperatives to perform an even greater role in the economy. This is a positive outcome. The key issue to resolve is their dual operational structure, through which the cooperative owns subsidiaries that operate as private enterprises. The Central Associations need to develop clear and enforceable guidelines that clarify when a subsidiary can and should be transformed into a cooperative. If they cannot be transformed into a cooperative, a framework should be established that defines what a cooperative must do to ensure that subsidiaries reflect cooperative values such as participation in the decision-making process, access to rebates and social welfare, and so on. The key issue here is not that workers are becoming capitalists and are exploiting other workers. This is prevented from taking place by the cooperative principles and values, legal requirements and application of the principle of equal pay for equal work. The key issue is not giving all workers the possibility of experiencing cooperative ownership and democratic management. These are two things that should always be encouraged.

11.5 Economics of the Cooperative Enterprise

The data presented in this book has confirmed the striking differences between cooperatives and private enterprises. The fundamental difference is that cooperatives are democratic economic organizations established by people to solve their basic needs, such as access to work, markets in which to sell their products, quality food at low prices and a family or business loan. In this endeavor, people raise capital to establish a cooperative to solve a need. Capital is a means to an end, not the end as it is with private enterprises. This is the key reason why cooperatives focus on the long-term interests of current and future members, while private enterprise focuses on the short-term interests of shareholders. Cooperatives are enterprises owned by employees where labor controls capital, whereas private enterprises are enterprises owned by shareholders where capital controls labor. Cooperatives retain most profits in the interest of current and future generations; private enterprises distribute most of the profits to shareholders. Cooperatives limit their distribution to capital; private enterprise maximizes returns to shareholders. Cooperative assets are community-owned and passed on from one generation to the next; in private enterprises, assets belong to capital, which can sell them for profit or transfer them to another country. Cooperatives placed people before profits during the GFC; private enterprise placed profits before people.

This study has also provided ample evidence that cooperatives do not under-employ or under-invest as classical economists have previously predicted. Cooperatives have behaved very rationally and have continued to invest in order to grow market share, diversify their products or their markets so they could provide more employment (via workers cooperatives), access a larger market for producers' products (via agricultural cooperatives) or offer consumers greater choice and lower food prices (via consumer cooperatives). The size of cooperatives and the continuous rise in employment levels support this view.

Also, cooperatives do not need to operate only in marginal areas of the economy where there has been a market or a state failure. They are successfully competing in all market sectors against private enterprises of all sizes, including multinational companies. Cooperatives have developed a genuine business model for the twenty-first century that ultimately promotes the common good and a more equal and just distribution of wealth between labor, capital and the community. This is in contrast to private enterprise's business model of profit maximization on behalf of shareholders leading to gross inequalities for society.[2]

11.6 Cooperatives and Public Policy

Cooperatives are a key component of a pluralist market economy and a potential partner to the State in key sectors of the economy. They invest their profits and equity capital to grow their business; are profitable; pay taxes; create jobs; promote economic democracy; distribute wealth equitably between capital, labor and the community; and build socially cohesive communities. Cooperatives are independently managed but act as a quasi-public service organization focusing on long-term goals and community needs. Areas where public-cooperative partnerships could develop or where the State could include cooperatives in its public policy initiatives are:

- Provision of social welfare services. States that outsource or that cannot meet the demand for social services could engage social cooperatives to perform these services. These cooperatives are led by people with a social motive or goals whose primary goal is to satisfy people's needs and not to make profits. Cooperatives in Italy have demonstrated that they can provide social services at home; manage aged care facilities, child care centers and medical centers; and provide health coverage as well. They can provide a holistic social welfare service.
- Job creation schemes to limit de-industrialization and promote inclusion. States could engage cooperatives to be a part of job creation schemes such as recuperating enterprises in crisis via WBOs, by employing the long-term unemployed and people with disabilities via Type B social cooperatives or by creating employment opportunities in high unemployment areas.

- Public infrastructure and maintenance. Cooperatives can build and operate all types of public infrastructure, including roads, highways, subways, public buildings, office building, public libraries, schools and universities.
- Community building. Cooperatives can rebuild communities in a holistic, cohesive and inclusive way by engaging all types of cooperatives, such as banks, insurance, housing, consumer, entertainment, social welfare, manufacturing and construction, agriculture, transport and so on. The cooperative development funds invest throughout Italy, making them a suitable partner.
- Small villages. The recently established community multi-sector cooperatives are the ideal type of organization that can provide a broad variety of services in remote or very small communities that have become too costly for the State to deliver and not profitable enough for the private sector to consider.

The State can support cooperative development through its role as a regulator, enabler, partner and investor. First, State laws and regulation need to reflect the economic, social and community needs of cooperatives. They need to provide the basis for cooperatives to grow, choose appropriate legal forms and access finance from a variety of sources while preserving cooperative identity. Demutualization should not be allowed. Second, the State should enable cooperatives to start and to grow via providing tax concessions subject to assets being indivisible, limited salary differentials and compliance with democratic principles. They could also provide 150 percent tax deductibility to all profits placed in the cooperative development funds as an incentive to increase the percentage of profits placed in these funds.[3] Third, the State can become a partner with cooperatives to promote economic development and the provision of public services. Previously, local governments have formed joint ventures with cooperatives to provide catering services at schools, worked with cooperatives to provide holistic services in cleaning, waste management and property services and have licensed cooperatives to build-own-operate-transfer child care centers. These types of partnerships could be formed in many other areas, including through managing libraries, public works, property maintenance at hospitals, schools, universities and other public buildings and the provision of IT services. Fourth, the State could also become a significant equity investor in cooperative enterprises and consortia. These are not grants, but equity investments designed to allow cooperatives to grow from small to medium and to large enterprises, to help cooperatives develop in nationally strategic priority areas or expand overseas. The state is already doing this via Invitalia, which invests in CFI and had also invested in Granarolo, and the Trento local government, which invested in Promosviluppo. This is little compared to the size and potential of the cooperative sector.

11.7 Economic Democracy: Toward a More Pluralist and Democratic Market Economy

Liberal/social democratic states have used progressive taxation systems, industrial relations laws, social security and social spending, consumer protection, health and safety regulations and anti-competition laws to humanize the market. A lot of progress has been made. The neo-liberal policies, however, have limited the role of the State in the economy, lowered tax revenues and used the market to provide many social services, education, housing and utilities. These policies have created less humane societies reflected in high unemployment, inequalities of wealth, unequal distribution of power in the enterprise and society, insecure communities and homelessness and poverty in western countries, and even more so in other parts of the world. In a global market where capital is free to move and labor freer to move than before, it is more difficult for the Nation States to govern as they compete with other States that wish to have a slice of international investments and trade. The promotion of economic democracy within liberal/social democratic pluralist economies is designed to build on the progress already made to humanize the market by giving people the opportunity to own their enterprises, direct investments and redistribute wealth.[4] Economic democracy is not seen as an end in itself, but a means through which people are given a chance to live in a society that allows everyone to fulfill their human potential and to feel and to be equal to everyone else.

The large, inter-sectoral and networked Italian cooperative sector is promoting its version of economic democracy within a liberal democratic state. It is promoting economic democracy at the enterprise level through worker cooperatives. The sector is practicing consumer democracy by giving consumers the power to choose the products that are sold at their local supermarkets. It is promoting producer democracy by giving producers the ability to market and manufacture their products to market through their consortia. Financial democracy is practiced by giving members the freedom to deposit and invest their money in financial consortia, cooperative development funds, local cooperative banks, ethical banks, cooperative-owned financial companies and insurance companies. The sector is improving the operation of the market by improving working conditions, giving employees more benefits than those offered in collective agreements. The sector is lowering prices and profits at supermarkets, tailoring insurance and banking products to meet everyone's real needs and having agricultural cooperatives helping small farmer-producers access markets, and in so doing preserving community life in rural areas. Cooperatives distribute wealth more equitably, with only a small percentage of the value-added amounts distributed to capital, leaving most of the surplus to be engaged in the cooperative and the local community.

The Italian cooperative sector can continue to grow and promote economic democracy through its inter-sectoral network and the ability of cooperatives to access external capital. The continued growth of cooperative development funds will further promote growth. The cooperative groups can become a key pillar of economic democracy on a world scale. Should the cooperative sector implement an appropriate external oversight framework, cooperatives would be in a better position to attract further investments from those people who wish to build a better economy and a society of equals. These investors need not only be local or national but can be international investors. Indeed, establishing international inter-cooperative linkages, investments and trade could lead to another phase of growth for the cooperative sector worldwide.

A more humane, pluralist and democratic economy is not hard to imagine, and is perhaps easier to achieve than first thought. Imagine government-owned public banks and local banks directing investments to cooperatives and socially responsible enterprises; public policy that provides incentives and rewards for cooperatives as well as socially responsible enterprises; cooperatives associating sole traders, professionals and retailers; small family businesses supported by their associations to cut their regulatory and business costs and achieve economies of scale; ethically and socially minded people shopping in consumer cooperatives, banking with cooperative banks and investing some of their superannuation savings into cooperatives; and superannuation funds working with cooperatives to provide affordable housing. This is already happening; it just requires more people to know about and support all enterprises that promote economic democracy.

11.8 Concluding Remarks

Much progress has been made toward building a more humane society. The political compromises made by Liberal Democrats, Social Democrats, Socialist/ Communists, Christian Democrats and, more recently, environmental groups have made significant progress. They have provided formal political equality, protection of basic human rights, a regulated market economy and a welfare state that addresses injustices and inequalities resulting from market failures. This political-economic system has led to economic growth and wealth creation, but inequalities, unemployment and insecurities have not been overcome. Continuing with this compromise will not bring further change because the fundamental cause of the problems is an economy dominated by profit maximizing firms alongside a State that can no longer provide for people's needs.

If countries are really serious about creating more just and equal societies and putting the needs of people before profits, then it is time for the development and implementation of policies and programs that support economic democracy and cooperative development. Cooperatives in Italy have demonstrated that economic growth can be reconciled with social responsibility and a fair and just distribution of the value added created. More importantly, cooperative sectors worldwide should consider those aspects of the Italian experience that may be transferable to their own countries in the hope that they will also develop unique and successful cooperative models.

Notes

1. Please refer to Chapter 8 for further information.
2. For information on the economics of the cooperative enterprise please see: (Ward 1958; Vanek 1975; Dow 2003; Zamagni and Zamagni 2010; Hansmann 2013; Perotin 2014; Mori 2014; Zanotti 2016; Borzaga and Tortia 2017).
3. These State measures could be available to all socially responsible businesses subject to their commitment to re-invest profits in the local economy; apply industrial relations agreements; limit salary differentials; protect the environment; pay all their taxes; and support their local community.
4. For information on the debate on economic democracy and the relationship between economic and political democracy, please refer to the works of Robert Dahl and Tom Malleson (Dahl 1985; Dahl 2000; Malleson 2014).

References

Borzaga, Carlo. 2015. "Introduzione e Sintesi." In *Economia Cooperativa: Terzo Rapporto Euriese*, edite by Carlo Borzaga 5–31. Trento: Euricse.

———, and Ermanno Tortia. 2017. "Co-operation as Co-ordination Mechanism: A New Approach to the Economics of Co-operative Enterprises." In *The Oxford Handbook of Mutual, Co-operative, and Co-owned Business*, edited by Jonathon Michie, Joseph R. Blasi and Carlo Borzaga, 55–75. Oxford: Oxford University Press.

Dahl, Robert. 1985. *A Preface to Economic Democracy*. Berkeley: University of California Press.

———. 2000. *On Democracy*. New Haven: Yale University Press.

Dow, Gregory K. 2003. *Governing the Firm*. Cambridge: Cambridge University Press.

Fondazione Censis. 2012. *Primo Rapporto sulla Cooperazione Italiana*. Economic Report, Rome: Alleanza Cooperative Italiane.

Hansmann, Henry. 2013. "All Firms Are Cooperatives—And so Are Government." *Journal of Entrepreneurial and Organizational Diversity*, 1–10.

Malleson, Tom. 2014. *Economic Democracy for the 21st Century*. Oxford: Oxford University Press.

Mori, Pier Angelo. 2014. *Economia Della Cooperazione e del Non-Profit*. Rome: Carocci Editore.

Perotin, Virginie. 2014. "Worker Cooperatives: Good, Sustainable Jobs in the Community." *Journal of Entrepreneurial and Organisational Diversity*, 34–47.

Vanek, Jaroslav. 1975. "The Basic Theory of Financing Participatory Firms." In *Self Management: Economic Liberation of Man*, edited by Jaroslav Vanek, 445–455. Harmondsworth: Penguin Books.

Ward, Benjamin. 1958. "The Firm in Illyria: Market Syndicalism." *The American Economic Review*, 566–589.

Zamagni, Stefano, and Vera Zamagni. 2010. *Cooperative Enterprise: Facing the Challenge of Globalisation*. Cheltenham: Edward Elgar Publishing Limited.

Zanotti, Antonio. 2016. *Cooperative e Imprese di Capitali: Quanto Sono Diverse e Quanto Sono Uguali?* Soveria Mannelli: Rubbettino Editore.

Index

Page numbers in italic indicate figures and in bold indicate tables on the corresponding pages.